Lecture Notes in Computer Science 5159

Commenced Publication in 1973
Founding and Former Series Editors:
Gerhard Goos, Juris Hartmanis, and Jan van Leeuwen

Willem Jonker   Milan Petković (Eds.)

Secure
Data Management

5th VLDB Workshop, SDM 2008
Auckland, New Zealand, August 24, 2008
Proceedings

 Springer

Volume Editors

Willem Jonker
Philips Research Europe
High Tech Campus 34, 5656 AE Eindhoven
and
University of Twente
Dept. of Computer Science
P.O. Box 217, 7500 AE Enschede, The Netherlands
E-mail: willem.jonker@philips.com

Milan Petković
Philips Research Europe
High Tech Campus 34, 5656 AE Eindhoven, The Netherlands
E-mail: Milan.Petkovic@philips.com

Library of Congress Control Number: Applied for

CR Subject Classification (1998): H.2.0, H.2, C.2.0, H.3, E.3, D.4.6, K.6.5

LNCS Sublibrary: SL 3 – Information Systems and Application, incl. Internet/Web and HCI

ISSN   0302-9743
ISBN-10   3-540-85258-1 Springer Berlin Heidelberg New York
ISBN-13   978-3-540-85258-2 Springer Berlin Heidelberg New York

Springer is a part of Springer Science+Business Media

springer.com

© Springer-Verlag Berlin Heidelberg 2008
Printed in Germany

Typesetting: Camera-ready by author, data conversion by Scientific Publishing Services, Chennai, India
Printed on acid-free paper   SPIN: 12452217   06/3180   5 4 3 2 1 0

Preface

Information and communication technologies are advancing fast. Processing speed is still increasing at a high rate, followed by advances in digital storage technology, which double storage capacity every year. Furthermore, communication technologies do not lag behind. The Internet has been widely used, as well as wireless technologies. With a few mouse clicks, people can communicate with each other around the world. All these advances have great potential to change the way people live, introducing new concepts like ubiquitous computing and ambient intelligence. Technology is becoming present everywhere in the form of smart and sensitive computing devices. They are nonintrusive, transparent and hidden in the background, but they collect, process, and share all kinds of information, including user behavior, in order to act in an intelligent and adaptive way.

These emerging technologies put new requirements on security and data management. As data are accessible anytime anywhere, it becomes much easier to get unauthorized data access. Furthermore, the use of new technologies has brought about some privacy concerns. It becomes simpler to collect, store, and search personal information, thereby endangering people's privacy. Therefore, research in secure data management is gaining importance, attracting the attention of both the data management and the security research communities. The interesting problems range from traditional topics, such as, access control and general database security, via privacy protection to new research directions, such as cryptographically enforced access control.

This year, the call for papers attracted 32 papers both from universities and industry. For presentation at the workshop, the Program Committee selected 11 full papers (34% acceptance rate) as well as 3 position papers. In addition, the program included a keynote by Sean Wang on "How Anonymous Is k- Anonymous? Look at Your Quasi-ID." The regular papers as well as the invited keynote paper are collected in this volume which we hope will serve you as useful research and reference material.

The regular papers in the proceeding are grouped into five sections. The first section focuses on database security, which remains an important research area. The papers in this section address mainly the issues around data disclosure detection and control. The second section changes the focal point to the topic of trust management. The papers in this section deal with data provenance, trust negotiations, and trust metrics. The third section focuses on privacy protection addressing the privacy issues around location-based services and access control on the Semantic Web. The fourth section collects the papers from the special session on privacy and security in healthcare. The papers in this section approach the problem of fine-grained access to healthcare data from two perspectives: (a) policy-driven access control models and (b) cryptographic enforcement of access control policies.

Finally, the last section presents three position papers whose topics range again from data disclosure control, via privacy protection to access control.

We wish to thank all the authors of submitted papers for their high-quality submissions. We would also like to thank the Program Committee members as well as additional referees for doing an excellent job. Finally, let us acknowledge Luan Ibraimi who helped in the technical preparation of the proceedings.

June 2008   Willem Jonker
                                                              Milan Petković

Organization

Workshop Organizers

Willem Jonker   Philips Research/University of Twente,
     The Netherlands
Milan Petković   Philips Research, The Netherlands

Program Committee

Gerrit Bleumer	Francotyp-Postalia, Germany
Ljiljana Branković	University of Newcastle, Australia
Sabrina De Capitani di Vimercati	University of Milan, Italy
Andrew Clark	Queensland University of Technology, Australia
Ernesto Damiani	University of Milan, Italy
Eric Diehl	Thomson Research, France
Lee Dong Hoon	Korea University, Korea
Jeroen Doumen	Twente University, The Netherlands
Jan Eloff	University of Pretoria, South Africa
Csilla Farkas	University of South Carolina, USA
Eduardo Fernández-Medina	University of Castilla-La Mancha, Spain
Elena Ferrari	Universitá degli Studi dell'Insubria, Italy
Simone Fischer-Hübner	Karlstad University, Sweden
Tyrone Grandison	IBM Almaden Research Center, USA
Dieter Gollmann	Technische Universität Hamburg-Harburg, Germany
Ehud Gudes	Ben-Gurion University, Israel
Marit Hansen	Independent Centre for Privacy Protection, Germany
Min-Shiang Hwang	National Chung Hsing University, Taiwan
Mizuho Iwaihara	Kyoto University, Japan
Sushil Jajodia George	Mason University, USA
Ton Kalker	HP Research, USA
Marc Langheinrich	Institute for Pervasive Computing ETH Zurich, Switzerland
Nguyen Manh Tho	Vienna University of Technology, Austria
Nick Mankovich	Philips Medical Systems, USA
Sharad Mehrotra	University of California at Irvine, USA
Stig Frode Mjølsnes	Norwegian University of Science and Technology, Norway
Eiji Okamoto	University of Tsukuba, Japan

Additional Referees

Table of Contents

Security and Privacy in Healthcare

Position Papers

How Anonymous Is k-Anonymous? Look at Your Quasi-ID*

Claudio Bettini[1], X. Sean Wang[2], and Sushil Jajodia[3]

[1] Dico, University of Milan, Italy
[2] Dept of CS, University of Vermont, USA
[3] CSIS, George Mason University, USA

Abstract. The concept of quasi-ID (QI) is fundamental to the notion of
k-anonymity that has gained popularity recently as a privacy-preserving
method in microdata publication. This paper shows that it is important
to provide QI with a formal underpinning, which, surprisingly, has been
generally absent in the literature. The study presented in this paper provides a first look at the correct and incorrect uses of QI in k-anonymization
processes and exposes the implicit conservative assumptions when QI is
used correctly. The original notions introduced in this paper include (1)
k-anonymity under the assumption of a formally defined external information source, independent of the QI notion, and (2) k-QI, which is an extension of the traditional QI and is shown to be a necessary refinement. The
concept of k-anonymity defined in a world without using QI is an interesting artifact itself, but more importantly, it provides a sound framework to
gauge the use of QI for k-anonymization.

1 Introduction

The concept of k-*anonymity*, used in the recent literature (e.g., [1, 7, 9, 12, 13]) to
formally evaluate the privacy preservation of published tables, was introduced in
the seminal papers of Samarati and Sweeney [12, 13] based on the notion of *quasi-
identifiers* (or QI for short). The process of obtaining k-anonymity for a given
private table is first to recognize the QIs in the table, and then to anonymize the
QI values, the latter being called k-*anonymization*. While k-anonymization is
usually rigorously validated by the authors, the definition of QI remains mostly
informal, and different authors seem to have different interpretations of the concept of QI.

The purpose of this paper is to provide a formal underpinning of QI and
examine the correctness and incorrectness of various interpretations of QI in our
formal framework. We observe that in cases where the concept has been used
correctly, its application has been conservative; this paper provides a formal
understanding of the conservative nature in such cases.

---

* Preliminary version appeared as [2]. Part of Bettini's work was performed at the
University of Vermont and at George Mason University. The authors acknowledge
the partial support from NSF with grants 0242237, 0430402, and 0430165, and from
MIUR with grant InterLink II04C0EC1D.

W. Jonker and M. Petković (Eds.): SDM 2008, LNCS 5159, pp. 1–15, 2008.

The notion of QI was perhaps first introduced by Dalenius in [4] to denote a set of attribute *values* in census records that may be used to re-identify a single or a group of individuals. To Dalenius, the case of multiple individuals being identified is potentially dangerous because of collusion. In [12, 13], the notion of QI is extended to a set of *attributes* whose (combined) values may be used to re-identify the individuals of the released information by using "external" sources. Hence, the appearance of QI attribute values in a published database table may give out private information and must be carefully controlled. One way to achieve this control is by anonymizing QI attribute values, through a k-anonymization process.

The k-anonymization process, as first defined in [12, 13], amounts to generalizing the values of the QI in the table so that the set of individuals, who have the same generalized QI attribute value combination, forms an anonymity set of size no less than k, following the pioneering work on *anonymity set* by Chaum [3]. (According to a later proposal for terminology [11], "Anonymity is the state of being identifiable within a set of subjects, the anonymity set.") The resulting table is said to be k-anonymous.

The notion of QI is hence fundamental for k-anonymity. In the original paper for k-anonymity [12], however, QI is only informally described. The paper seems to assume that all attributes that may be available from external sources should be part of QI. Recent papers (e.g., [1, 9]) appear to use a similar informal definition, but with a variety of interpretations (see below). We will formally establish that the use of such a QI is correct, albeit conservatively correct.

The only formal definition of QI that we are aware of appears in [13]. The definition is rather complicated, but from that definition, we understand that a set of attributes Q_T in a table T is a QI if there exists a specific individual r_i, such that, only based on the combination of the values for Q_T associated with r_i, it is possible to re-identify that specific, *single* individual.

From the above formal definition emerges that what really characterizes a QI is the ability to associate a combination of its values with a single individual. The same notion seems to be captured by Def. 2.1 of [8]. We shall call the QI defined this way 1-QI (the number 1 intuitively indicates the number of individuals identified by the QI). This formal definition seems to deviate from the original idea of Dalenius [4] which gave importance to the identification of *groups* of individuals. Although Dalenius was only concerned about collusion, the identification of groups of individuals is closely related to the anonymity set concept and should not be ignored. This deviation actually leads to incorrectness as we shall show in this paper.

Many studies on k-anonymization have since appeared in the literature. However, different authors seem to interpret the concept of QI differently. In addition to the original interpretation of QI as (1) the set of all the attributes that appear in external sources [12], and (2) a set of attributes that we call 1-QI [13], we found the following use of QI in k-anonymization: (3) use the minimum QI, i.e., the minimum set of attributes that can be used to re-identify individuals [6, 7], and (4) anonymize the multiple minimum QIs in the same table [14] since the minimum QI is found not unique.

Through a formal study of the notion of QI, we conclude in this paper that the use of QI as in category (1) is correct but conservative, while the use of QI as in the other three categories is incorrect. Hence, the contribution of this paper is: (a) the concept of QI and its role in k-anonymity are clarified, and (b) the conservative nature of the techniques in the recent papers is better understood. Point (b) above can further lead to (c) new possibilities for more focused data anonymization to avoid over conservativeness.

The remainder of this paper is organized as follows. Section 2 gives some preliminary definitions. Section 3 introduces a new formalization of k-anonymity, and Section 4 defines the notion of QIs and links the QI with k-anonymity. Section 5 shows k-anonymity using QI other than all the external attributes is problematic, and Section 6 formalizes in our framework the conservative assumption currently used for k-anonymization and provides evidence that the approach is sufficient but not necessary. Section 7 concludes the paper.

2   Preliminary Definitions

Following the convention of the k-anonymity literature, we assume a relational model with the bag semantics (or multiset semantics). We assume the standard bag-semantic definitions of database relation/table, attribute and tuple, as well as the standard bag-semantic definitions of the relational algebra operations. In particular, under the bag semantics, relations allow duplicate tuples and operations keep duplicates [10].

We shall use T (possibly with subscripts) to denote relational tables, t (possibly with subscripts) to denote tuples in tables, and $Attr[T]$ to denote the attribute set of table T. We shall also use A and B (possibly with subscripts) to denote both sets of attributes and single attributes as the difference will be clear from the context.

To prevent private information from leaking, the k-anonymization approach is to generalize the values in a table. For example, both ZIP codes "22033" and "22035" may be generalized to the value "2203*", an interval value [22000–22099], or a general concept value "Fairfax, Virginia". The idea is that each "generalized" value corresponds to a set of "specific" values, and the user of the table can only tell from the general value that the original value is one of the specific values in the set.

The set of specific values that corresponds to a general value can be formally specified with a decoding function. This decoding function, denoted $Dec()$, maps a value to a non-empty set of values. The domain of $Dec()$ is said to be the *general values*, denoted D_G, and the range of $Dec()$ is the non-empty subsets of the *specific values*, denoted D_S. As such, all attributes in our relational tables will use the same domain, either D_G (for generalized tables) or D_S (for specific tables). We assume that D_S is a subset of D_G and decoding of a D_S value is the set consisting of the value itself. We call a tuple using only specific values a *specific tuple*. In addition, we assume that the decoding function is *publicly known* and hence all the privacy protection is from the uncertainty provided by the set of values decoded from a single one.

The decoding function is trivially extended to tuples, by decoding each of the attribute values in a tuple. More specifically, given a tuple t with generalized values on attributes $A_1, \ldots, A_n$, $Dec(t)$ gives the set of tuples $Dec(t[A_1]) \times \cdots \times Dec(t[A_n])$, i.e., the cross product of the decoding of each attribute. In other words, the decoding of a tuple t gives rise to the set of all specific tuples that would be generalized to t. The decoding function is similarly extended to tables, yielding a set $Dec(T)$ of tables from a given T. Specifically, given a table $T = t_1, \ldots, t_n$, a table $T' = t'_1, \ldots, t'_n$ is in $Dec(T)$ if t'_i is in $Dec(t_i)$ for each $i = 1, \ldots, n$.

In the k-anonymization literature, tables may be generalized using a *local encoding* or *global encoding* [7]. (*Encoding* refers to the process of obtaining the general value from a specific one.) The difference is that in global encoding, the different appearances of a specific value (or tuple) are generalized to the same generalized value (or tuple), while in local encoding, they may be generalized to different generalized values. The use of different classes of generalization affects the set of possible generalized tables from an input one, with local recoding more flexible but computationally harder. The formalization with $Dec()$ function is oblivious to this difference, and is correct in the sense that with either approach, the original table is in $Dec(T)$. The $Dec()$ approach is justified as we are not concerned in this paper with specific anonymization techniques.

3   The World and k-Anonymity

In this section, we formally define the notion of k-anonymity without using QIs. We will introduce the QI concept in the next section. The approach is in contrast to defining k-anonymity based on the concept of QI as traditionally done. We note that our approach is a logical one since only when we can define k-anonymity independently of QI, we may prove the correctness of a particular definition of QI.

3.1   The World

To start with, we model all the external sources that can be used to re-identify individuals as a *world*. A world W conceptually is a blackbox that uses attribute values for re-identification. That is, given a tuple t on some of the attributes of W, the world W will give back the set of individuals that have the attribute values given by t. Formally,

Definition 1. *A world W is a pair $(Attr[W], ReID_W)$, where $Attr[W]$ is a set of attributes, and $ReID_W$ is a function that maps the tuples on the schemas that are non-empty subsets of $Attr[W]$, with domain values from D_S, to the finite sets of individuals.*

In other words, given a relation schema $R \subseteq Attr[W]$ and a tuple t on R with values from D_S, $ReID_W(t)$ gives the set of individuals that possess the attribute values given in t. We say that an individual in $ReID_W(t)$ is an individual *re-identified with t by W*, or simply *re-identified with t* when W is understood. In this case, we may also say that tuple t re-identifies the individual.

Since the $ReID_W$ function re-identifies individuals with their attribute values, two properties naturally follow. The first is the *unique value property*, meaning that each individual only has one specific value under one attribute. This property has the implication that if given two tuples $t_1 \neq t_2$ on $R \subseteq Attr[W]$ with specific values (i.e., no generalized values), then $ReID_W(t_1) \cap ReID_W(t_2) = \emptyset$.

The second property we call "supertuple inclusion" should also hold. For example, if a person is in the set P of individuals re-identified with ZIP code 22032 together with gender male, then this person should be in the set P' re-identified with ZIP code 22032 alone, i.e., $P \subseteq P'$. On the other hand, if a person is in P', then there must be a value of gender (either male or female) so that the person must be re-identified with ZIP code 22032 and gender male (or female) together. More generally, supertuple inclusion property means that if we add more attributes to a tuple t resulting in a "supertuple", then the set of individuals re-identified will be a subset of those identified with t, and at the same time, each individual re-identified with t will be re-identified with a particular supertuple of t. Formally, we have:

Definition 2. *A world* $W = (Attr[W], ReID_W)$ *is said to satisfy the super-tuple inclusion* property *if for each tuple t on attribute set* $A \subseteq Attr[W]$ *and each attribute set B, with* $A \subseteq B \subseteq Attr[W]$, *there exist a finite number of tuples* $t_1, \ldots, t_q$ *on B such that (1) $t_i[A] = t[A]$ for each $i = 1, \ldots, q$, and (2) $ReID_W(t) = ReID_W(t_1) \cup \cdots \cup ReID_W(t_q)$.*

In the sequel, we shall assume all the worlds satisfy the supertuple inclusion property.

We also assume that, in the sequel, each world we consider is a *closed world*, in which all the relevant individuals are included. That is, the set of individuals identified by $ReID_W(t)$ consists of *all* the individuals who have the attribute values given by t.

A world is called a *finite world* if $ReID_W$ maps only a finite number of tuples to non-empty sets. In the sequel, we assume all worlds are finite worlds.

In summary, we assume in the sequel all the worlds (1) satisfy the unique value and supertuple inclusion properties, (2) are closed, and (3) are finite.

The function $ReID_W$ in a world W is naturally extended to a set of tuples.

The above conceptual, blackbox worlds may be concretely represented as finite relations. In particular, a world $W = (Attr[W], ReID_W)$ can be represented as a relation W on $Attr[W]$ with domain D_S, having the condition that W includes attributes, such as SSN, that directly point to an individual. In this case, function $ReID_W$ will simply be a selection followed by a projection. For example, if SSN is the attribute to identify individuals, then $ReID_W(t)$ is defined as $\pi_{SSN}\sigma_{R=t}(W)$, where R is the schema for tuple t.

In this relational view of W, table W may be considered as a universal relation storing for each individual all the associated data that are publicly known. As in previous work on this topic, for the sake of simplicity, we also assume that the information of one individual is contained in at most one tuple of W. We also assume that one tuple of W contains information of only one individual. Furthermore, we assume there is a public method that links a tuple of W with the individual that the tuple corresponds to. This public method may be as simple as an attribute, such as the social security number, in W that directly points to a particular individual.

For example, W may contain the attributes SSN, Name, Birth Date, Gender, Address, Voting record, etc. Each tuple of W corresponds to one individual pointed by the SSN. Other attributes give the other property values of the individual.

Note that the unique value and supertuple inclusion properties are automatically satisfied by any relational world.

3.2 k-Anonymity in W

In our environment, to provide privacy in a published table is to avoid any attacker from using the world W to re-identify the individuals in the published table. The k-anonymity in W is stronger, namely, it avoids any attacker from using the world W to re-identify the individual to be among less than k individuals. This intuition is captured more formally in Definition 4 below.

In order to simplify notation, in the following we use $PAttr[T]$ to denote the *public* attributes of T, formally defined as $Attr[W] \cap Attr[T]$ when the world W is understood.

In the above discussion, the case of 0 individuals re-identified is a special case. This is the case when a tuple $\pi_{PAttr[T]}(T)$ does not re-identify anyone by W, it would actually be a mistake since T is supposed to represent information of some individuals and the world is assumed to be closed. If this 0 individuals case happens, it must mean that the closed world we have is not "consistent" with the table in our hand. This observation leads to the following:

Definition 3. *Given a table T, a world W is said to be* consistent *with T if $|\bigcup_{t' \in Dec(t)} ReID_W(t')| > 0$ for each tuple t in $\pi_{PAttr[T]}(T)$.*

A consistent world for a table T is one that can re-identify all the individuals whose information is represented in T. In the sequel, we assume the world is consistent with the tables under discussion.

We are now ready to define k-anonymity in W.

Definition 4. *Let $k \geq 2$ be an integer, W a world, and T a table with $PAttr[T] \neq \emptyset$. Then T is said to be k-anonymous in W if there exist (1) pairwise disjoint subsets $G_1, \ldots, G_l$ of the tuples in W, with $|G_j| \geq k$ for all j, and (2) a partition $T_1, \ldots, T_l$ of the tuples in T, such that for each j and each t in T_j $\bigcup_{t' \in Dec(t)} ReID_W(t') \supseteq G_j$.*

In the above definition, the $Dec()$ function is implicitly assumed as public knowledge, and $\bigcup$ is the set union that removes duplicates. Each subset G_j of individuals is called an *anonymity group*. Intuitively, the definition says that T is

k-anonymous in W if each tuple t in $\pi_{PAttr[T]}(T)$ re-identifies (through $Dec()$ and $ReID_W()$) at least all the individuals in one of the anonymity groups. In addition, we require that the anonymity groups be pairwise disjoint to provide a form of indistinguishability (cf. [15]). A discussion of safety of k-anonymity in W follows the example below.

As an example, assume the table in Figure 1(a) is the world W, in which the ID attribute is one that directly connects to actual individuals. Table T in Figure 1(b) is 2-anonymous in W since we can partition the tuples in T into T_1 and T_2, each with tuples having ZIP=20033 and 20034, respectively, and partition the tuples in W into $G_1 = \{Id1, Id3\}$ and $G_2 = \{Id2, Id4\}$. Now the tuples in T_j will re-identify all individuals in G_j for $j = 1, 2$. We note that the size of T_j is no greater than that of G_j, for $j = 1, 2$. For table T', the decoding function will map name J* to the set of all names that start with J. We partition the T' into T_1 and T_2, each with tuples have FirstName=J* and Jane, respectively. Hence $|T_1| = 2$ and $|T_2| = 1$. We also partition the world into $G_1 = \{Id1, Id2\}$ and $G_2 = \{Id3, Id4\}$. We can conclude that also T' is 2-anonymous in W. Note that neither T nor T' is considered k-anonymous according to the original definition of k-anonymity.

ID	FirstName	ZIP
Id1	John	20033
Id2	Jeanne	20034
Id3	Jane	20033
Id4	Jane	20034

ZIP	Disease
20033	D1
20033	D2
20034	D3

FirstName	Bonus
J*	$10K
J*	$100K
Jane	$20K

(a) The world W (b) A table T (c) Another table T'

Fig. 1. The world W and two published tables

3.3   Safety of k-Anonymity in W under Different Adversary Models

There are different adversary models that have been considered in the literature. The difference among them lies in the external knowledge the adversary may have and use to re-identify the individuals that the tuples in T correspond to.

Consider a first adversary having no external knowledge other than W and what we have assumed in our definitions. In particular, he does not know that any specific individual in the world is among the respondents in the table T, and doesn't know whether different tuples in T correspond to different respondents. This is the weakest form of adversary. The only way for this adversary to re-identify an individual is through the use of $Dec()$ and $ReID_W()$. By definition, if T is k-anonymous in W, for each j, at least k individuals in G_j can potentially be the respondents for each tuple in T_j, and the adversary has no way of excluding any individual in G_j from being a candidate respondent for any tuple in T_j. Therefore, the respondents in T are safe.

A more common adversary studied in the literature is the second one we consider who is the same as the first adversary, except that this second adversary knows that each different tuple in T corresponds to a different respondent. But still, he does not know any particular individual in the world who is among the respondents in T. In order to deal with this case, we need to add a constraint to the definition to require each T_j set is at most of the same size as G_j in order to avoid attacks by applying a form of "pigeon hole" principle (cf. [5]). Since this will be the adversary we will assume in this paper if not explictly mentioned otherwise, we repeat the definition k-anonymity in W with the constraint built in.

Definition 5. *Let $k \geq 2$ be an integer, W a world, and T a table with $PAttr[T] \neq \emptyset$. Then T is said to be k-anonymous in W against the second adversary if there exist (1) pairwise disjoint subsets G_1, ..., G_l of the tuples in W, with $|G_j| \geq k$ for all $j = 1, \ldots, l$, and (2) a partition T_1, ..., T_l of the tuples in T with $|T_j| \leq |G_j|$ for all $j = 1, \ldots, l$, such that for each j and each t in T_j, $\bigcup_{t' \in Dec(t)} ReID_W(t') \supseteq G_j$.*

Comparing with the safety against the first adversary, we note that a defense from the the second adversary is more challanging since some kind of "pigeon hole" principle can be exploited. More specifically, if G_j includes only k individuals, but the number of tuples in T_j is more than k, then some of the tuples in T_j must use individuals in other groups, and thus reduce the anonymity of tuples in other groups. For example, assume $T_1 = \{t_1, t_2, t_3\}$, $T_2 = \{t_4\}$, $G_1 = \{i_1, i_2\}$ and $G_2 = \{i_3, i_4\}$, and let the three tuples in T_1 all re-identify i_1, i_2 and i_3, while the tuple in T_2 re-identifies i_3 and i_4. By Definition 4, T is 2-anonymous in W. However, since the adversary knows that the four tuples t_1–t_4 correspond to four different individuals, he can deduce that t_4 must re-identify i_4 since i_3 has to be "used" by the tuples in T_1, a privacy leak. By Definition 5, T is not 2-anonymous in W. In fact, with Definition 5, the adversary cannot deny logically that each individual in G_j can be the respondent for each tuple in T_j. Therefore, with the addition of the constraints $|T_j| \leq |G_j|$, the definition of k-anonymity in W is safe against the second adversary.

A third adversary is assumed to know some particular individuals in the world W are respondents of tuples in table T, in addition to what the second adversary knows. In this case, we need to add a condition in the k-anonymity definition saying that the union of the G_j groups must contain these individuals.

A fourth adversary is even stronger than the third adversary by knowing exactly the subset of individuals in W that are the respondents of tuples in T (cf. [5]). In this case, we add a constraint to the k-anonymity definition such that the union of the G_j groups must be exactly the same set of individuals who are the respondents in T. Note that the fact that a table T is k-anonymous against the first adversary does not necessarily imply that T is k-anonymous against the second adversary, since the possible ways to form the groups G_j become fewer. The same can be said comparing the second and the third adversaries, as well as the third and the fourth.

In the sequel, we only consider the second adversary in our exposition if not explicitly mentioned otherwise, and we use Definition 5 for our k-anonymity in W. However, results should not change significantly regarding the other adversaries.

3.4 Practical Considerations

As observed in [12, 13], in practice it is very difficult to check k-anonymity on external sources, mainly due to the difficulty, if not impossibility, of knowing the closed world W that represents the complete knowledge of the external world. Indeed, it is not what we are proposing to do in this paper from an algorithmic point of view. Instead, we use this formal definition to clarify the role of quasi-identifiers, to give a precise semantics to k-anonymity, and to study the conservative nature of generalization algorithms reported in the literature.

On the other hand, from a practical point of view, it is possible that some global constraints exist on the world, and that they could be exploited by k-anonymization algorithms. For example, if we know from census data that the combination ⟨ZIP, Gender⟩ has always no less than 500 individuals, any table T_S with $PAttr[T_S] \subseteq \langle$ZIP, gender$\rangle$ is automatically k-anonymous for any $k \leq 500$. Further investigation of such a technique is beyond the scope of this paper.

4 Quasi-identifiers and k-Anonymity

In order to understand the relationship between the notion of QI and k-anonymity we formally define QI, or more precisely k-QI, where $k \geq 1$ is an integer. We then provide a sufficient and necessary condition for k-anonymity in W based on these notions. Intuitively, a set of attributes is a k-QI of a world W if a certain combination of values for these attributes can only be found in no more than k individuals of W, i.e., if that combination identifies a group of no more than k individuals.

Definition 6. *Given a world W and positive integer k, an attribute set $A \subseteq Attr[W]$ is said to be a k-QI of W if there exists a specific tuple t on A such that $0 \neq |ReID_W(t)| \leq k$.*

For example, in the relational world W in Figure 1(a), ZIP is a 2-QI, FirstName is a 1-QI, and ⟨FirstName, ZIP⟩ combination is a 1-QI.

Clearly, each set of attributes $A \subseteq Attr[W]$ is a k-QI for some k for a given finite world W.

Note that the notion of QI formalized in [13] and informally defined in other works is captured by our definition of 1-QI. Indeed, assume some values of QI uniquely identify individuals using external information. That is, if external information is represented by a world W, QI is any set of attributes $A \subseteq Attr[W]$ such that $|ReID_W(t)| = 1$ for at least one specific tuple t on A. It can be easily seen that this is equivalent to the notion of 1-QI of W.

Proposition 1. *If a set of attributes is a k-QI, then it is an s-QI for each $s \geq k$.*

Thus, we know that each 1-QI is a k-QI for $k \geq 1$. It is clear that the inverse does not hold, i.e., if $k \geq 2$ there exist k-QI that are not 1-QI. For example, ZIP in the world W of Figure 1(a) is a 2-QI, but not a 1-QI.

Definition 7. *A set A of attributes is said to be a proper k-QI if it is a k-QI but it is not an s-QI for any $s < k$.*

The following results directly from the supertuple inclusion property of the worlds:

Proposition 2. *If a set A of attributes is a k-QI, then any $A' \supseteq A$ is a k-QI.*

Note that the special case of Proposition 2 for 1-QI has been independently proved in [7].

The following sufficient condition for k-anonymity says that if the full set of attributes appearing in external sources is a proper s-QI, then the table is k-anonymous for each $k \leq s$.

Theorem 1. *A table T is k-anonymous in a world W if $PAttr[T]$ is a proper s-QI in W with $k \leq s$.*

The above theorem holds because by definition, an attribute set $A \subseteq PAttr[W]$ is a proper k-QI if for each specific tuple t on A either $|ReID_W(t)| = 0$ or $|ReID_W(t)| \geq k$. Hence, if $PAttr[W]$ is a proper s-QI we know that for each specific tuple t on $PAttr[W]$, we have either $|ReID_W(t)| = 0$ or $|ReID_W(t)| \geq s$. As we have always assumed that W is consistent with T, we know $|ReID_W(t)| \geq s$. For k-anonymity, it is enough that we have $s \geq k$. Note we can form the pairwise-disjoint groups G_j required in our k-anonymity definition by picking (arbitrarily) one of the tuples t' in $Dec(t)$ for each $t \in T$, and use $ReID_W(t')$ as such a group. Due to value uniqueness, we know that each obtained group is either equal to one previously obtained or disjoint from all the others. The tuples in T can be partitioned as follows: if t'_1 and t'_2 have been picked for t_1 and t_2, respectively, and they both re-identify the same group G_j (i.e., $t'_1 = t'_2$), then t_1 and t_2 belong to the same T_j in the partition of T. By Definition 4, T is k-anonymous in W. If we consider the second adversary, i.e., for Definition 5, then in the above process, we will need to use a tuple t' in $Dec(t)$ that yields a largest $ReID_W(t')$ in terms of size among all the tuples in $Dec(t)$. In this case, since we assume a different tuple in T must correspond to a different person, it is easy to verify that the size of T_j as constructed this way is indeed at most as that of G_j.

By the above theorem, if the general constraints on the external world ensure that $PAttr[T]$ is an s-QI with $s > k$, then there is no need to anonymize table T if k-anonymity in W is the goal.

Now we can state the relationship between the k-anonymity in W notion and the k-QI notion.

Theorem 2. *A table T is k-anonymous in a world W if and only if $\pi_A(T)$ is k-anonymous in W for each k-QI A of W, with $A \subseteq PAttr[T]$.*

From the results of this section, we may have the following observations and conclusions. Given a table T, if any subset A of $PAttr[T]$ is a k-QI, then $PAttr[T]$ itself is k-QI. Hence, we need to make sure that the values on $PAttr[T]$, not just a proper subset of $PAttr[T]$, are general enough to gain k-anonymity. On the other hand, if we have values on $PAttr[T]$ general enough to have k-anonymity, then the values of any proper subset of $PAttr[T]$ will also be general enough due to the supertuple inclusion property. Therefore, for k-anonymization, we should only be concerned with the attribute set $PAttr[T]$, not any proper subset of it. In the next section, we show, in fact, that limiting the consideration to any or all proper subsets of $PAttr[T]$ will lead to privacy leaking.

5   Incorrect Uses of QI in k-Anonymization

As mentioned in the introduction, k-anonymity in a published table can be obtained by generalizing the values of QI in the table. This process is called k-anonymization. As mentioned also in the introduction, at least four different uses of QI in k-anonymization have appeared in the literature. In this section, we point out the incorrectness of cases (2)–(4). We defer the study of case (1) to Section 6.

5.1   Use 1-QI only

Firstly, we note that the use of 1-QI (e.g., the QI as defined in [13] and [8]) instead of k-QI in the definition of k-anonymity can lead to incorrect results. Indeed, accordingly to the current anonymization techniques, if an attribute is not in any QI, then the attribute is not considered for k-anonymity or k-anonymization (see Def. 2.2 in [8]).

However, if QI is interpreted as 1-QI, as done in [8, 13], a released table may be incorrectly considered as k-anonymous.

Consider the table T in Figure 1(b) for 3-anonymity. The public attribute of T is ZIP only, which is *not* a 1-QI. If we only consider 1-QI for table T, then we may incorrectly conclude that the table does not need any generalization (on ZIP values) in order to protect privacy. However, we know T is not 3-anonymous (but is 2-anonymous) against W in the same figure. In order to achieve 3-anonymity, we will need to generalize the ZIP values in T.

Therefore, the k-anonymity requirements based only on 1-QI fail to protect the anonymity of data when $k \geq 2$. We can correct this problem by considering all k-QIs, not just 1-QIs.

5.2   Use a Subset of $PAttr[T]$

The public attributes of a table is given by $PAttr[T]$. A few papers seem to imply that only a subset of $PAttr[T]$ needs to be considered. For example, [6, 7] define QI as the *minimum* subset of $PAttr[T]$ that can be used to identify individuals, and [14] proposes to generalize all such minimum QIs. Even if we take QI as k-QI, the use of the minimum subset is incorrect. We have the following important result.

Theorem 3. *Given an arbitrary T, an integer $k \geq 2$, and a world W, the fact that $\pi_B(T)$ is k-anonymous in W for each proper subset B of $PAttr[T]$ does not imply that T is k-anonymous in W.*

ID	Name	ZIP
Id1	John	20033
Id2	Jeanne	20034
Id3	Jane	20033
Id4	Jane	20034

ID	ZIP	Disease
Id1	20033	D1
Id2	20034	D2
Id3	20033	D3
Id4	20034	D4

ID	ZIP	Disease
[Id1–Id2]	20033	D1
[Id1–Id2]	20034	D2
[Id3–Id4]	20033	D3
[Id3–Id4]	20034	D4

(a) The world W (b) Original table T (c) T' with generalized ID

Fig. 2. Example without proper generalization

By Theorem 3, we understand that we cannot simply apply generalization techniques on a proper subset of attributes of $PAttr[T]$. As an example, consider table T and its generalized version T' in Figure 2. Attribute ID is a 1-QI, while ZIP is not a 1-QI (however the combination of ID and ZIP is). To generalize the minimum 1-QI, we would probably generalize table T to T' to make sure there are two appearance for each (generalized) ID value. However, it is clear that T' does not provide 2-anonymity in the world W given in the same figure.

6   Conservativeness of Previous Approaches

In practical scenarios, we do not know exactly what the world W is. In such scenarios, we may want to define k-anonymity referring to all "possible" worlds, to guarantee "conservative" k-anonymity. Indeed, this is the view taken by [12] and other researchers. In this subsection, we provide a formal correctness proof of the standard k-anonymity notion by showing it is more "conservative" than k-anonymity in W defined in this paper. (Here, "conservative" means "we would rather err on overprotection".)

The standard k-anonymity is defined as follows. Given a relational table T, assume each tuple contains information about a single, different individual. And assume that the public attributes that can be used to identify the individuals in T are $PAttr[T]$. Then T is *standard k-anonymous* if for each tuple t in T, the value $t[PAttr[T]]$ appears in at least k tuples in T. (Note that in the literature, the attributes $PAttr[T]$ above is replaced with the "QI attributes", which would be a mistake if "QI attributes" do not mean $PAttr[T]$ as shown in the previous section.)

In contrast to the definition of k-anonymity in W (Definition 5), in standard k-anonymity, no external world is mentioned. We shall show below that, in fact, the standard k-anonymity is rather "conservative" from two perspectives.

The first is that the standard k-anonymity is equivalent to k-anonymity in W with the following assumptions: Given a table T that is a generalization of T' (consisting of specific tuples) such that T is standard k-anonymous, assume $W = (\pi_{PAttr[T]}(T'), Id)$ is the world, where Id is the identity function, and each individual in the world is a respondent in T (i.e., the fourth adversary). Now we can see that T is k-anonymous in W with the additional constraint that the union of G_j groups is exactly the same as all the individuals in this world

W. Indeed, in this case, a group G_j can be formed by the tuples in the world W corresponding to the set of tuples T_j that have the same $PAttr[T]$ attribute values. Now $|G_j| = |T_j|$, and each tuple in T_j will re-identify each individual in G_j, and the union of the individuals in all G_j is exactly the individuals in W. Since standard k-anonymity requires that each $PAttr[T]$ value in T appears at least k times, then $|G_j| \geq k$. It is also clear that G_j are pairwise disjoint.

Another view of the standard k-anonymity is through the perspective of all "possible" worlds. As we observe in standard k-anonymity, there is an additional assumption that each tuple of T is for a different individual. That is, the second adversary is assumed. Therefore, the requirement of a consistent world for such a table need to be upgraded. Earlier, we only needed a consistent world to be able to re-identify each tuple in $\pi_{PAttr[T]}(T)$ with at least one individual. Here, since each tuple of T is assumed to be for a different individual, a consistent world must be able to re-identify each tuple in $\pi_{PAttr[T]}(T)$ with a different individual.

Definition 8. *A world W is said to be* individualized consistent *with a table T with n tuples if there exist n individuals $i_1, \ldots, i_n$ such that there exists $T' = t'_1, \ldots, t'_n$ in $Dec(T)$ satisfying the condition that i_j is in $ReID_W(\pi_{PAttr[T]}(t'_j))$ for each $j = 1, \ldots, n$.*

Intuitively, this means that T could be generalized from a table T' such that each tuple may be used to re-identify a different individual by W.

The fact that a world W is individualized consistent with a table T basically confirms the assumption that each tuple of T can indeed re-identify a different individual. All other worlds are going to be "impossible" for table T since the assumption that a different tuple T is for a different individual cannot hold with such worlds. We can now capture the notion of conservative anonymity for such tables.

Definition 9. *A table T is said to be* conservatively k-anonymous *if it is k-anonymous in each W that is individualized consistent with T.*

We use the term "conservative" also to indicate the fact that we do not use any knowledge of the world, even if we have any, when k-anonymity is considered.

We are now ready to state that the standard k-anonymity is correct, if $PAttr[T]$ is taken as QI for a given table T.

Theorem 4. *Let T be a table such that there exists a world that is individualized consistent with T. Then T is conservatively k-anonymous if for each tuple t in T, there exist at least $k-1$ other tuples $t_1, \ldots, t_{k-1}$ in T such that $t_i[PAttr[T]] = t[PAttr[T]]$ for $i = 1, \ldots, k-1$.*

Theorem 4 shows that in general, if $PAttr[T]$ is taken as the QI, the standard k-anonymization appeared in the literature is sufficient under the assumption that we have no knowledge of the world.

The inverse of Theorem 4 does not hold. Indeed, consider T' in Figure 1(c). If the $Dec()$ function is such that $Dec(J*) = \{Jane\}$ and $Dec(Jane) = \{Jane\}$, then it is clear that T' is 3-anonymous in all the worlds that are individualized consistent with T' because in any of these worlds, there must be at least 3 individuals with the first name Jane. However, in T' we do not have three tuples with the same First name attribute values.

The above example may be dismissed as using a strange decoding function. However, for any $Dec()$, we can always construct a table T such that the inverse of Theorem 4 does not hold. Formally,

Theorem 5. *For any decoding function, the inverse of Theorem 4 does not hold.*

In Theorem 3, we showed that k-anonymization of any or all proper subsets of $PAttr[T]$ is no guarantee in obtaining k-anonymity from T. We may extend the result to the conservative case.

Theorem 6. *Given an arbitrary T and integer $k \geq 2$, the fact that $\pi_B(T)$ is conservatively k-anonymous for each proper subset B of $PAttr[T]$ does not imply that T is conservatively k-anonymous.*

As a final remark of this section, we note that if we do have some knowledge about the world and the $Dec()$ function, we can in some cases do better than this conservative approach. For example, for table T' in Figure 1(c), if we know that $Dec(J*)$ includes Jane, and there are at least 3 Jane's in the world, then T' is 3-anonymous for T'. Without such assumptions, we will have to generalize Jane to J* in order to achieve 3-anonymity. The investigation of how to take advantage of such knowledge in anonymization is beyond the scope of this paper.

7   Discussion and Conclusion

In summary, we have formally analyzed the notion of quasi-identifier as it is essential to understand the semantics of k-anonymity. We have shown that improper formal definitions of QI as well as misinterpreted informal definitions, may lead to respondent re-identification, and hence to privacy violations. We have also formally proved the correctness of using all attributes that appear in external data sources as QI, and point out precisely what conservative assumptions are made along the way.

We have provided a new formal framework for k-anonymity that, by clarifying the role of quasi-identifiers, allows the designers of anonymization techniques to prove the formal properties of their solutions. The presented framework can also serve as the basis for generalization methods with more relaxed, or different assumptions. Indeed, the new notion of k-anonymity in W enables improvements when assumptions can be made on the external information sources. Even if global constraints can only be specified on the set of possible "worlds", in some cases, our results can lead to more specific, hence more useful, released data while providing the same privacy guarantee as the standard k-anonymity.

References

1. Bayardo Jr., R.J., Agrawal, R.: Data privacy through optimal k-anonymization. In: Proceedings of the 21st International Conference on Data Engineering, pp. 217–228. IEEE Computer Society Press, Los Alamitos (2005)
2. Claudio Bettini, X., Wang, S., Jajodia, S.: The role of quasi-identifiers in k-anonymity revisited. ACM Computing Research Repository (CoRR) (November 2006) arXiv:cs/0611035v1
3. Chaum, D.: The dining cryptographers problem: Unconditional sender and recipient untraceability. J. Cryptology 1(1), 65–75 (1988)
4. Dalenius, T.: Finding a needle in a haystack - or identifying anonymous census record. Journal of Official Statistics 2(3), 329–336 (1986)
5. Gionis, A., Mazza, A., Tassa, T.: k-anonymization revisited. In: ICDE, pp. 744–753. IEEE, Los Alamitos (2008)
6. LeFevre, K., DeWitt, D., Ramakrishnan, R.: Workload-aware anonymization. In: ACM SIGKDD International Conference on Knowledge Discovery and Data Mining (2006)
7. LeFevre, K., DeWitt, D.J., Ramakrishnan, R.: Incognito: efficient full-domain k-anonymity. In: SIGMOD 2005: Proceedings of the 2005 ACM SIGMOD international conference on Management of data, pp. 49–60. ACM Press, New York (2005)
8. Machanavajjhala, A., Gehrke, J., Kifer, D., Venkitasubramaniam, M.: l-Diversity: Privacy beyond k-anonymity. In: ICDE (2006)
9. Meyerson, A., Williams, R.: On the complexity of optimal k-anonymity. In: Proceedings of the Twenty-third ACM Symposium on Principles of Database Systems, pp. 223–228. ACM Press, New York (2004)
10. Mumick, I.S., Pirahesh, H., Ramakrishnan, R.: The magic of duplicates and aggregates. In: VLDB (1990)
11. Pfitzmann, A., Köhntopp, M.: Anonymity, unobservability, and pseudonymity - a proposal for terminology. In: Federrath, H. (ed.) Designing Privacy Enhancing Technologies. LNCS, vol. 2009, pp. 1–9. Springer, Heidelberg (2001)
12. Samarati, P.: Protecting respondents' identities in microdata release. IEEE Trans. Knowl. Data Eng. 13(6), 1010–1027 (2001)
13. Sweeney, L.: k-anonymity: a model for protecting privacy. International Journal on Uncertainty, Fuzziness in Knowledge-based Systems 10(5), 557–570 (2002)
14. Wang, K., Fung, B.C.M., Yu, P.S.: Handicapping attacker's confidence: An alternative to k-anonymization. Knowledge and Information Systems: An International Journal 11(3), 345–368 (2007)
15. Yao, C., Wang, L., Wang, X.S., Jajodia, S.: Indistinguishability: The other aspect of privacy. Secure Data Management, 1–17 (2006)

Simulatable Binding: Beyond Simulatable Auditing

Lei Zhang, Sushil Jajodia, and Alexander Brodsky

Center for Secure Information Systems
George Mason University, Fairfax, VA, U.S.A.

Abstract. A fundamental problem in *online query auditing* is that an outside attacker may compromise database privacy by exploiting the sequence of query responses and the information flow from the database state to the auditing decision. Kenthapadi et al. [14] proposed the *simulatable auditing* model to solve this problem in a way that completely blocks the aforementioned information flow. However, the security does not come for free. The simulatable auditing model actually suffers from unnecessary data utility loss.

We assert that in order to guarantee database privacy, blocking the information flow from the true database state to the auditing decision is sufficient but far from necessary. To limit the loss in data utility, we suggest an alternative approach that controls, instead of blocks, such information flow. To this end, we introduce a new model, called *simulatable binding*, in which the information flow from the true database state to the auditing decision is provably controlled by a selected *safe binding*. We prove that the proposed simulatable binding model provides a sufficient and necessary condition to guarantee database privacy, and therefore, algorithms based on our model will provide better data utility than algorithms based on the simulatable auditing model. To demonstrate the strength and practicality of our model, we provide two efficient algorithms for the max query and sum query auditing, respectively. For the ease of comparison, each algorithm is built by applying our simulatable binding model, and is compared to an algorithm applying the simulatable auditing model. Clear improvements are shown through experiments.

1 Introduction

Let $X = \{X_1, X_2, \ldots, X_n\}$ be a statistical database consisting of n variables. Generally, X_i are all real numbers. We use the vector $x = (x_1, x_2, \ldots, x_n)$, where $x_i \in R (1 \leq i \leq n)$, to denote a database state. All queries over X take the form $q : R^n \to R$.

The following problem is known as the *online query auditing problem* ([10,19,5]): Suppose that a set of queries $q_1, q_2, \ldots, q_{T-1}$ has already been posed and the corresponding answers $a_1, a_2, \ldots, a_{T-1}$ have been given, where each answer $a_i, 1 \leq i < T$, is either the true answer to the query or "denied". Given a new query q_T, the database should give the true answer if the privacy of the database is not breached (i.e., an x_i cannot be determined); otherwise, it should give "denied" as the answer.

W. Jonker and M. Petković (Eds.): SDM 2008, LNCS 5159, pp. 16–31, 2008.
© Springer-Verlag Berlin Heidelberg 2008

1.1 The Failure of a Simple Strategy

A simple strategy, denoted as A_{simple}, is to deny q_T if database privacy may be breached when true answer of q_T is given, and provide the true answer otherwise. Surprisingly, as observed recently by Kenthapadi, Mishra, and Nissim [14], the privacy of the database could still be breached if A_{simple} is applied.

To see this, consider the following example: we have a database consisting of four variables $x = (x_1, x_2, x_3, x_4)$, all of which are integers. Suppose that the first query $q_1 : max(x_1, x_2)$ has been posed and the true answer, say $a_1 = 5$, has been given. Suppose the next query is $q_2 : max(x_2, x_3, x_4)$. Based on the strategy A_{simple}, if the true answer happens to be $a_2 \geq 5$, then the database will return the true answer a_2 for q_2 because the database privacy will not be breached. On the other hand, if the true answer is $a_2 < 5$, the database will deny q_2 because by giving a_2, database will disclose the the true value of x_1.

Unfortunately, this is not enough to protect the database privacy. The problem is that if q_2 gets "denied", an outside attacker can still determine that $x_1 = 5$. This is because the only reason for the denial of q_2 under such condition is that $a_2 < 5$, which leads to the fact that $x_1 = 5$.

1.2 The Idea of Simulatable Auditing

Intuitively, the reason that the simple strategy A_{simple} fails is that it does not take into consideration the information flow from the true database state to the auditing decision. The *simulatable auditing* model proposed by Kenthapadi, Mishra, and Nissim [14] guarantees that the decision making process does not leak any information. This is because whether to answer a newly posed query is decided based on knowledge that an attacker has already acquired, including all posed queries and all given answers.

In general, the strategy of a *Simulatable Auditor*, denoted as A_{sa}, can be stated as the following: Given a set $\mathcal{X}$ of all possible database states that are consistent with previously posed queries $(q_1, q_2, \ldots, q_{T-1})$ and their answers $(a_1, a_2, \ldots, a_{T-1})$, a newly posed query q_T will be denied if:

$\exists x' \in \mathcal{X}$, the privacy of x' will be breached if the true answer a_T of $q_T(x')$ is given.

If we apply A_{sa} to the example shown in Figure 1, q_2 will always be denied no matter what possible answer a_2 is.

1.3 Unnecessary Loss of Utility in Simulatable Auditing

Although strategy A_{sa} prevents the information flow from the true database state to the decision making process during auditing, it does so at a large cost

$$x = (x_1,\ x_2,\ x_3,\ x_4)$$
$$q_1: max(x_1,\ x_2) \qquad\qquad = 5$$
$$q_2: max \qquad (x_2,\ x_3,\ x_4) \quad = ?$$

Fig. 1. Answering Two Max Queries

of data utility, much of which is unnecessary. In the example shown in Figure 1, in order to protect the data privacy, A_{sa} will always deny q_2. Later we will show that we should be able to do much better than this.

The situation gets much worse when the simulatable auditing model is applied to sum queries. When there exist some database constraints, which happens in most cases, A_{sa} could become a strategy that will refuse all queries [14]. For example, in a database $x = (x_1, x_2, \ldots, x_n) \in R^n$, if we have the database constraints $x_i \geq 0, (1 \leq i \leq n)$, for any sum query $q : \sum_{i=0}^{n} b_i x_i, (b_i \in \{0, 1\})$, we will give a "denied" answer based on A_{sa} because there always exists a possible database state $x' = (0, 0, \ldots, 0)$ that if the true answer $a = q(x')$ is given, some x_i will be disclosed.

The problem of information disclosure can be regarded as an optimization problem, i.e., to maximize the data utility of the disclosed data under the constraint that data privacy must be guaranteed. This key observation leads to the problem of finding the sufficient and necessary condition to guarantee database privacy, which is the main focus of our paper.

Indeed, the model of simulatable auditing model only provides a sufficient condition that is far from necessary. Such a sufficient condition may lead to significant and unnecessary data utility loss, as discussed above. We will show that, by applying the technique proposed in this paper, such unnecessary utility loss can be completely avoided.

1.4   Contribution and Organization

In this paper, we propose a new model called *simulatable binding*. The intuition is to find a set of database states and bind them together when "denied" is the answer to a posed query, under the condition that the binding set is "large" enough to protect the privacy of its elements.

To illustrate, consider the example shown in Figure 1 we have discussed. The strategy A_{simple} fails to guarantee the database privacy because the denial of q_2 will leads to the fact that $a_1 = 5$. The strategy A_{sa} of the simulatable auditing model deny q_2 unconditionally to protect the privacy of all possible database states. However, what we can do is to deny q_2 not only when the true answer of q_2 satisfies $a_2 < 5$, but also when $a_2 = 5$. Therefore, an outside attacker cannot determine any of the $\{x_1, x_2, x_3, x_4\}$ if he gets "denied" when posing query q_2.

The result of such a strategy, denoted as A_{sb}, is shown in the following table with comparisons:

a_2	A_{simple}	A_{sa}	A_{sb}
$a_2 < 5$	Deny	Deny	Deny
$a_2 = 5$	Answer	Deny	Deny
$a_2 > 5$	Answer	Deny	Answer
Privacy Guarantee?	No	Yes	Yes

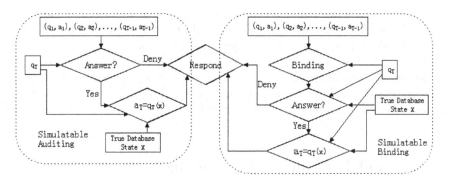

Fig. 2. Comparison of Simulatable Binding and Simulatable Auditing Frameworks

Both A_{sa} and A_{sb} guarantee privacy. However, A_{sb} is able to answer the query q_2 in more cases than A_{sa} does. Note that although a binding set can protect the privacy of its element database states, the decision process for determining such a set may contain additional information about the true database state.

Therefore we need to make sure this binding decision is made based on the knowledge that is already known to the outside attacker, leading to the name of *simulatable binding*. Conceptually, the framework of our simulatable binding model compared to the simulatable auditing model is shown in Figure 2. We emphasize that the fundamental differences between our model and the simulatable auditing model are as follows:

- Under the simulatable auditing model, a decision to whether answer a newly posed query is made solely based on the knowledge that has already been disclosed.
- Under our simulatable binding model, selection of a safe binding for a newly posed query is made solely based on the knowledge that has already been disclosed; however, the decision to whether answer the newly posed query is based on not only the disclosed knowledge and the safe binding, but the secret and true database state also.

It is clear that our model provides a more relaxed condition for answering queries. However, we will prove that, the condition provided by our simulatable binding model is not only sufficient but also necessary to guarantee database privacy in the online auditing problem. As a consequence, we prove that the algorithms applying the simulatable binding model always provide better utility than algorithms applying the simulatable auditing model. It is worth noting that our model is independent of the concerned privacy property, i.e., any privacy property can be applied to our model, which makes our model widely applicable.

In order to show the practicality and efficiency of our model, we present two algorithms for max query online auditing and sum query online auditing, respectively. Each of those algorithms is built in a way that is comparable to an algorithm applying the simulatable auditing model considering the same privacy property. We conduct experiments to show the improved data utility of our model over the simulatable auditing model.

The remainder of this paper is organized as follows. In section 2, we introduce the *simulatable binding* model along with an illustrative graphical example, and provide the aforementioned proofs. In section 3, we discuss two particular online auditing problems for max query and sum query, respectively, and construct a simulatable binding algorithm for each of the problems. Experimental results of the proposed algorithms are provided to demonstrate the performance in section 4. We discuss the related work in section 5 and conclude the paper in section 6.

2   The Model of Simulatable Binding

To build intuition, we introduce the *simulatable binding* model through the following simple graphical example:

- Consider a database state as a point and the current knowledge of an outside attacker as a set of points $\mathcal{X}$. Intuitively, $\mathcal{X}$ contains exactly all database states that are possible from the point of view of an outside attacker.
- We state the database privacy requirement as that an outside attacker cannot determine any point in $\mathcal{X}$ to be the true database state. Therefore, a set of possible database states $\mathcal{X}'$ is safe if $|\mathcal{X}'| > 1$. We assume that $\mathcal{X}$ is safe at the beginning, which means that $|\mathcal{X}| > 1$.
- A newly posed query q over the database is a partition of $\mathcal{X}$, $q = \{s_1, s_2, \ldots, s_n\}$. The true answer to q is s_i, $1 \le i \le n$ such that $x \in s_i$. The database auditor has to decide whether to give the true answer for q, or to deny it.

Note that, in this toy example, we consider a very naive privacy requirement. In the general problem setting, the privacy property can regarded as a predicate p and we say a set of possible database states $\mathcal{X}$ is safe if $p(\mathcal{X}) = true$.

As an example, let $\mathcal{X} = \{b_1, b_2, \ldots, b_6\}$. Figure 3(A) shows a potential query $q_1 = \{\{b_1, b_2, b_6\}, \{b_3, b_4, b_5\}\}$. In (B) $q_2 = \{\{b_1, b_4\}, \{b_2, b_3\}, \{b_5, b_6\}\}$ denotes another potential query.

If we follow the traditional simple strategy for online auditing problem, we will give the true answer for a newly posed query q if the size of the true answer, being a set, is safe. In this case, the simple strategy can be stated as:

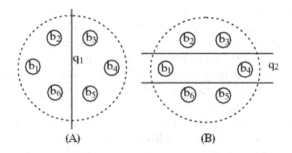

(A)   (B)

Fig. 3. Queries as Partitions

A_{simple}: Given $\mathcal{X}$, x and a newly posed query q, let a denote the true answer for q: (1) a "denied" answer is given if the set $\mathcal{X} \cap a$ is not safe; (2) a is given otherwise.

In this example, the safety of a set means its size is larger than 1. Clearly, in both cases (A) and (B), if the true answer of the newly posed query is given, an outside attacker still cannot determine the true database state. Thus, we will give the true answer for q_1 and q_2 in the two cases, respectively.

The database privacy will certainly be guaranteed in any case where A_{simple} returns the true answer for the newly posed query. In fact, all algorithms we discuss in this paper will meet this requirement.

However, the safety of a strategy requires guaranteeing privacy not only when the true answer is given, but also when "denied" is given. Let $\eta_{(A,\mathcal{X},q)}$ denote the subset of possible database states in $\mathcal{X}$ where q will be denied by a strategy A. We have the following definition.

Definition 1 (deny-safe). *A strategy A is said to be* deny-safe *if:*
$$\forall \mathcal{X}, \forall q, |\mathcal{X}| > 1 \Rightarrow \eta_{(A,\mathcal{X},q)} = \phi \vee \eta_{(A,\mathcal{X},q)} \text{ is safe}$$

Unfortunately, A_{simple} is not a *deny-safe* strategy. Figure 4 shows a situation, where $|\eta_{(A_{simple},\mathcal{X},q_3)}| = 1$. In this case, if the newly posed query q_3 is denied, an outside attacker would determine the true database state to be b_1.

Now we consider the strategy of the simulatable auditing model:

A_{sa}: Given $\mathcal{X}$, x and a newly posed query q: (1) a "denied" answer is given if $\exists s \in q, \mathcal{X} \cap s$ is not safe; (2) the true answer of q is given otherwise.

It is clear that, in the situation in Figure 4, q_3 will always be denied no matter which point represents the true database state.

Theorem 1. *A_{sa} is* deny-safe.

This is an obvious result because the definition of A_{sa} naturally implies that $\eta_{(A,\mathcal{X},q)} = \phi$ or $\eta_{(A,\mathcal{X},q)} = \mathcal{X}$, where $\mathcal{X}$ is safe as assumed. But A_{sa} denies more queries than what is necessary. Instead, a better way is described as follows.

- We select another query (partition) $q' = \{\{b_1, b_6\}, \{b_2, b_3\}, \{b_4, b_5\}\}$ on $\mathcal{X}$;
- Let a and a' denote the true answer for q_3 and q', respectively. We will deny q_3 not only if "a *is not safe*" but also if "$a' \cap \eta_{(A_{simple},\mathcal{X},q_3)} \neq \phi$"

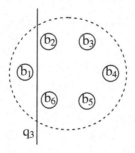

Fig. 4. A Query that A_{simple} Cannot Answer Safely

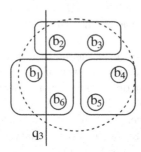

Fig. 5. A Safe Binding for Query q_3

As illustrated in Figure 5, by applying the above strategy, if q_3 gets denied, an outside attacker still cannot determine whether b_1 or b_6 is the true database state. This illustrates the idea of a binding strategy. And the safety of such a strategy depends on the selected query q'.

Definition 2 (safe binding). *Given a set $\mathcal{X}$ and a query q, a safe binding q' is a partition of $\mathcal{X}$ such that:*

(1) $\forall s' \in q'$, s' is safe, and
(2) $\forall s \in q$, if s is safe, then $s \setminus s^*$ is either ϕ or a safe set, where $s^* = \bigcup_{s' \in q', s' \cap \eta_{(A_{simple}, \mathcal{X}, q)} \neq \phi} s'$.

A binding strategy can be stated as follows:

A_b: Given $\mathcal{X}$, x, a safe binding q', and a newly posed query q, let a' denotes the true answer for q':
(1) a "denied" answer is given for q if $a' \cap \eta_{(A_{simple}, \mathcal{X}, q)} \neq \phi$
(2) the true answer for q is given otherwise.

Note that a safe binding q' protects the privacy of the true database state because $\eta_{(A_b, \mathcal{X}, q)}$ is determined by "safe" elements of q'. However, in order to prevent inference about the true database state, we still need to be aware of the potential information flow from the true database state to the selection of q'.

Definition 3 (simulatable binding). *A binding strategy is said to be simulatable, if the safe binding is selected based on $\mathcal{X}$ and the newly posed query.*

Theorem 2. *If the desired safety property satisfies:*

$$\forall \mathcal{X}' \subseteq \mathcal{X}'', \mathcal{X}' \text{ is safe} \Rightarrow \mathcal{X}'' \text{ is safe}$$

A simulatable binding, denoted as A_{sb}, is deny-safe.

Proof: For any set $\mathcal{X}$, any query q, let q' denote the safe binding of A_{sb}. Suppose that $\eta_{(A_{sb}, \mathcal{X}, q)} \neq \phi$. Then there exists a possible database state $b \in \mathcal{X}$ such that $b \in \eta_{(A_{sb}, \mathcal{X}, q)}$. Based on the definition of a binding strategy, there exists $s \in q'$ such that $b \in s \wedge s \subseteq \eta_{(A_{sb}, \mathcal{X}, q)}$. Because q' is a safe binding, we have that s is safe. Therefore $\eta_{(A_{sb}, \mathcal{X}, q)}$ is safe.
We slightly extend this as follows:

Definition 4 (ultimate simulatable binding). *A simulatable binding is said to be* ultimate *if any selected safe binding q' based on $\mathcal{X}$ and q satisfies:*

$$\exists s \in q', \eta_{(A_{simple}, \mathcal{X}, q)} \subsetneq s$$

The following theorem is straightforward:

Theorem 3. *An* ultimate simulatable binding, *denoted as A_{usb}, is* deny-safe.

Until now, we have proven that both A_{sa} and A_{sb} are *deny-safe*. Also, they are both safe in the case when true answer are given for a posed query. For A_{sb}, this is guaranteed by the condition (2) in the definition of a "safe binding".

However, the data utility provided by these two models is quite different. Next, we prove that any A_{sb} provides more data utility than A_{sa} by means of the following theorem.

Theorem 4. *Given $\mathcal{X}$ and a query q:$\eta_{(A_{sb}, \mathcal{X}, q)} \subseteq \eta_{(A_{sa}, \mathcal{X}, q)}$*

Proof: Because $\eta_{(A_{sa}, \mathcal{X}, q)}$ is either an empty set or the set $\mathcal{X}$ itself, it is sufficient to prove that $\eta_{(A_{sa}, \mathcal{X}, q)} = \phi \Rightarrow \eta_{(A_{sb}, \mathcal{X}, q)} = \phi$. This is a natural implication by the definition of A_{sa}. Because if $\eta_{(A_{sa}, \mathcal{X}, q)} = \phi$, there will be no $b \in \mathcal{X}$ for which A_{simple} will output "denied". Thus the condition for A_{sb} to deny q will never be satisfied. Thus we will have $\eta_{(A_{sb}, \mathcal{X}, q)} = \phi$.

In the example shown in Figure 5, A_{sa} will deny to answer q_3 no matter what the true database state is and A_{sb} will deny to answer q_3 only if the true database state $x = b_1$ or $x = b_6$. Furthermore, we can prove that:

Theorem 5. *Given any strategy A, $\mathcal{X}$, and a newly posed query q, if for any $x \in \mathcal{X}$, to disclose the answer for q based on A does not violate the safety of the database, then:*

(1) there exists a safe binding q', such that A is identical to a binding strategy A_b based on q' with respect to the knowledge that any outside attacker could obtain, and

(2) q' is independent of the true database state.

Proof: To prove (1), we construct q' as the follows:

- Let $s_1 = \eta_{(A, \mathcal{X}, q)}$ and $s_1 \in q'$;
- Let $s^* = \mathcal{X} \setminus s_1$;
- While $s^* \neq \phi$:
  - Select $x \in \mathcal{X} \setminus s_1$, let s_x be the set of all possible database states that an outside attacker could obtain after the true answer for query q based on A is given, and $s_x \in q'$;
  - Let $s^* = s^* \setminus s_x$;

Because A is safe, it is clear that q' is a safe binding and (1) is true. (2) is also clear because the following condition must be satisfied when considering an attacker's knowledge: $\forall x, x' \in \mathcal{X}, x' \in s_x \Leftrightarrow x \in s_{x'}$

With Theorem 5, we have shown that the simulatable binding model provides not only a sufficient, but also a necessary condition to guarantee the database privacy for the online auditing problem.

However, we can see that, the process of selecting a safe binding is only required to be simulatable, which means that the safe binding that can be selected is not unique. Therefore, the performance of a simulatable binding can be influenced by the way that a safe binding is "simulatably" selected. The problem is that "what is the best safe binding given $\mathcal{X}$ and q" can not be uniformly defined. Because a "safe binding" naturally creates a dependency between different possible database states within the set $\mathcal{X}$, such preference in dependency really depends on the real-time application and the users' requirements.

Generally, there are two different ways to select a "safe binding" in a simulatable binding with respect to the treatment to the set $\eta_{(A_{simple}, \mathcal{X}, q)}$:

- Bind the entire set $\eta_{(A_{simple}, \mathcal{X}, q)}$ together with other selected possible database states in $\mathcal{X} \setminus \eta_{(A_{simple}, \mathcal{X}, q)}$.
- Bind the elements in the set $\eta_{(A_{simple}, \mathcal{X}, q)}$ separately with different selected possible database state in $\mathcal{X} \setminus \eta_{(A_{simple}, \mathcal{X}, q)}$.

The first way represents the preference that tries to remain the data utility that can be safely provided by the simple strategy A_{simple} for the elements in the set $\mathcal{X} \setminus \eta_{(A_{simple}, \mathcal{X}, q)}$. The second way represents the preference that tries to obtain a more balanced result, i.e., to provide better utility for the possible database states in the original none-guaranteed set $\eta_{(A_{simple}, \mathcal{X}, q)}$ than the first way, by sacrificing a little more data utility for other possible database states.

In next section, we discuss applications of these two different ways in two particular online auditing problems.

3   Two Practical Algorithms

In this section, we provide algorithms based on the *simulatable binding* model for the problems of auditing max query and auditing sum query, respectively. Note that, when considering a practical problem, two changes are noticeable: 1) the set $\mathcal{X}$ is no longer a static set, but defined by all the previously posed queries and their answers; 2) the privacy property may be quite different and involved in different applications. In fact, we consider two different privacy properties for the two cases.

3.1   A Simulatable Binding Algorithm for Max Query Auditing

We consider the following online auditing problem of max query. This is the same problem setting used in [14].

1. The database consists of n variables, all of which are real-valued, where a database state is denoted as a vector $x = (x_1, x_2, \ldots, x_n) \in R^n$;

2. The database privacy is said to be guaranteed if an outside attacker cannot determine the value of any variable in the database. We say that a set of possible

database states $\mathcal{X}'$ is safe if: $\forall i, 1 \leq i \leq n, \exists x', x'' \in \mathcal{X}', x'_i \neq x''_i$. Note that, here $\forall \mathcal{X}' \subseteq \mathcal{X}''$, $\mathcal{X}'$ is safe implies that $\mathcal{X}''$ is safe.

3. A query q over the database is to ask the maximum value of a set of the variables in the database. Let Q denote the corresponding set, the true answer a for q is computed as $a = max\{x_i | x_i \in Q\}$.

4. The problem is: Given a set of queries $q_1, q_2, \ldots, q_{T-1}$ and their answers, how to answer a newly posed query q_T, providing as much data utility as possible, while the database privacy is also guaranteed.

Theorem 6. *There exists a simulatable binding algorithm for the max query auditing problem above that runs in $O(T \sum_{i=1}^{T} |Q_i|)$ time where $|Q_i|$ represents the number of variables in q_i.*

We prove this theorem by providing Algorithm 1, which is built comparable to the algorithm proposed in [14] for the same problem setting. We adopt the process that is proposed in the work [15], which has already solved the off-line max auditing problem. Some of the parameters are set as follows: Let $q'_1, q'_2, \ldots, q'_{T-1}$ be the previous queries with $a'_1 \leq \ldots \leq a'_{T-1}$ as the corresponding true answers. Let $a'_L = a'_1 - 1$ and $a'_R = a'_{T-1} + 1$. Let $\alpha[1..2T+1]$ be a array which takes the value of the sequence $(a'_L, a'_1, \frac{a'_1 + a'_2}{2}, a'_2, \frac{a'_2 + a'_3}{2}, a'_3, \ldots, a'_{T-2}, \frac{a'_{T-2} + a'_{T-1}}{2}, a'_{T-1}, a'_R)$. Let $\beta[1..2T+1]$ be a boolean array with default values of "false".

In [14], the authors have already shown that in order to check whether $\eta_{(A,\mathcal{X},q)} \neq \phi$ for such a problem setting, it is sufficient to check whether it is not safe to answer q_T under the condition that the true answer for q_T is any one of the values listed in the array $\alpha[1..2T+1]$. Thus, the algorithm they proposed based on the simulatable auditing model is to deny q_T if $\eta_{(A,\mathcal{X},q)} \neq \phi$.

Algorithm 1. MAX simulatable binding

For $i = 1$ to $2T + 1$ do
    Let a_T be $\alpha[i]$;
    If a_T is consistent with previous answers $a_1, a_2, \ldots, a_{T-1}$ AND
    there exists $1 \leq j \leq n$ such that x_j is uniquely determined (using [15])
        then set $\beta[i]$ to "true";
If all the $\beta[i]$, $(1 \leq i \leq 2T + 1)$ have been set to "true"
    then return "denied";
Select the least $k \in [1..2T + 1]$ such that $\beta[k] =$ "false";
Let a_T be the true answer for q_T;
If there does not exist $1 \leq j \leq n$ such that x_j is uniquely determined (using [15])
AND $a_T \neq \alpha[k]$
    then return the true answer a_T;
If all the $\beta[i]$, $(1 \leq i \leq 2T + 1)$ remain "false"
    then return the true answer a_T;
Record the the answer for q_T as $\alpha[k]$ (*);
Return "denied";

---
*: This record serves only for future auditing.

Comparably, the Algorithm 1 we propose based on the simulatable binding model applies the way to select a safe binding that binds the entire set $\eta_{(A,\mathcal{X},q)}$ together with the set of possible true database states which is consistent with $\mathcal{X}$ and the least "safe" answer $\alpha[k]$ for q_T. For other possible database states, the true answer will be given for the query q_T. Clearly, this applies the first kind of strategy to select a safe binding as we have discussed in previous section.

Note that by selecting a safe binding in this way, we need to log the returned answer of q_T as $\alpha[k]$ (in Algorithm 1) while the actually returned answer is "denied". The logged answer is used to define a new $\mathcal{X}'$ representing the knowledge contained in the denial for future auditing. In order to guarantee the safety of the binding, in future auditing, the answers have to be consistent not only with $q_1, q_2, \ldots, q_{T-1}$ and their answers, but also with q_T and its answer $\alpha[k]$.

The selection of the $\alpha[k]$, bound with "denied", is based on the order of α and independent from the true database state. Thus we have that:

Lemma 1. *Algorithm 1 is a* simulatable binding.

Proof Sketch: Clearly, the selection of binding in Algorithm 1 is based on $q_1, \ldots, q_T$ and $a_1, \ldots, a_{T-1}$. It suffices to prove that the binding in Algorithm 2 is a safe binding. Algorithm 1 tends to bind the entire denial set of A_{simple} with a set that already satisfies the privacy requirement. Therefore, the proof of safe binding requires: (1) the desired safety property satisfies that $\forall \mathcal{X}' \subseteq \mathcal{X}''$, $\mathcal{X}'$ is safe implies that $\mathcal{X}''$ is safe and (2) it is sufficient to check values in the array $\alpha[1..2T + 1]$ to determine $\eta_{(A_{simple}, \mathcal{X}, q_T)}$. (1) is clear and (2) has already been proved in the work [14]. Besides, the complexity of Algorithm 1, $O(T \sum_{i=1}^{T} |Q_i|)$ can be computed from the algorithm itself including the process from [15]. In fact, we have illustrated the result of Algorithm 1 in Section 1.4, when applying to the example we discussed in the introduction.

3.2   A Simulatable Binding Algorithm for Sum Query Auditing

We consider the following online auditing problem of sum query:

1. The database consists of n variables, all of which are real-valued, where a database state is denoted as a vector $x = (x_1, x_2, \ldots, x_n) \in R^n$.

2. There is a set of constraints $\mathcal{C}$: for each x_i: $c_{i,l} \leq x_i \leq c_{i,r}, (c_{i,l}, c_{i,r} \in R, c_{i,r} - c_{i,l} \geq 1)$.

3. We adopt the similar privacy requirement used in [16]. The database privacy is said to be guaranteed if an outside attacker cannot determine the value of any variable within an interval of 1. We say that a set of possible database states $\mathcal{X}'$ is safe if: $\forall i, (1 \leq i \leq n), \exists x', x'' \in \mathcal{X}', |x_i' - x_i''| \geq 1$. Note that, here $\forall \mathcal{X}' \subseteq \mathcal{X}''$, $\mathcal{X}'$ is safe implies that $\mathcal{X}''$ is safe.

4. A query q over the database asks the sum value of a set of the variables in the database. Let Q denote the corresponding set, the true answer a for q is computed as $a = sum\{x_i | x_i \in Q\}$.

5. The problem is: Given a set of queries $q_1, q_2, \ldots, q_{T-1}$ and their answers, how to answer a newly posed query q_T, providing as much data utility as possible, while the database privacy is also guaranteed?

Theorem 7. *There exists a simulatable binding algorithm for the sum query auditing problem above that runs in polynomial time w.r.t. n, T.*

We provide Algorithm 2 based on the following two tests:

Test 1: Given a set of sum queries $q_1, q_2, \ldots, q_{T-1}$ and their corresponding answers $a_1, a_2, \ldots, a_{T-1}$, a set of constraints $\mathcal{C} = \{c_{i,l} \le x_i \le c_{i,r}, (1 \le i \le n)\}$, and a new query q_T, a real value $r \in R$ satisfies Test 1 if: there exists $x \in R^n$ such that x satisfies $\mathcal{C}$ and x is consistent with the set of sum queries $q_1, q_2, \ldots, q_T$ and their corresponding answers $a_1, a_2, \ldots, a_T$, where $a_T = r$.

Test 2: Given a set of sum queries $q_1, q_2, \ldots, q_{T-1}$ and their corresponding answers $a_1, a_2, \ldots, a_{T-1}$, a set of constraints $\mathcal{C} = \{c_{i,l} \le x_i \le c_{i,r}, (1 \le i \le n)\}$, and a new query q_T, a real value $r \in R$ satisfies Test 2 if each of the values $r - 1$, r, $r + 1$ satisfies Test 1, given the same setting.

As we have mentioned in the introduction, the problem to decide whether a variable can be determined by a sequence of answered sum queries, under the condition that there is no constraint on the database state, has been solved in [7]. For the sake of simplicity, in Algorithm 2 we adopt the process proposed in [7] when checking the same problem. On the other hand, when constraints exist, any simulatable auditing algorithm that guarantees the safety of the entire database will never answer a single query.

In algorithm 2, we apply our simulatable binding model using the following way to select a safe binding: we bind the set of possible database states which is consistent with an "unsafe" answer r', i.e., it does not satisfy Test 2, with another set of possible database states which is consistent with a "safe" answer $r' + 1$ or $r' - 1$, i.e., it does satisfy Test 2. Note that when r' is an "unsafe" answer, at most one of $r' + 1$ or $r' - 1$ could possibly be a "safe" answer. Similar to Algorithm 1, we need to log the returned answer of q_T as $r' + 1$ or $r' - 1$ (corresponding to r in Algorithm 2) while the actually returned answer is "denied". The logged answer is used to define a new $\mathcal{X}'$ representing the knowledge contained in the denial for future auditing. That is, in order to guarantee the safety of the binding, in future auditing, the answers have to be consistent not only with $q_1, q_2, \ldots, q_{T-1}$ and their answers, but also with q_T and its answer as logged.

Also, it is clear that this selection applies the second kind of strategy to select a safe binding as we have discussed in previous section. And we have that:

Lemma 2. *Algorithm 2 is a simulatable binding.*

Proof Sketch: Clearly, the selection of binding in Algorithm 2 is based only on $q_1, \ldots, q_T$ and $a_1, \ldots, a_{T-1}$. It suffices to prove the binding in Algorithm 2 is a safe binding. As shown in Algorithm 2, in the deny set $\eta_{(A_{sb}, \mathcal{X}, q_T)}$, where $\mathcal{X}$ is defined by $q_1, q_2, \ldots, q_{T-1}$ and their corresponding answer $a_1, a_2, \ldots, a_{T-1}$, there always exist two set of database states and a real value r'' such that (1) one set of database states is consistent with $\mathcal{X}$, q_T and its corresponding answer r'' and (2) the other set of database states is consistent with $\mathcal{X}$, q_T and its corresponding answer $r'' + 1$. In each set, because the database privacy has not been breached before q_T is posed, regardless to q_T and its answer, none of x_i can be determined within an interval of 1. Thus, for any i, there always exists

---
Algorithm 2. SUM simulatable binding

Use [7] to decide q_T without considering $\mathcal{C}$:

　　If [7] denies q_T then return "denied";

　　Let r be the true answer for q_T computed from x;

　　If r satisfies Test 2 do

　　　　If both $r - 1$ and $r + 1$ satisfy Test 2, do

　　　　　　Let $a_T = r$, return a_T;

　　　　Else do

　　　　　　Record the answer for q_T as r (*);

　　　　　　Return "denied";

　　Else do

　　　　If $\exists r', r' = r - 1 \lor r' = r + 1$, such that r' satisfies Test 2, do

　　　　　　Record the answer for q_T as r' (*);

　　　　　　Return "denied";

　　　　Else do

　　　　　　Return "denied";

---
*: This record serves only for future auditing.

---

two possible database states, $x' = (x'_1, x'_2, \ldots, x'_n)$ and $x'' = (x''_1, x''_2, \ldots, x''_n)$, in the two sets above, respectively, such that $|x''_i - x'_i| = 1$.

The complexity of Algorithm 2 depends on Test 1, which is a linear programming problem, and the process we adopt from [7]. Both of them have been proved to be polynomial w.r.t. n, T.

4   Experiments

We conduct experiments to show the better performance of the above two algorithms than that of algorithms based on the simulatable auditing model.

For MAX query, Algorithm 1. The size of the database, n, is selected from 1000 to 2000. Each variable, as an integer, is randomly selected from $[1..n]$ with uniform distribution. The sequence of queries $q_1, q_2, \ldots$ is also randomly selected from all possible max queries such that the corresponding set $|Q_i| \leq \frac{n}{10}$. In Figure 6, we show the large performance improvement of Algorithm 1 compare to the reference algorithm based on the simulatable auditing model in average of 50 tests (performance of the unsafe A_{simple} is also listed as reference). In Figure 6,

- Plot (A) shows the number of answered queries before the first denial.
- Plot (B) shows the number of answered queries for total 200 posed queries.
- Plot (C) shows the number of answered queries when different number of queries are posed (from 50 to 250), in a data set with the fixed size 1000.

In above experiments, more than 50% sacrificed data utility (unnecessarily denied queries) by the algorithm based on the simulatable auditing model is regained by Algorithm 1 based on our simulatable binding model.

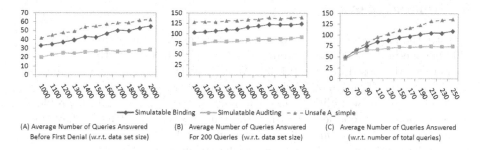

Performance of Algorithm 1 (Max Query Auditing)

For SUM query, Algorithm 2. The size of the database, n, is selected from 1000 to 2000. Each real number variable is randomly selected from $[0, 10]$ with uniform distribution. The database constraint is a set $\{0 \leq x_i \leq 10, (1 \leq i \leq n)\}$. The sequence of queries $q_1, q_2, \ldots, q_{n-1}$ is randomly selected from all possible sum queries such that all these $n-1$ queries are independent and can be answered by the algorithm in [7], without considering the existence of the constraints.

In this case, because an algorithm based on the simulatable auditing model cannot even answer a single query, Figure 7 shows that the number of answered queries by Algorithm 2 based on our simulatable binding model is very close to the upper bound determined by the original A_{simple}, which is safe in no-constraint case, but not safe in this case.

One may argue that we should compare our Algorithm 2 with the algorithm proposed in [14], based on their compromised privacy definition: $(\lambda, \delta, \alpha, T)$-Private. However, we claim that:

(1) The utilities of all these algorithms are bound by the utility provided by the unsafe A_{simple}.
(2) More importantly, the algorithm based on the aforementioned probabilistic private definition, is not a safe algorithm. It is not able to guarantee the safety of all the possible database states, and therefore not comparable to our safe algorithm with data utility.

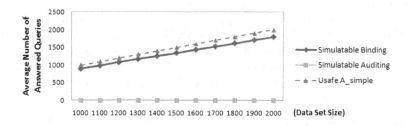

Performance of Algorithm 2 (Sum Query Auditing)

5   Related Work

To solve the problem of protecting the data privacy in a statistical database [1], different methods have been introduced. One way is to perturb the data in the answers for the posed queries [9,11,6]. Another choice is to perturb the data in the database itself before answering the posed queries [20,3,12,4,17].

Besides these noise-addition based approaches, works on the auditing problem, where responses to queries are either the true answers or "denied", have also been proposed. An *off-line auditing problem* [15,8,13,7,2] is to decide whether the database privacy has been breached based on a set of posed queries and their answers. Complexity analysis on specific problems on max/min [7,15] and sum [7,13,8] queries are given.

In [10,19,5], the authors target the *online auditing problem*, that is, to decide whether the database privacy will be breached by giving true answer to a newly posed query based on a set of posed queries and their answers. [5] also provides a logic-oriented model for the online auditing problem that combines modified answers and denials to enforce the database privacy.

Recently, in [14], the authors uncover that the database privacy may be breached by an attacker with the help of information leaked in the online auditing process, i.e., to decide how to answer a posed query. The authors also provide a model called *simulatable auditing* [14,18] to prevent information leakage in a auditing process. However, because the conditions provided by the simulatable auditing model is far from necessary to guarantee the database privacy, the huge data utility loss in their solutions inspired our work.

6   Conclusion

We address the fundamental issue in an online auditing problem that the decision on how to reply a posed query may leak information about the true database state. The newly proposed *simulatable auditing* model can get around the problem, but do have a huge data utility loss when applied. We suggest that it would be much better to control this information leakage instead of totally denying it.

We propose a new model, called *simulatable binding*, which controls the information leakage and is proved to provide a not only sufficient but also necessary condition to guarantee the database privacy. Two practical *simulatable binding* algorithms are also given for max query and sum query, respectively. Related experimental results are provided to show the regaining, by our algorithms, of great and unnecessary utility loss by previous models. As future work, we believe that our model can be applied to many other online auditing problems, including more sophisticated queries, besides those we have discussed in this paper.

Acknowledgements

This material is partially supported by the National Science Foundation under grants CT-0716567, CT-0627493, IIS-0242237, and IIS-0430402.

References

1. Adam, N., Wortmann, J.: Security-control methods for statistical databases: a comparative study. ACM Computing Surveys 21(4), 515–556 (1989)
2. Agrawal, R., Bayardo, R., Faloutsos, C., Kiernan, J., Rantzau, R., Srikant, R.: Auditing compliance with a hippocratic database. In: Proceedings of ACM VLDB, pp. 516–527 (2004)
3. Agrawal, R., Srikant, R.: Privacy-preserving data mining. In: Proceedings of ACM SIGMOD, pp. 439–450 (2000)
4. Agrawal, R., Srikant, R., Thomas, D.: Privacy-preserving olap. In: Proceedings of ACM SIGMOD, pp. 251–262 (2005)
5. Biskup, J., Bonatti, P.A.: Controlled query evaluation for known policies by combining lying and refusal. Annals of Mathematics and Artificial Intelligence 40(1-2), 37–62 (2004)
6. Blum, A., Dwork, C., McSherry, F., Nissim, K.: Practical privacy: the sulq framework. In: Proceedings of ACM PODS, pp. 128–138 (2005)
7. Chin, F.: Security problems on inference control for sum, max, and min queries. Journal of ACM 33(3), 451–464 (1986)
8. Chin, F., Ozsoyoglu, G.: Auditing for secure statistical databases. In: Proceedings of ACM 1981 conference, pp. 53–59 (1981)
9. Dinur, I., Nissim, K.: Revealing information while preserving privacy. In: Proceedings of ACM PODS, pp. 202–210 (2003)
10. Dobkin, D., Jones, A.K., Lipton, R.J.: Secure databases: protection against user influence. ACM Transactions on Database Systems 4(1), 97–106 (1979)
11. Dwork, C., Nissim, K.: Privacy-preserving data mining on vertically partitioned databases. In: Franklin, M. (ed.) CRYPTO 2004. LNCS, vol. 3152, pp. 528–544. Springer, Heidelberg (2004)
12. Evfimievski, A., Gehrke, J., Srikant, R.: Limiting privacy breaches in privacy preserving data mining. In: Proceedings of ACM PODS, pp. 211–222 (2003)
13. Kam, J.B., Ullman, J.D.: A model of statistical database and their security. ACM Transactions on Database Systems 2(1), 1–10 (1977)
14. Kenthapadi, K., Mishra, N., Nissim, K.: Simulatable auditing. In: Proceedings of ACM PODS, pp. 118–127 (2005)
15. Kleinberg, J., Papadimitriou, C., Raghavan, P.: Auditing boolean attributes. Journal of Computer and System Sciences 66(1), 244–253 (2003)
16. Li, Y., Wang, L., Wang, X., Jajodia, S.: Auditing interval-based inference. In: Pidduck, A.B., Mylopoulos, J., Woo, C.C., Ozsu, M.T. (eds.) CAiSE 2002. LNCS, vol. 2348, pp. 553–568. Springer, Heidelberg (2002)
17. Mishra, N., Sandler, M.: Privacy via pseudorandom sketches. In: Proceedings of ACM PODS, pp. 143–152 (2006)
18. Nabar, S.U., Marthi, B., Kenthapadi, K., Mishra, N., Motwani, R.: Towards robustness in query auditing. In: Proceedings of ACM VLDB, pp. 151–162 (2006)
19. Reiss, S.P.: Security in databases: A combinatorial study. Journal of ACM 26(1), 45–57 (1979)
20. Warner, S.: Randomized response: A survey technique for eliminating error answer bias. Journal of American Statistical Association 60(309), 63–69 (1965)

ARUBA: A Risk-Utility-Based Algorithm for Data Disclosure

M.R. Fouad[1], G. Lebanon[2], and E. Bertino[1,*]

[1] Department of Computer Science,
Purdue University, West Lafayette, IN 47907-2107
{mrf,bertino}@cs.purdue.edu
[2] Department of Statistics and School of Electrical and Computer Engineering,
Purdue University, West Lafayette, IN 47907-2107
lebanon@stat.purdue.edu

Abstract. Dealing with sensitive data has been the focus of much of recent research. On one hand data disclosure may incur some risk due to security breaches, but on the other hand data sharing has many advantages. For example, revealing customer transactions at a grocery store may be beneficial when studying purchasing patterns and market demand. However, a potential misuse of the revealed information may be harmful due to privacy violations. In this paper we study the tradeoff between data disclosure and data retention. Specifically, we address the problem of minimizing the risk of data disclosure while maintaining its utility above a certain acceptable threshold. We formulate the problem as a discrete optimization problem and leverage the special monotonicity characteristics for both risk and utility to construct an efficient algorithm to solve it. Such an algorithm determines the optimal transformations that need to be performed on the microdata before it gets released. These optimal transformations take into account both the risk associated with data disclosure and the benefit of it (referred to as utility). Through extensive experimental studies we compare the performance of our proposed algorithm with other date disclosure algorithms in the literature in terms of risk, utility, and time. We show that our proposed framework outperforms other techniques for sensitive data disclosure.

Keywords: Privacy, Security, Risk Management, Data Sharing, Data Utility, Anonymity.

1 Introduction

Maximizing data usage and minimizing privacy risk are two conflicting goals. Disclosing the minimum amount of information (or no information at all) is compelling specially when organizations try to protect the privacy of individuals. To achieve such goal, the organizations typically try to (1) hide the identity

---

* The work reported here has been supported by the NSF grants IPS-0712846 "Security Services for Healthcare Applications" and IPS-0712856 "Decision Theoretic Approaches to Measuring and Minimizing Customized Privacy Risk".

W. Jonker and M. Petković (Eds.): SDM 2008, LNCS 5159, pp. 32–49, 2008.
© Springer-Verlag Berlin Heidelberg 2008

of individual to whom data pertains, and (2) apply a set of transformations to the microdata before releasing it. These transformations include data suppression, data generalization, and data perturbation. Data suppression refers to suppressing certain attribute values (or equivalently disclosing the value $\perp$). Data generalization [15] refers to releasing a less specific variation of the original data; for example, releasing 479** for the zip code instead of 47906. In data generalization a value generalization hierarchy (VGH) for each attribute is constructed and consulted whenever a generalization is to take place (see Fig. 1(a) for an example of the VGH for the *city* attribute). Data perturbation [10] adds noise directly to the original data values; for example, perturbing a numeric value such as a salary by a Gaussian noise. In this paper, we focus on the technique of data generalization which includes data suppression as a special case.

We measure the harmful effect due to the disclosure of private data using the notion of an expected loss or a risk. This loss could be incurred, for example, as a result of privacy violations, financial loss due to identity theft, and security breaches. On the other hand, releasing data has its own merits. Released data could be useful for data mining and research purposes, data sharing, and improved service provisioning. Examples of risk-utility conflicts include, but not limited to, (i) medical research benefits vs. fear of patients' privacy violation, (ii) detecting purchasing patterns of customers vs. privacy of customers transactions, and (iii) benefits of disclosing sensitive geospatial data (for example, maps) vs. threats to national security.

Releasing more general information seems to have a diminishing effect on both risk and utility. However, the fact that we have opposite goals for risk and utility (minimizing the risk and maximizing the utility) raises the following crucial question: "Up to what level of generalization can we tolerate?". Indeed, without the help of powerful models that asses the risk and utility of a given information item, answering the above question is impossible. Many models have been proposed to quantify data utility all of which show that data generalization has negative impact on how useful data is. Xiao et al. [17] define the information loss of a more general attribute value v^* in terms of the number of values that

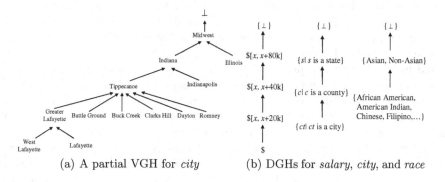

(a) A partial VGH for *city*   (b) DGHs for *salary*, *city*, and *race*

Fig. 1. Value generalization hierarchy (VGH) and domain generalization hierarchy (DGH)

it represents. Under the approach by Bayardo and Agrawal [1], a penalty cost is assigned to a generalized or suppressed tuple to reflect the information loss in such transformations. Fung et al. [3] define a tuple information in terms of the number of records that could be generalized to this tuple. An entropy-based model to assess information gain/loss is adopted in the approach by Wang et al. [16]. From the proposed models it is evident that when the released records are generalized to a greater extent, a larger information loss is incurred.

Assessing the risk of releasing a given information item has also been the subject of recent research. Assessing the risk is a more challenging task than quantifying the utility and there exist only very few models for assessing risk. Intuitively, releasing more specific information will incur a higher risk than releasing general information. Cheng et al. [2] model the risk of a tuple in terms of the value of information contained in it. A privacy risk model has been proposed by Lebanon et al. [7] that takes into account both the entity identification and the sensitivity of the disclosed information.

In this paper we propose an efficient algorithm (ARUBA) to address the trade-off between data utility and data privacy. ARUBA operates on the microdata to identify the optimal set of transformations that need to be applied in order to minimize the risk and in the meantime maintain the utility above a certain threshold.

The rest of the paper is organized as follows. The problem statement is presented in Section 2. Section 3 introduces the basic definitions and terminology used throughout the paper. Different risk and utility models are discussed in Section 4. In section 5, we develop an efficient scalable algorithm for data disclosure. Experimental results that show the superiority of our proposed algorithm over existing algorithms are reported in Section 6. Section 7 surveys related work. Finally, Section 8 presents concluding remarks and outlines future work.

2   Problem Statement

In this paper we consider the problem of identifying the optimal set of transformations which, when carried out on a given table, generate a resulting table that satisfies a set of optimality constraints. The optimality constraints are defined in terms of a preset objective function as well as risk and utility conditions.

The relationship between the risk and expected utility is schematically depicted in Fig. 2 which displays different instances of a disclosed table by their 2-D coordinates (r, u) representing their risk and expected utility, respectively. In other words, different data generalization procedures pose different utility and risk which lead to different locations in the (r, u)-plane. The shaded region in the figure corresponds to the set of feasible points (r, u) (i.e., the risk and utility are achievable by a certain disclosure policy) whereas the unshaded region corresponds to the infeasible points. The vertical line corresponds to all instances whose risk is fixed at a certain level. Similarly, the horizontal line corresponds to all instances whose expected utility is fixed at a certain level. Since the disclosure goal is to obtain both low risk and high expected utility, we are naturally most

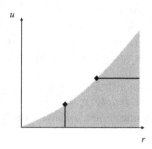

Fig. 2. Space of disclosure rules and their risk and expected utility. The shaded region correspond to all achievable disclosure policies.

interested in disclosure policies occupying the boundary of the shaded region. Policies in the interior of the shaded region can be improved upon by projecting them to the boundary.

The vertical and horizontal lines suggest the following two ways of resolving the risk-utility tradeoff. Assuming that it is imperative that the risk remains below a certain level, we can define the problem as

$$\text{maximize } u \quad \text{subject to} \quad r \leq c. \tag{1}$$

Alternatively, insisting on having the expected utility to be no less than a certain level we can define the problem as

$$\text{minimize } r \quad \text{subject to} \quad u \geq c. \tag{2}$$

A more symmetric definition of optimality is given by

$$\text{minimize } (r - \lambda u) \tag{3}$$

where $\lambda \in \mathbb{R}_+$ is a parameter controlling the relative importance of minimizing risk and maximizing utility.

In this paper, without loss of generality, we model our problem as in (2). Specifically, we address the problem of identifying the optimal transformations that produce the minimum risk and lower bound the utility above a given threshold. Given a specific tuples $a = \langle a_1, a_2, \cdots, a_i, \cdots, a_k \rangle$, the following problem has to be solved:

$$t^* = \arg\min_t r(t) \text{ subject to } u(t) \geq c \tag{4}$$

where t is a generalization of a.

3   Notations and Definitions

Throughout the paper, we will usually refer to an arbitrary record as a or b and to a specific record in a particular database using a subscript a_i. Attributes are denoted by A_i (or simply A). Attribute values of A are represented using the notation $[a]_j$ (or $[a_i]_j$) or just a_j (or a_{ij}). Note the "**bold**" typesetting representing vector notation and the "non-bold" typesetting representing attribute values. A collection of n records such as a database is denoted by $(a_1, \ldots, a_n)$.

Definition 1. *The* depth *of an attribute value a_i corresponding to attribute A, denoted by $depth(a_i)$, is the length of the path from a_i to $\perp$ in the VGH corresponding to A, that is, the maximum possible number of generalization steps applicable to this value.*

Example 1. In the VGH shown in Fig. 1(a), $depth$(Greater Lafayette) $= 4$.

Definition 2. *The* generalization set *of an attribute value a_i corresponding to attribute A, $GE(a_i)$, is the set of all ancestors of a_i in the VGH corresponding to A. We denote any element in $GE(a_i)$ as $\hat{a}$. The* parent *of a_i is the immediate ancestor and is denoted by $parent(a_i)$. On the other hand, the* specialization set *of an attribute value a_i, $SP(a_i)$, is the set of all descendants of a_i in the VGH corresponding to A. That is, $\forall_{a_i \in SP(\hat{a}_i)} \hat{a}_i \in GE(a_i)$. The* child *of a_i is the immediate descendent and is denoted by $child(a_i)$.*

Example 2. In the VGH shown in Fig. 1(a), GE(Lafayette) $= \{$Greater Lafayette, Tippecanoe, Indiana, Midwest, $\perp\}$, and SP(Greater Lafayette) $= \{$West Lafayette, Lafayette$\}$.

Definition 3. *An* immediate generalization *of a record $\mathbf{a} = \langle a_1, a_2, \cdots, a_i, \cdots, a_k \rangle$ with respect to an attribute a_i is a transformation on this record in which the value a_i is replaced by $parent(a_i)$ from the corresponding VGH. It is denoted by $ig_{a_i}(\mathbf{a})$, that is, $ig_{a_i}(\mathbf{a}) = \langle a_1, a_2, \cdots, parent(a_i), \cdots a_k \rangle$. The set of all immediate generalizations of a record $\mathbf{a}$ is denoted by $IG(\mathbf{a}) = \bigcup_{i=1}^{k} ig_{a_i}(\mathbf{a})$.*

Lemma 1. *The risk and utility associated with a record $\mathbf{a}$ ($r(\mathbf{a})$ and $u(\mathbf{a})$, respectively) have the following property:*

$$r(\mathbf{a}) \geq r(ig_{a_i}(\mathbf{a})) \text{ and } u(\mathbf{a}) \geq u(ig_{a_i}(\mathbf{a})), \ \forall i : 1, 2, \ldots, k.$$

This property, which we refer to as the *monotonicity property*, can be easily verified for most standard definitions of utility and risk.

Definition 4. *An* immediate specialization *of a record $\mathbf{a} = \langle a_1, a_2, \cdots, a_i, \cdots, a_k \rangle$ with respect to an attribute a_i is a transformation on this record in which the value a_i is replaced by $child(a_i)$ from the corresponding VGH. It is denoted by $is_{a_i}(\mathbf{a})$, that is, $is_{a_i}(\mathbf{a}) = \langle a_1, a_2, \cdots, child(a_i), \cdots a_k \rangle$. The set of all immediate specializations of a record $\mathbf{a}$ is denoted by $IS(\mathbf{a}) = \bigcup_{i=1}^{k} is_{a_i}(\mathbf{a})$. Note that $|IG(\mathbf{a})| \leq k$ and $|IS(\mathbf{a})| \leq k$.*

Example 3. In Fig. 3(a), $IG(\langle$Chinese, Tippecanoe$\rangle) = \{\langle$Asian, Tippecanoe$\rangle$, $\langle$Chinese,Indiana$\rangle\}$ and $IS(\langle$Chinese, Tippecanoe$\rangle) = \{\langle$Chinese,Dayton$\rangle\}$.

Definition 5. *A generalization lattice for a given record* $\boldsymbol{a} = \langle a_1, a_2, \cdots, a_i, \cdots, a_k \rangle$ *is the lattice formed by the immediate generalization relation on the set* $\left(\{a_1\} \cup GE(a_1)\right) \times \left(\{a_2\} \cup GE(a_2)\right) \cdots \times \left(\{a_k\} \cup GE(a_k)\right)$. *It is a graph* (V, E) *where* $V = \left(\{a_1\} \cup GE(a_1)\right) \times \left(\{a_2\} \cup GE(a_2)\right) \cdots \times \left(\{a_k\} \cup GE(a_k)\right)$ *and* $E = \{(v_1, v_2) | \ v_1, v_2 \in V \ \wedge \ v_1 \in IG(v_2) \cup IS(v_2)\}$. *The* dimension *of the lattice is the number of attributes of the initial record, that is,* k.

Lemma 2. *The generalization lattice for a given record* $\boldsymbol{a} = \langle a_1, a_2, \cdots, a_i, \cdots, a_k \rangle$ *has* $\Pi_{i=1}^{k} \left(depth(a_i) + 1\right)$ *nodes.*

Definition 6. *A* border node *$\boldsymbol{a}$ is a lattice vertex that satisfies the following condition:* $|IG(\boldsymbol{a})| < k$ *or* $|IS(\boldsymbol{a})| < k$. *It is the node in which at least one of the attributes cannot be further generalized or cannot be further specialized. Otherwise, if* $|IG(\boldsymbol{a})| = |IS(\boldsymbol{a})| = k$, *$\boldsymbol{a}$ is called an* inner node.

Example 4. In Fig. 3(a), $\langle$Chinese, Tippecanoe$\rangle$ is a border node whereas $\langle$Asian, Indiana$\rangle$ is an inner node.

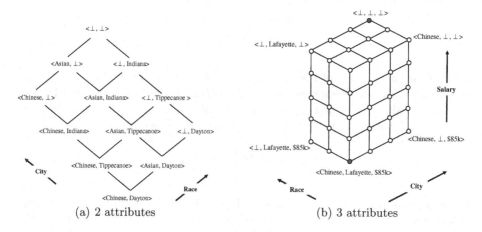

(a) 2 attributes   (b) 3 attributes

Fig. 3. Example of 2D and 3D lattices

Fig. 1(b) shows examples of domain generalization hierarchies for the *race*, *city*, and *salary* attributes. Using these hierarchies, two lattices representing specific records with different number of attributes are depicted in Fig. 3. Notice that moving in one dimension is equivalent to generalizing the attribute that corresponds to this dimension. Moreover, the dimension of the lattice is the number of attributes and the size of each dimension is the number of generalization steps for the corresponding attribute.

Definition 7. *A* feasible node *is the lattice vertex that satisfies all the given constraints that are mentioned in equations (1) and (2). Otherwise, it is called* infeasible node. *The best feasible node is called the* optimal node.

Note that all the children of a feasible node are also feasible and all the parents of an infeasible node are also infeasible.

4   Risk and Utility Computation

Our proposed algorithms make use of existing tools to quantify the utility and risk of a given tuple. In order to determine whether a tuple a is feasible, one needs to compute $u(a)$. On the other hand, the proposed algorithms consider the objective function of minimizing the risk. Therefore, it is imperative that, given a tuple a, a tool for quantifying risk $r(a)$ exists. In this section, we describe some models that have been proposed in the literature for utility and risk assessment. It is worth to note that all these models intuitively adhere to the fact that both risk and utility increase as the disclosed data becomes more specific and decrease as the disclosed data becomes more general.

4.1   Utility Assessment Models

Utility assessment models are often specified in terms of the number of leaves of the VGH subtree rooted at each attribute value. Specifically, one way to assess the utility of a record $\mathbf{a} = \langle a_1, a_2, \cdots, a_i, \cdots, a_k \rangle$ is

$$u(\mathbf{a}) = \sum_{i=1}^{k} 1/n_i, \tag{5}$$

where n_i is the number of leaf nodes of the VGH rooted at a_i. Note that, this model has a few disadvantages. According to this model, a non-zero (although minimum) value is assigned to the most general node and the utility of the leaf nodes is k. A variation of (5) is to use a logarithmic function as in

$$u(\mathbf{a}) = \sum_{i=1}^{k} \ln(m_i/n_i), \tag{6}$$

where m_i and n_i are the total number of leaf nodes of the VGH and the number of leaf nodes of the VGH subtree rooted at a_i, respectively. In agreement with our intuition, equation (6) assigns zero utility for the most general node.

Instead of taking into account the number of leaf nodes as a metric for utility assessment, one may consider attribute depths as defined in Definition 1, for example $\sum_{i=1}^{k} depth(a_i)$ (the sum of the heights of all VGHs *minus* the number of lattice generalization steps that are performed to obtain the record **a**). As data gets more specific, its depth increases and, accordingly, so does the utility. As in the previous case, the utility of the most general node ($\langle \bot, \bot, \cdots, \bot \rangle$) is zero.

In some cases, information loss, denote by $\triangle u$, can be used in lieu of utility. Maximizing the utility u is analogous to minimizing the information loss $\triangle u$ and, therefore, it is straightforward to transfer the optimization problem from one of these utility measures to the other. Xiai and Tao [17] defined the information loss as follows: $\triangle u(\mathbf{a}) = \sum_{i=1}^{k}(n_i - 1)/m_i$, where m_i and n_i are defined as above. Likewise, Iyengar [4] proposes the LM loss metric which is based on summing up normalized information losses for each attribute i.e. LM $= \triangle u(\mathbf{a}) = \sum_{i=1}^{k}(n_i - 1)/(m_i - 1)$.

4.2   Risk Assessment Models

Lebanon et al. [7] have proposed an analytical model to quantify the privacy risk. The risk of disclosing a record **a** is decomposed into two parts: (i) the user-specified data sensitivity $\Phi(\mathbf{a})$, and (ii) the attacker's probability of identifying the data owner based on **a** and side information θ. Data sensitivity is a subjective and personalized measure, for example $\Phi(\mathbf{a}) = \sum_{i\,:\,a_i \neq \perp} w_i$, where w_i represents the sensitivity of the attribute value a_i to the user who owns this data. The second component of the risk corresponding to the attacker's probability of identifying the data owner is given by $1/|\rho(\mathbf{a}, \theta)|$ where $|\rho(\mathbf{a}, \theta)|$ is the number of entries in the database θ consistent with the disclosed data **a** (anonymity number). Multiplying the two components we obtain

$$r(\mathbf{a}, \theta) = \frac{\Phi(\mathbf{a})}{|\rho(\mathbf{a}, \theta)|},$$

The database θ is assumed to be the side information available to the attacker but, assuming it is unknown, replacing it with the original database of pre-disclosed records provides an upper bound of the risk.

In this paper we consider as risk a more general combination of the data sensitivity Φ and anonymity number $|\rho|$ given by an arbitrary function

$$r(\mathbf{a}, \theta) = f(\Phi(\mathbf{a}), |\rho(\mathbf{a}, \theta)|).$$

Three examples which we concentrate on are:

Model I: $f_1(x, y) = x/y$ which leads to the risk proposed by Lebanon et al. [7].
Model II: $f_2(x, y) = 1/y$ which leads to non-personalized and constant data sensitivity.
Model III: $f_3(x, y) = x \log(1/y)$ corresponding to an entropic measure emphasizing small values of $1/|\rho|$.

5   Algorithms for Optimal Data Disclosure

Taking into account the special nature of the optimization problem at hand as well as the monotonicity property of both risk and utility, the discrete optimization problem (4) reduces to the following problem: Given a record **a**, it is required to

$$\text{minimize } r(\boldsymbol{a}^{(x_1, x_2, \ldots, x_i, \ldots, x_k)})$$

subject to

$$u(\boldsymbol{a}^{(x_1, x_2, \ldots, x_i, \ldots, x_k)}) \geq c, \quad 0 \leq x_i \leq h_i, \quad \forall i : 1, 2, \ldots, k$$

where: $h_i = depth(a_i)$, x_i represents the number of generalization steps applied on the ith attribute value of the record **a**, and $\boldsymbol{a}^{(x_1, x_2, \ldots, x_i, \ldots, x_k)}$ is the resulting record after applying these generalization steps. Moreover, the risk and utility satisfy the following:

$$r(a^{(x_1,x_2,\ldots,x_i,\ldots,x_k)}) \geq r(a^{(x_1,x_2,\ldots,x_i+1,\ldots,x_k)}),$$
$$u(a^{(x_1,x_2,\ldots,x_i,\ldots,x_k)}) \geq u(a^{(x_1,x_2,\ldots,x_i+1,\ldots,x_k)}), \; \forall i : 1, 2, \ldots, k.$$

A brute-force method for obtaining the optimal transformations is to try all possible combinations of attribute values and their generalizations and select the transformation that produces a feasible anonymized table which poses the minimum risk. Note that: (1) a crucial difference between our algorithm and most of the other anonymization algorithms is that we apply the transformations on a record-by-record basis instead of dealing with sets of equivalent records and we capture record similarities by means of the number of consistent records, $|\rho(a, \theta)|$, that is embedded in the risk models; (2) the proposed algorithms do not require the construction of the lattice beforehand; (3) the risk and utility functions are called as needed; (4) checking whether a node v has been visited (i.e., $v \in V$) can be implemented by inserting the nodes in V in a hash table and checking if v, when hashed using the same hashing function, collides with any existing node; and (5) the proposed algorithms can be easily extended to handle the dual problem of maximizing the utility subject to a risk constraint.

5.1   Basic Top-Down Algorithm (BTDA)

In this section we propose a modification of the brute-force algorithm that uses the *priority queue* data structure to navigate through lattice nodes until it reaches the optimal point.

Definition 8. *A priority queue is a linked list of lattice nodes sorted by risk in ascending order.*

Algorithm 1. BTDA Algorithm

Input: A record $a = \langle a_1, a_2, \cdots, a_i, \cdots, a_k \rangle$, a utility threshold c, and risk and utility functions $r(a), u(a)$, respectively.
Output: The optimal node a^*
BTDA()
(1)   initialize Q, V
```
/* Q is priority queue where r() is used to insert a node, where
nodes are sorted such that the front of Q always holds the node
with the minimum risk. V is the set of visited nodes. Inserting
a node v in Q is done according to r(v). */
```

(2)   insert $\langle \perp, \perp, \cdots, \perp \rangle$ in both Q and V
(3)   **while** (The front node, call it v, of Q is infeasible, i.e. $u(v) < c$)
(4)   delete v from Q
(5)   insert $IS(\mathbf{v}) - V$ in Q and V

(6)   `/* v is the first feasible node with min risk */`

         return v

Theorem 1. *Algorithm 1 generates the optimal node.*

Proof. We prove the theorem by contradiction. Assume that the front node of Q, say v, is feasible but not optimal. This implies that the optimal node is one of the nodes already inserted in Q after v or one of their children yet to be inserted. Since children nodes have higher risk than their parents and the parents have higher risk than v (because they are inserted after v in the priority queue), the optimal node a^* has higher risk than v which contradicts with the optimality definition. $\qquad\square$

5.2 ARUBA

In this section we propose an efficient algorithm, referred to as A Risk-Utility Based Algorithm (ARUBA), to identify the optimal node for data disclosure. The algorithm scans a significantly smaller subset of nodes (the so called *frontier nodes*) that is guaranteed to include the optimal node.

Definition 9. *A* frontier node *is a lattice vertex that is feasible and that has at least one infeasible immediate generalization.*

Theorem 2. *The optimal node is a frontier node.*

Proof. First, it is evident that the optimal node, say a^*, is feasible. Second, we prove that all its immediate generalizations are infeasible by contradiction. Assume that at least one of its parents, say $b \in IG(a^*)$, is feasible. Since $r(b) \leq r(a^*)$ and b is feasible, then b is better than a^* which contradicts the fact that a^* is the optimal node. Therefore, all immediate generalizations of a^* are infeasible and a^* is thus a frontier node. $\qquad\square$

Definition 10. *An* adjacency cube *associated with a lattice vertex* $\mathbf{v} = \langle v_1, v_2, \cdots, v_i, \cdots, v_k \rangle$ *is the set of all nodes* $\Big\{ \langle u_1, u_2, \cdots, u_i, \cdots, u_k \rangle | u_i \in \{v_i, parent(v_i), child(v_i)\} \forall i : 1, 2, \cdots, k \Big\} \setminus \{\langle v_1, v_2, \cdots, v_i, \cdots, v_k \rangle\}$. *The number of nodes in the adjacency cube is* $\leq 3^k - 1$.

Example 5. In Fig. 4 the adjacency cube associated with f is $\{a, b, c, d, e, g, h, i\}$.

Theorem 3. *Let* $\mathcal{L}$ *be a generalization lattice of dimension* k. *Except for border nodes, a frontier node* $f \in \mathcal{L}$ *has at least* k *frontier neighbors in the adjacency cube associated with it.*

Proof. We prove the theorem for the case of 2D lattice. A more general proof is provided in the appendix. Fig. 4 shows a general section of a 2D lattice. Assume that the node f is a frontier node. There are 2 cases:

- Both c and e are infeasible. If b is feasible, then it is a frontier node (since c is infeasible). Otherwise, c is a frontier node. The same argument applies to nodes e, g, and h.
- One of c and e is infeasible. Assume, without loss of generality, that c is infeasible and e is feasible. Since c is infeasible, then d is infeasible and, therefore, e is a frontier node. Moreover, if b is feasible, then it is a frontier node (since c is infeasible). Otherwise, a is a frontier node.

Algorithm 2. ARUBA Algorithm

Input: A record $a = \langle a_1, a_2, \cdots, a_i, \cdots, a_k \rangle$, a utility threshold c, and risk and utility functions $r(a), u(a)$, respectively.
Output: The optimal node a^*.
ARUBA()
```
(1)     initialize S, V
        /* S is the set of uninvestigated frontier nodes, V is the set
        of visited nodes. */

(2)     locate an initial frontier node f, update V
(3)     set r* = r(f)
(4)     set a* = f
(5)     S = S ∪ f
(6)     while (S ≠ Φ)
(7)          extract v from S
(8)          if r(v) ≤ r*
(9)               set r* = r(v)
(10)              set a* = v
(11)         locate the set of uninvestigated neighboring frontier nodes in the
             adjacency cube associated with v, call it NF
(12)         update V
(13)         S = S ∪ NF

(14)    /* All frontier nodes are scanned and a* is the node with min
        risk */

        return a*
```

In both cases, the frontier node f has two frontier neighbors in its adjacency cube.

$\square$

Theorem 4. *Algorithm 2 generates the optimal node.*

Proof. The proof follows directly from Theorem 3 in that all frontier nodes will have been visited when Algorithm 2 terminates. Since the optimal node is a frontier node (from Theorem 2), Algorithm 2 will generate the optimal node. $\square$

The initial frontier node may be obtained by (i) using binary search to locate the node with a utility closest to c given the maximum utility (utility for the most specific node), or (ii) navigating through a random path.

5.3   Example

For the sake of illustration, consider the simple 2D lattice in Fig. 5. The subscripts assigned to each node are hypothetical risks and utilities satisfying the monotonicity property. The figure shows the feasible nodes with the frontier nodes underlined and the optimal node identified as e^*. We assume a risk minimization problem subject to $u \geq 18$.

First, we apply Algorithm 1 on the displayed lattice. Fig. 6 shows the status of the priority queue Q and the set of visited nodes V after the execution of each iteration of the algorithm (steps 3,4,5). The algorithm starts off by inserting the most general node t in Q and V. Due to the fact that it is infeasible, t is removed from Q and its unvisited immediate specializations are inserted in Q in ascending order of risk (s then r). The algorithm goes on until the node at the front of Q is feasible (node e in iteration #16). At the end of the execution the queue contains the frontier nodes and the number of visited nodes is 18.

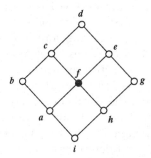

Fig. 4. Neighboring frontier nodes

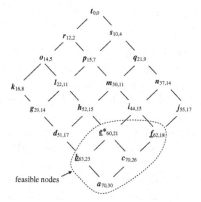

Fig. 5. Illustrative example for $\min r$ s.t. $u \geq 18$ (the feasible nodes are shown, the frontier nodes are underlined, the subscripts of each node give the hypothetical risk and utility, respectively)

Iter. #	Front of Q $\downarrow$				Visited nodes V
1	$t_{0,0}$				t
2	$s_{10,4}$	$r_{12,2}$			$t\ s\ r$
3	$r_{12,2}$	$p_{15,7}$	$q_{21,9}$		$t\ s\ r\ p\ q$
4	$o_{14,5}$	$p_{15,7}$	$q_{21,9}$		$t\ s\ r\ p\ q\ o$
5	$p_{15,7}$	$k_{16,8}$	$q_{21,9}$	$l_{22,11}$	$t\ s\ r\ p\ q\ o\ k\ l$
$\vdots$					
15	$j_{55,17}$	$e_{60,21}$	$f_{62,18}$	$b_{63,23}$	$t\ s\ r\ p\ q\ o\ k\ l$ $m\ g\ n\ h\ d\ i\ j$ $e\ f\ b$
16	$e_{60,21}$	$f_{62,18}$	$b_{63,23}$		$t\ s\ r\ p\ q\ o\ k\ l$ $m\ g\ n\ h\ d\ i\ j$ $e\ f\ b$

Iter. #	Unvisited frontier nodes S	Visited nodes V
0	f	$a\ c\ f\ j$
1	e	$a\ c\ f\ j\ e\ i\ n$
2	b	$a\ c\ f\ j\ e\ i\ n\ b\ d\ h\ m$
3		$a\ c\ f\ j\ e\ i\ n\ b\ d\ h\ m$

Fig. 6. For the lattice shown in Fig. 5, a list of visited visited nodes at different iterations of Algorithm 1 (left) and Algorithm 2 (right)

We also apply Algorithm 2 on the same lattice. The algorithm starts from node a and assumes that the first frontier node to be visited is f. Along the path to f, the nodes a, c, f, j are visited before determining that f is a frontier node. Node f is inserted in S. In the next iteration, the uninvestigated nodes in the adjacency cube of f are visited (nodes e, i, n) where it is determined that e is a frontier node and needs to be inserted in S. The algorithm continues until S is empty. Fig. 6 shows the status of the set of uninvestigated frontier nodes S and the set of visited nodes V after the execution of each iteration of the algorithm (steps 6 through 13). At the end of execution, the algorithm has visited all frontier nodes and determined that f is the optimal node. The number of visited nodes in this case is 11 which is, considering the small scale of the lattice, still a good improvement over Algorithm 1.

6   Experiments

We conducted our experiments on a real Wal-Mart database. An `item description` table of more than 400,000 records each with more than 70 attributes is used in the experiments. Part of the table is used to represent the disclosed data whereas the whole table is used to generate the attacker's dictionary. Throughout all our experiments, the risk components are computed as follows. First, the identification risk is computed by using the Jaro distance function [5] to identify the dictionary items consistent with a released record to a certain extent (we used 80% similarity threshold to imply consistency.) Second, the sensitivity of the disclosed data is assessed by means of an additive function and random weights that are generated using a uniform random number generator. The heights of the generalization taxonomies VGHs are chosen to be in the range from 1 to 5.

We use a modified harmonic mean to compute the sensitivity of a parent node w_p with l immediate children given the sensitivities of these children w_i: $w_p = \frac{1}{\sum_{1 \leq i \leq l} \frac{1}{w_i}}$ with the exception that the root node (corresponding to suppressed data) has a sensitivity weight of 0. Clearly, the modified harmonic mean satisfies the following properties: (i) the sensitivity of any node is greater than or equal to zero provided that the sensitivity of all leaves are greater than or equal to zero, (ii) the sensitivity of a parent node is always less than or equal (in case of 1 child) the sensitivity of any of its descendent nodes, and (iii) the higher the number of children a node has the lower the sensitivity of this node is. For example, given a constant city weight w_c, the weight of the `County` node j in the VGH for the `City` is $\frac{1}{\sum_{1 \leq i \leq l_j} \frac{1}{w_c}} = \frac{w_c}{l_j}$, where l_j is the number of cities in the county j. Moreover, the sensitivity of the `State` node in the same VGH is $\frac{1}{\sum_{1 \leq j \leq m} \frac{1}{w_c/l_j}} = \frac{w_c}{\sum_{1 \leq j \leq m} l_j} = \frac{w_c}{n}$, where m is the number of counties in the state and $n = \sum_{1 \leq j \leq m} l_j$ is the number of cities in the state. Due to the randomness nature of the sensitivity weights, each of the obtained result points is averaged over 5 runs.

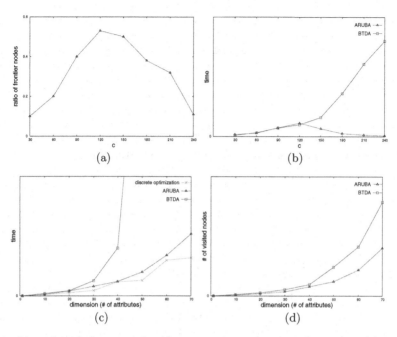

Fig. 7. Algorithms behavior with increasing utility threshold c (subfigures (a) and (b)) and with increasing dimension (subfigures (c) and (d))

We use a simplified utility function $u(\mathbf{a})$ to capture the information benefit of releasing a record $\mathbf{a} : u(\mathbf{a}) = \sum_{i=1}^{k} depth(a_i)$. For each record $\mathbf{a}$, the minimum risk is obtained subject to the constraint $u(\mathbf{a}) \geq c$. The impact of varying the utility threshold c while maintaining a full set of attributes is shown in Fig. 7(a) and Fig. 7(b). The percentage of frontier nodes is plotted as c varies from 30 to 240 in Fig. 7(a). It is evident that the number of frontier nodes is not directly proportional to c. When c is large, all lattice nodes tend to be infeasible leading to zero or a small number of frontier nodes. Likewise, when c is too small, all lattice nodes tend to be feasible leading to zero or small number of frontier nodes (refer to the definition of frontier nodes in Section 5). In Fig. 7(b), the running time for both algorithms is measured at various values of c. The experimental results show that ARUBA almost always outperforms BTDA especially for large values of c. Intuitively, as c increases towards the high extreme, the number of frontier nodes rapidly decreases (as shown in Fig. 7(a)) and, consequently, ARUBA converges very quickly. On the other hand, for large values for c more lattice nodes will be visited by BTDA before the optimum is reached. Therefore, the performance of BTDA deteriorates as c increases. Interestingly, for small values of c, there is no significant difference between ARUBA and BTDA. The reason is that the number of frontier nodes decreases rapidly as c approaches the lower extreme as well and ARUBA tends to perform well.

Throughout the following set of experiments, we fix the utility threshold c at a certain level which is intentionally chosen to be midway through the lattice

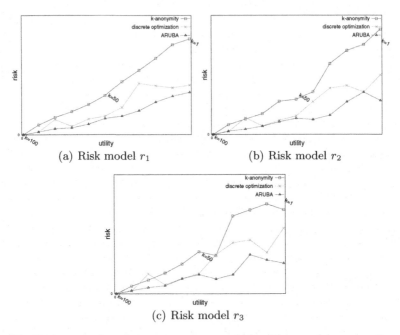

(a) Risk model r_1 (b) Risk model r_2

(c) Risk model r_3

Fig. 8. A comparison between our proposed algorithms and k-anonymity

(i.e., $c = \frac{1}{2}\sum_{i=1}^{k} h_i$) where ARUBA tends to perform the worst. We implement a heuristic discrete optimization algorithm, Branch and Bound [6], to obtain the heuristic optimum disclosure rule. Fig. 7(c) and Fig. 7(d) show that ARUBA outperforms BTDA in terms of both execution time and number of lattice visited nodes. Moreover, ARUBA exhibits a comparable performance with the discrete optimization algorithm in terms of time as shown in Fig. 7(c) but with a lower risk as shown in Fig. 8.

We compare the risk and utility associated with a disclosed table based on our proposed algorithm and arbitrary k-anonymity rules for k from 1 to 100. At each value of k, we generate a set of 10 k-anonymous tables and then compute the average utility associated with these tables using the simplified utility measure mentioned earlier. For each specific utility value c, we run both our proposed algorithm and the discrete optimization algorithm to identify the table that has not only the minimum risk but also a utility greater than or equal to c. We use each of the three risk models when solving these optimization problems. In Fig. 8 we plot the utility and risk of ARUBA (optimally selected disclosure policies), discrete optimization algorithm, and standard k-anonymity rules for different risk models. It is clear that ARUBA consistently outperforms both of the discrete optimization algorithm and standard k-anonymity rules regardless the nature of the model used to compute the risk. It is worth mentioning that a crucial difference between our algorithm and most of the other anonymization algorithms is that we apply the transformations on a record-by-record basis instead of dealing with sets of equivalent records and we capture record similarities by means of the number of consistent records, $|\rho(\mathbf{a}, \theta)|$, that is embedded in the risk models.

7 Related Work

Much of the research carried out on data transformations focused on anonymizing a disclosed table so that every record that belongs to it is made indistinguishable from as many other released records as possible [14,9,11,1,8]. This approach, although may sometimes achieve privacy, does not address the privacy-utility tradeoff.

Samarati et al. [13] introduced the concept of minimal generalization in which k-anonymized tables are generated without distorting data more than needed to achieve k-anonymity. Such approach, although it tries to minimize suppressions and generalizations, does not take into account sensitivity and utility of different attribute values at various levels of the generalization hierarchies.

The tradeoff between privacy and utility is investigated by Rastogi et al. [12]. A data-perturbation-based algorithm is proposed to satisfy both privacy and utility goals. However, they define privacy based on a posterior probability that the released record existed in the original table. This kind of privacy measure does not account for sensitive data nor does it make any attempt to hide the identity of the user to whom data pertains. Moreover, they define the utility as how accurate the results of the $count()$ query are. Indeed, this definition does not capture many aspects concerning the usefulness of data.

A top-down specialization algorithm is developed by Fung et al. [3] that iteratively specializes the data by taking into account both data utility and privacy constraints. A genetic algorithm solution for the same problem is proposed by Iyengar [4]. Both approaches consider classification quality as a metric for data utility. However, to preserve classification quality, they measure privacy as how uniquely an individual can be identified by collapsing every subset of records into one record. The per-record customization nature of our algorithm makes it much more practical than other algorithms in terms of both privacy and utility.

A personalized generalization technique is proposed by Xiao and Tao [17]. Under such approach users define maximum allowable specialization levels for their different attributes. That is, sensitivity of different attribute values are binary (either released or not released). In contrast, our proposed scheme provides users with the ability to specify sensitivity weights for their attribute values.

8 Conclusions

In this paper we propose an efficient algorithm to address the tradeoff between data utility and data privacy. Maximizing data usage and minimizing privacy risk are two conflicting goals. Our proposed algorithm (ARUBA) deals with the microdata on a record-by-record basis and identifies the optimal set of transformations that need to be applied in order to minimize the risk and in the meantime keep the utility above a certain acceptable threshold. We use predefined models for data utility and privacy risk throughout different stages of the algorithm. We show that the proposed algorithm is consistently superior in terms of risk when compared with k-anonymity and discrete optimization algorithm without a significant sacrifice in the execution time.

As future work, we plan to elaborate more on the impact of different risk and utility models on the performance of our algorithm. Estimating the dictionary of the attacker and the required set of transformations based on incremental disclosure of information is also a subject of future research. Finally, as an ongoing work, we are working on improving the scalability of the proposed algorithm.

References

1. Bayardo, R.J., Agrawal, R.: Data privacy through optimal k-anonymization. In: ICDE 2005: Proceedings of the 21st International Conference on Data Engineering, Washington, DC, USA, pp. 217–228. IEEE Computer Society Press, Los Alamitos (2005)
2. Cheng, P.-C., Rohatgi, P., Keser, C., Karger, P.A., Wagner, G.M., Reninger, A.S.: Fuzzy multi-level security: An experiment on quantified risk-adaptive access control. In: SP 2007: Proceedings of the 2007 IEEE Symposium on Security and Privacy, Washington, DC, USA, pp. 222–230. IEEE Computer Society Press, Los Alamitos (2007)
3. Fung, B.C.M., Wang, K., Yu, P.S.: Top-down specialization for information and privacy preservation. In: Proc. of the 21st IEEE International Conference on Data Engineering (ICDE 2005), Tokyo, Japan, April 2005, pp. 205–216. IEEE Computer Society Press, Los Alamitos (2005)
4. Iyengar, V.S.: Transforming data to satisfy privacy constraints. In: KDD 2002: Proceedings of the eighth ACM SIGKDD international conference on Knowledge discovery and data mining, pp. 279–288 (2002)
5. Jaro, M.: UNIMATCH: A record linkage system, user's manual. In: U.S. Bureau of the Census (1978)
6. Lawler, E.L., Wood, D.E.: Branch-and-bound methods: A survey. Operations Research 14(4) (1966)
7. Lebanon, G., Scannapieco, M., Fouad, M.R., Bertino, E.: Beyond k-anonymity: A decision theoretic framework for assessing privacy risk. In: Domingo-Ferrer, J., Franconi, L. (eds.) PSD 2006. LNCS, vol. 4302. Springer, Heidelberg (2006)
8. LeFevre, K., DeWitt, D.J., Ramakrishnan, R.: Incognito: Efficient full-domain k-anonymity. In: SIGMOD Conference, pp. 49–60 (2005)
9. Li, T., Li, N.: t-closeness: Privacy beyond k-anonymity and l-diversity. In: Proc. of ICDE (2007)
10. Liu, L., Kantarcioglu, M., Thuraisingham, B.: The applicability of the perturbation based privacy preserving data mining for real-world data. Data Knowl. Eng. 65(1), 5–21 (2008)
11. Machanavajjhala, A., Gehrke, J., Kifer, D., Venkitasubramaniam, M.: l-diversity: Privacy beyond k-anonymity. In: ICDE (2006)
12. Rastogi, V., Suciu, D., Hong, S.: The boundary between privacy and utility in data publishing. In: VLDB 2007: Proceedings of the 33rd international conference on Very large data bases, pp. 531–542 (2007)
13. Samarati, P.: Protecting respondents' identities in microdata release. IEEE Trans. Knowl. Data Eng. 13(6), 1010–1027 (2001)

14. Samarati, P., Sweeney, L.: Generalizing data to provide anonymity when disclosing information. In: Proc. of PODS (1998)
15. Sweeney, L.: Privacy-enhanced linking. ACM SIGKDD Explorations 7(2) (2005)
16. Wang, K., Yu, P.S., Chakraborty, S.: Bottom-up generalization: A data mining solution to privacy protection. In: ICDM 2004, pp. 249–256. IEEE Computer Society, Los Alamitos (2004)
17. Xiao, X., Tao, Y.: Personalized privacy preservation. In: Proc. of SIGMOD (2006)

Appendix: Proof of Theorem 3 for the Case of 3D Lattice

Proof. Consider the section of the 3D lattice shown in Fig. 9 and assume that f is a frontier node. There are 3 cases:

- All nodes in $IG(f) = \{a, b, c\}$ are infeasible. Consider the node e. If $ig_{a_1}(e)$ is infeasible, then e is a frontier node. Otherwise, $ig_{a_1}(e)$ a frontier node. The exact same argument applies to nodes d and g.
- Exactly two nodes in $IG(f)$ are infeasible. Assume, without loss of generality, that these two nodes are a and b. Since c is feasible and $ig_{a_1}(c) = ig_{a_3}(a)$ is infeasible (since a is infeasible), then c is a frontier node. Now, consider the node e. If $ig_{a_1}(e)$ is infeasible, then e is a frontier node. Otherwise, $ig_{a_1}(e)$ a frontier node. The exact same argument applies to node d.
- Exactly one node in $IG(f)$ are infeasible. Assume, without loss of generality, that this node is c. Since a is feasible and $ig_{a_1}(c) = ig_{a_3}(a)$ is infeasible (since c is infeasible), then a is a frontier node. Likewise, it can be proved that b is a frontier node. Now, if $ig_{a_3}(e)$ is infeasible, then e is a frontier node. Otherwise, $ig_{a_3}(e)$ is a frontier node since $c = ig_{a_2}(ig_{a_3}(e))$ is infeasible.

In all of the above cases, f has at least 3 neighboring frontier nodes.   □

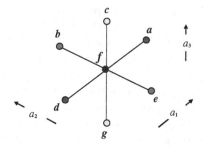

Fig. 9. Proof for Theorem 3 for 3D lattice

Responding to Anomalous Database Requests

Ashish Kamra, Elisa Bertino, and Rimma Nehme

Purdue University

Abstract. Organizations have recently shown increased interest in database activity monitoring and anomaly detection techniques to safeguard their internal databases. Once an anomaly is detected, a response from the database is needed to contain the effects of the anomaly. However, the problem of issuing an appropriate response to a detected database anomaly has received little attention so far. In this paper, we propose a framework and policy language for issuing a response to a database anomaly based on the characteristics of the anomaly. We also propose a novel approach to dynamically change the state of the access control system in order to contain the damage that may be caused by the anomalous request. We have implemented our mechanisms in PostgreSQL and in the paper we discuss relevant implementation issues. We have also carried out an experimental evaluation to assess the performance overhead introduced by our response mechanism. The experimental results show that the techniques are very efficient.

1   Introduction

Recently, we have seen an interest in solutions that continuously monitor a database system and report any relevant suspicious activity [6]. Gartner research has identified Database Activity Monitoring (DAM) as one of the top five strategies that are crucial for reducing data leaks in organizations [11,13]. Such step-up in data vigilance by organizations is partly driven by various government regulations concerning data management such as SOX, PCI, GLBA, HIPAA and so forth [12]. Organizations have also come to realize that current attack techniques are more sophisticated, organized and targeted than the broad-based hacking days of past. Often, it is the sensitive and proprietary data that is the real target of attackers. Also, with greater data integration, aggregation and disclosure, preventing data theft, from both *inside* and *outside* organizations, has become a major challenge. Standard database security mechanisms, such as access control, authentication, and encryption, are not of much help when it comes to preventing data theft from insiders [2]. Such threats have thus forced organizations to re-evaluate security strategies for their internal databases [12]. Monitoring a database to detect any potential abnormal user behavior is a crucial technique that has to be part of any comprehensive security solution for high-assurance database security. Today there are several commercial products for database monitoring against intrusions [6]. These products are crucial in the line of defense against data theft, but a common shortcoming they all have is

W. Jonker and M. Petković (Eds.): SDM 2008, LNCS 5159, pp. 50–66, 2008.

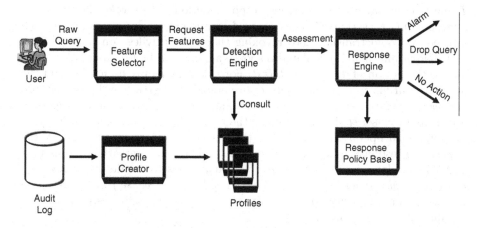

Fig. 1. System Architecture

their inability to issue a suitable *response* to an ongoing attack. The response can either be *aggressive* and the anomalous request may be dropped, or *conservative* and only an alarm may be raised, letting the anomalous request go through.

So what more can a DBMS do to respond to an anomalous request? Standard security violations in the context of a DBMS are dealt with simple and intuitive responses. For example, if a user tries to exercise an unassigned privilege, the access control mechanism will deny the access request. However, it is not trivial to develop a response mechanism capable of automatically taking actions when abnormal database behavior is detected. Let us illustrate this with the following example. Consider a database system with several users, each having the *data-reader* and the *data-writer* role in the database[1]. Although users have the necessary read/write privileges to all database objects, they typically exercise only a subset of those privileges to carry out their "normal" day-to-day work. The key approach to detect abnormal behavior here is to "learn" profiles of users based on their day-to-day (normal) interaction with the database system. Then, behavior deviating from normal behavior is flagged as malicious. For such purpose, we consider a database monitoring system in place that builds database user profiles based on SQL queries submitted by the users (see Figure 1) [2]. Suppose that a user $\mathcal{U}$, who has never accessed table $\mathcal{T}$, issues a query that accesses all columns in $\mathcal{T}$. The detection mechanism flags this request as anomalous for $\mathcal{U}$. The major question is what should the system do next once a request is marked as anomalous by the detection mechanism. Since the anomaly is detected based on the learned profiles, it may well be a false alarm. It is easy to see then there are no simple intuitive response measures that can be defined for such security-related events. The system should take different response actions depending on the details of the anomalous request and the request context. If

---

[1] SQL Server 2000/2005 has the fixed database roles, *db_datareader* and *db_data writer* [14].

[2] More algorithmic details on this system can be found in [8].

$\mathcal{T}$ contains sensitive data, a strong response action is to revoke the privileges corresponding to actions that are flagged as anomalous. In our example, such a response would translate into revoking the *select* privilege on table $\mathcal{T}$ from $\mathcal{U}$. Different and more articulated response actions can be formulated by introducing the notion of *"privilege states"*. For example, as we discuss later in the paper, the privilege corresponding to an anomalous action may be moved into a *suspended* state until a remedial action, such as a 2nd-factor authentication, is executed by user $\mathcal{U}$ [17]. However, if the user action is a one-time action part of a bulk-load operation, when all objects are expected to be accessed by the request, no response action may be necessary. The key observation here is that a DBMS needs to be instrumented with capabilities to decide *which response measure to take under a given situation*. Therefore, a *response policy* is required by the database security administrator to specify appropriate response actions for different circumstances.

In this paper, we present the design and implementation details of a *Database Anomaly Response Framework* (*DARF*). *DARF* is an anomaly response framework integrated inside a DBMS server that stores response policies and automatically performs response actions. The two main issues that we address in the context of response policies are the *expressiveness* and *overhead* of these policies. To the best of our knowledge, this is the first solution addressing the problem of developing intrusion response policies in the context of a DBMS. We also propose a novel approach to dynamically change the state of the access control system as a response to an anomalous request. The main contributions of this paper can be summarized as follows:

1. A policy language for specifying response policies to anomalous behavior in a DBMS.
2. A taxonomy of response actions that can be taken in the context of a detected anomalous action.
3. A scheme for efficiently storing and retrieving response policies in a DBMS.
4. A prototype implementation of privilege states in PostgreSQL's access control system.
5. An experimental evaluation assessing the overhead incurred by the policy selection mechanism.

1.1   Paper Road Map

The rest of the paper is as follows. Section 2 explains our detection methodology. Section 3 presents the response framework. Section 4 explains the details of the system implemented in PostgreSQL and presents the experimental results. Section 5 gives an overview of related work in the area of database activity monitoring and response. We conclude in Section 6 with directions for future work.

2   Background: Detection Methodology

Before proceeding with the introduction of *DARF*, we give some background on the intrusion detection task in the context of a DBMS. We first start with a general categorization of threats to databases. They can be broadly categorized as follows [9]:

1. **Privilege Elevation.** Elevated privileges may be obtained by an attacker by: *Exploiting software vulnerabilities,* vulnerabilities in the database server code can be exploited to launch arbitrary programs; *SQL Injection,* Web applications and database stored procedures that do not sanitize user input can be exploited to gain elevated privileges.

2. **Privilege Abuse.** This is the insider threat scenario. In this case, a malicious user uses his/her privileges for performing actions that do not conform to its *expected* day-to-day behavior.

To defend against privilege elevation due to software vulnerabilities, the DBMS must be patched regularly [9]. Our detection and response framework addresses the problem of SQL Injection and the privilege abuse behavior. The key idea underlying our approach is to model both SQL Injection attacks and the privilege abuse behavior as an *anomaly detection* problem. The detailed approach is as follows [5,8,4]. We learn profiles of users and applications that submit queries and updates to the DBMS. For this purpose, either the DBMS audit data can be used or the system can be trained online. The profile information can vary depending on the detection task at hand. For example, in order to support the detection of anomalous access patterns, the profile contains information on database objects accessed by the SQL queries submitted to the DBMS [8]. To detect SQL Injection attacks, we build application profiles that contain a query fingerprint consisting of association rules between the projection and the selection clause of the SQL queries [4]. Over a period of time, these profiles describe the normal baseline behavior of the users/applications. This is the learning phase of the system. After the learning phase, the detection phase begins. In the detection phase, every user/application request is monitored and matched against the learned profile. A significant deviation from the profile is classified as anomalous by the detection engine. In what follows, we give some examples of anomalous actions that can be detected by profiling users and applications interacting with a DBMS:

1. User $\mathcal{U}$ has read access to table $\mathcal{T}$. Normally on a daily basis, $\mathcal{U}$ accesses only a fraction of records in $\mathcal{T}$. One day, $\mathcal{U}$ issues a query to read all the data from all columns of $\mathcal{T}$.

2. A DBA logs in from an IP address from which he/she has never logged in before.

3. A backup DBA issues select queries on the application data tables.

4. A database application issues malformed queries that result in database errors on a regular basis. This may be an indication of the information gathering phase of a SQL Injection attack.

5. A malicious employee writes code that reads all credit card numbers from a production database table and sends these sensitive data across to a remote development database.

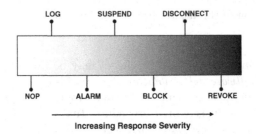

Fig. 2. Immediate Response Actions

3   Database Anomaly Response Framework (DARF)

The problem we focus in this paper is the following: once an anomaly has been detected, what actions should the DBMS perform to address the anomaly? As we can infer from the examples given in Section 2, there is no single universal correct response measure to all anomalous events. The response must be tailored to the context and the details of the detected anomaly. To address such requirement, our detection engine submits to the response engine an *anomaly characterization* along with anomaly indication. Our approach thus supports the definition of response policies, taking into account the anomaly characteristics, for guiding the actions of the response engine. Note that the strategy of *detect-all-respond-few* is applied here. We do not specify policies for the detection engine in order to guide its detection strategy. The detection engine, instead, uses machine learning algorithms to detect anomalies [5,4]. Once the anomaly is detected, the process of deciding how to respond (or not respond) is driven by user-defined policies based on the anomaly characteristics. This arrangement allows for a loose coupling between the detection and the response mechanisms.

The next section describes the taxonomy of response actions that can be taken in context of a DBMS and which are supported by our response engine.

3.1   Response Actions

There are two types of response actions supported by our system. The first type is a **immediate** response action, that is, an action that produces an immediate result. The various immediate response actions that can be taken are listed in Figure 2. The are further described in Table 1 where they are specified in an increasing order of *severity*. Actions such as $SUSPEND$, $BLOCK$, $DISCONNECT$, and $REVOKE$ directly affect the user associated with the anomalous request. Other actions such as NOP, LOG and $ALARM$ are immediate but their effect is transparent to the user. The second type of response action is a **delayed** response action. Such a response is transparent to the user, leads to a change in the state of the database system and specifically to changes in attributes characterizing the state. Such attributes can then be used by policies to specify other immediate response actions later on; and hence the reason for calling them delayed responses. An important delayed response action is based on the notion of *privilege state* discussed in what follows.

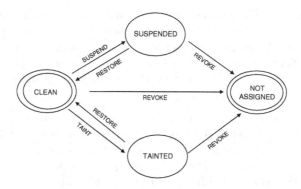

Fig. 3. Privilege State Transitions

Table 1. Immediate Response Actions

Severity Level	Action	Description
0	$\mathcal{NOP}$	No OPeration. This option can be used to filter unwanted alarms.
1	$\mathcal{LOG}$	The anomaly details are logged.
2	$\mathcal{ALARM}$	A notification is sent to the security administrator.
3	$\mathcal{SUSPEND}$	The user request is suspended.
4	$\mathcal{BLOCK}$	The user request is dropped.
5	$\mathcal{DISCONNECT}$	The user session is disconnected.
6	$\mathcal{REVOKE}$	The user privileges corresponding to actions in the anomalous request are revoked.

Current DBMSs essentially follow a discretionary access control model with some features from role based access control to simplify administration of privileges [16]. Thus, in a general sense, a permission on a database object is either assigned to a user or not assigned to it[3]. Therefore, an object permission (or privilege) exists in a binary state for a particular user. To support delayed response actions to anomalous activities, we introduce the notion of privilege states. The basic design change is that privileges assigned to a user on a database object can now exist in different states. We identify three states that are sufficient for issuing a response to an anomaly. The state transitions are shown in Figure 3. Assume a user logs on to the database for the first time. At this time, all its assigned permissions start in a $\mathcal{CLEAN}$ state. If a user submits a request that is detected as anomalous by the detection engine, the response engine is invoked. Based on the response policy, the response engine can either $\mathcal{TAINT}$, $\mathcal{SUSPEND}$ or $\mathcal{REVOKE}$ the privileges associated with the request. We now describe privilege tainting and suspension in detail:

---

[3] An exception is SQL Server 2000/2005 that supports a DENY statement. DENY puts an assigned privilege in a denied state. [15]

Privilege Tainting. The privilege state for a user can be changed to *tainted* as a delayed response. All current and future requests using a tainted privilege are still allowed. Privilege tainting is essentially a lesser form of response measure that does not affect access control decisions but can act as a stepping stone to further response actions. A response policy can then make use of the tainted privilege state to take a stronger response.

Privilege Suspension. It is a more severe form of response and its effect is immediate. When a privilege state is changed to suspended for a user on a database object, any access request using that privilege is put on hold till a confirmation action as defined by a response policy is taken. An example of a confirmation action is a second factor authentication [17].

Note that a sequence of response actions can also be specified as a valid response action. For example, $\mathcal{LOG}$ can be issued before $\mathcal{ALARM}$ in order to log the anomaly details as well as send a notification to the security administrator. Also the *severity level of the policy* in case of a sequence of response actions is the severity level of the final response action.

3.2   Response Policy Language

The detection of an anomaly by the detection engine can be considered as a system event. The attributes of the anomaly then correspond to the environment surrounding such an event. Intuitively, a policy can be specified taking into account the anomaly attributes to guide the response engine in taking a suitable action. Keeping this in mind, we propose an **Event-Condition-Action** (ECA) language for specifying response policies. Later in this section, we extend the ECA language to support novel response semantics. ECA rules have been widely investigated in the field of active databases [19]. An ECA rule is typically organized as follows:

```
ON   {Event}
IF   {Condition}
THEN {Action}
```

As it is well known, its semantics is as follows: if the *event* arises and the *condition* evaluates to true, the specified *action* is executed. In our context, an event is the detection of an anomaly by the detection engine. A condition is specified on the attributes of the detected anomaly and on the attributes representing the internal state of the DBMS. An action is the response action executed by the engine. In what follows, we use the term ECA policy instead of the common terms ECA rules and triggers to emphasize the fact that our ECA rules specify policies driving response actions. We next discuss in detail the various components of our language for ECA policies.

Policy Attributes. Response policy conditions can be specified against two types of attributes: *anomaly attributes*, characterizing the detected anomaly, and *state attributes*, characterizing certain aspects of the system state that are relevant for response actions.

Table 2. Anomaly Attributes

Attribute	Description
CONTEXTUAL	
User	The user associated with the anomalous request
Role	The role associated with the anomalous request
Session	Session ID of the request
Client App	The client application associated with the anomalous request
Source IP	The IP address associated with the anomalous request
Date Time	Date/Time of the anomalous request
STRUCTURAL	
Database	The database referred to in the anomalous request
Schema	The schema referred to in the anomalous request
Obj Type	The type of the database objects referred to in the request such as table, view, stored procedure
Obj(s)	The database object name(s) referred in the request
SQL Cmd	The SQL Command associated with the request
Obj Attr(s)	The attributes of the object(s) referred in the request. For example, if object type is 'table' then the table columns are the object attributes.

Anomaly Attributes. The anomaly detection mechanism provide its assessment of the anomaly using the anomaly attributes. We have identified two main categories for those attributes. The first category, referred to as *contextual category*, includes all attributes describing the context of the anomalous request such as user, role, source, and time. The second category, referred to as *structural category*, includes all attributes conveying information about the structure of the anomalous request such as SQL command, and accessed database objects. Details concerning these attributes are reported in Table 2. The detection engine submits its characterization of the anomaly using the anomaly attributes. Therefore, the anomaly attributes also act as an interface for the response engine, thereby hiding the internals of the detection mechanism.

State Attributes. We support only one state attribute in the current version of our system, that is, the *Privilege State*. This attribute conveys the state of a specific user privilege. The possible state values for this attribute are *clean, tainted*, and *suspended* (cfr. Section 3).

Policy Conditions. An ECA policy condition is a conjunction of atomic predicates where each predicate is specified against a single anomaly attribute or on a state attribute. Examples of such predicates are given below:

```
Role != DBA , Source IP ~ 192.168.[0-255].[0-255]
Objs IN {dbo.*} , Privilege State = tainted
```

Policy Examples. We now present two comprehensive examples illustrating the various components of our response policies.

POLICY 1: If there is an anomalous write to tables in the 'dbo'
schema from un-privileged users inside the organization's internal
network, the user should be disconnected.

```
ON      ANOMALY DETECTION IF      Role != DBA
and
        Source IP ~ 192.168.[0-255].[0-255]  and
        Obj Type = table                     and
        Objs IN {dbo.*}                      and
        SQL Cmds IN {Insert, Update, Delete}
THEN    disconnect User
```

POLICY 2: Ignore all anomalies from privileged uses originating
from the internal network during normal business hours

```
ON      ANOMALY DETECTION IF      Role = DBA
and
        Source IP ~ 192.168.[0-255].[0-255] and
        Date Time BETWEEN {0800-1800}
THEN    No OPeration
```

Extended ECA Policies. An ECA policy is sufficient to trigger simple response measures such as disconnecting users, dropping anomalous request, and
raising an alarm. In some cases, however, we need to engage in interactions
with users. For example, suppose that upon an anomaly, we put the anomalous
privileges in a suspended state as our initial action. Then we ask the user to
authenticate with a second authentication factor as the next action. In case the
authentication fails, the user is disconnected. Otherwise, the request proceeds.
As ECA policies are unable to support such sequence of actions, we extend them
with the following two constructs:

Confirmation Action. A confirmation action is the second course of action after
the initial response action. Its purpose is to interact with the user to resolve the
effects of the initial action. If the confirmation action is successful, the request
proceeds, otherwise the alternate action is executed.

Alternate Action. An alternate action is the action to be taken in case the confirmation action fails.

Thus, a response policy in our framework can be symbolically represented as[4]:

```
ON       {Event}
IF       {Condition}
THEN     {Initial Action}
CONFIRM  {Confirmation Action}
ELSE     {Alternate Action}
```

----
[4] Note that in case where an interactive response with the user is not required, the
confirmation/alternate actions may be omitted from the policy.

An example of an extended ECA policy is as follows.

POLICY 3: Reauthenticate un-privileged users who are logged from inside the organization's internal network with a second password for write anomalies to tables in the dbo schema

```
ON        ANOMALY DETECTION IF      Role != DBA
and
          Source IP ~ 192.168.[0-255].[0-255] and
          Obj Type = table                    and
          Objs IN {dbo.*}                     and
          SQL Cmds IN {Insert, Update, Delete}
THEN      suspend privilege CONFIRM authenticate with second
password /*Confirmation Action*/ ELSE    disconnect User
/*Alternate Action*/
```

The above example illustrates an interactive response ECA policy. The initial action is to suspend the user privilege(s) associated with the anomalous request. As a confirmation action, the user is prompted for the second factor of authentication such as a second password or a biometrics. If the confirmation action fails, the alternate action is to disconnect the user.

Policy Matching and Selection. When an anomaly is detected, the policy database is searched to find the policies that match[5] the anomaly. In the event of multiple policies matching an anomaly, we must provide for a resolution scheme to determine the response to be issued. We present the following two rank-based selection options that are based on the severity level of the response actions:

1. **Most Severe Policy (MSP).** Since the severity level of a policy is determined by the severity level of its response action, this strategy selects the most severe action from the set of all applicable response actions. Note that the immediate response actions described in Section 3 are ordered according to their severity level. Also, in case of a sequence of confirmation and alternate actions, the severity of the policy is taken as the severity level of the alternate action.
2. **Least Severe Policy (LSP).** This strategy, unlike the MSP strategy, selects the least severe action.

4   Implementation and Experiments

To show the feasibility of our approach and identify the key implementation issues, we have developed a prototype implementation of the response mechanism in PostgreSQL. Two important implementation issues are related to the efficient strategy for storage and selection of policies in a DBMS, and to the efficient implementation of the notion of privilege states (cfr. Section 3). We have

---

[5] Matching here means that the policy is applicable to an anomaly.

Table 3. Policy selection time for the simple scheme

No. of policies = 1000	
Anomaly w/o Objs(ms)	**Anomaly with Objs (ms)**
2	130

also performed an experimental evaluation of the response policy implementation and analyzed the overhead of our solution. We begin our discussion with implementation details about policy storage and selection.

Policy Storage. Our strategy is to store policies according to a relational table format and use native DBMS functionality to retrieve them efficiently. We store the information describing each policy in a table called $\mathcal{PG\_POLICY}$. Such table contains two sets of columns. The first set contains the *Predicate* columns recording predicate constants in the policy condition that correspond to the anomaly attributes specified in Table 2. Some predicate constants corresponding to attributes, such as Role(s) and Obj(s) may contain multiple values. They are stored as PostgreSQL arrays. The second set contains the *Action* columns recording the implementation function for carrying out the actual response actions[6]. Note that the domain of all predicate columns in $\mathcal{PG\_POLICY}$ is finite. Thus storing only the predicate constants enables us to support both equality and inequality predicates. For example, suppose that there are four roles in the system, that is, R_1, R_2, R_3 and R_4. If a policy predicate specifies Role ! = 'R_1', we convert this predicate into an semantically equivalent predicate Role IN (R_2, R_3, R_4) before storing the array (R_2, R_3, R_4) in the $\mathcal{PG\_POLICY}$ table.

Policy Matching and Selection. The response system includes a table, called $\mathcal{ANOMALY\_ATTRS}$, for logging the anomaly details submitted by the detection engine. Upon detection of an anomaly, the detection engine inserts a row into the $\mathcal{ANOMALY\_ATTRS}$ table. There is a row-level insert trigger defined on this table. A simple scheme to retrieve the matching policies is to gather the anomaly details from the inserted row and issue a SQL query on the $\mathcal{PG\_POLICY}$ table. The policy selection time of such scheme is reported in Table 3. We observe that if the anomaly attribute Objs (see Section 3.2) is not null, the time taken for policy retrieval significantly increases. The reason is that with multiple object values in anomaly details, the policy matching SQL query on $\mathcal{PG\_POLICY}$ has to repeatedly perform set containment checks for the policy objects, which leads to a higher execution time. To address this issue, we employ the following mechanism. We create two additional tables (see Table 4). We further define a primitive called "Policy_Control_List" ($\mathcal{PCL}$). A $\mathcal{PCL}$ is a bit string data type of length equal to the number of policies. It is attached to every policy predicate constant to indicate which policies are applicable to the constant. For example, if the kth policy is applicable to Role R_1, the kth bit of

---

[6] The response functions are encoded as PostgreSQL functions.

Table 4. $\mathcal{PCL}$ tables

Table	Description
$\mathcal{PG\_PCL}$	Stores the policy control list on the policy predicate constants.
$\mathcal{PG\_SOURCE\_PCL}$	Stores the policy control list on the Source IP predicate constants.

R_1's $\mathcal{PCL}$ is set to 1. The Source IP predicate constants and their corresponding $\mathcal{PCL}$s are stored in $\mathcal{PG\_SOURCE\_PCL}$ table while the rest of the predicate constants and their $\mathcal{PCL}$s are stored in $\mathcal{PG\_PCL}$[7]. An example of a policy storage scheme with a partial listing of $\mathcal{PG\_POLICY}$ columns is presented in Table 5. We create a B+tree index on both the $\mathcal{PG\_PCL}$ and $\mathcal{PG\_SOURCE\_PCL}$ tables for efficient retrieval of $\mathcal{PCL}$s. The steps of working of policy selection algorithm using $\mathcal{PCL}$s are reported in Table 6.

Table 5. Policy Storage Example

$\mathcal{PG\_POLICY}$					
Policy Num	Roles	Source IP	Objs	SQL Cmds	Severity
1	R_1, R_2	192.168.168.[0 − 255]	T_1, T_2	Select	3
2	R_1	192.168.168.[0 − 255]	T_2	Select,Insert,Update	6

$\mathcal{PG\_PCL}$	
Predicate Constant	PCL
R_1	00011
R_2	00001
T_1	00001
T_2	00011
Select	00011
Insert	00010
Update	00010

$\mathcal{PG\_SOURCE\_PCL}$	
Predicate Constant	PCL
192.168.168.[0 − 255]	00011

4.1   Experimental Results

We begin with describing the experimental set-up. The experiments are performed on a Pentium dual-core processor machine with 2 GB RAM running openSUSE 10.3. The programming language used is PostgreSQL's procedural language i.e. pl/pgsql. For the DBMS installation, we create 10 databases, 50

---

[7] This distinction is made because Source IP predicate constants are stored as PostgreSQL native datatype 'inet' while the other predicate constants are stored as 'text'. Storing Source IP as inet type enables us to perform IP address specific operations such as checking whether an IP belongs to a subnet or not, and so forth.

Table 6. Policy Selection Algorithm using $\mathcal{PCL}$s

Step	Description
1	Determine all PCLs matching the anomaly Source IP from $\mathcal{PG\_SOURCE\_PCL}$.
2	Determine all PCLs matching the rest of the anomaly attribute values from $\mathcal{PG\_PCL}$.
3	Combine all applicable PCLs to get the final $\mathcal{PCL}$.
4	Determine applicable policy ids from the final $\mathcal{PCL}$.
5	Determine the response action functions from $\mathcal{PG\_POLICY}$ corresponding to the policy ids
6	Execute the MSP or LSP depending upon the policy selection strategy.

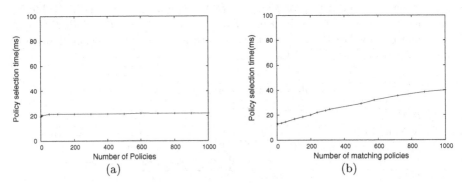

Fig. 4. Policy selection experiments

tables per database, 50 users and 5 roles. The number of client applications is set to 10 and the source IP values are generated in the $192.168.[0 - 255].[0 - 255]$ range. The policy generation procedure randomly generates the predicates for each policy condition, stores them in the $\mathcal{PG\_POLICY}$ table and also updates the $\mathcal{PG\_PCL}$ and $\mathcal{PG\_SOURCE\_PCL}$ tables with the $\mathcal{PCL}$s. We have performed two sets of experiments on the policy selection algorithm using $\mathcal{PCL}$s.

In the *first experiment*, we vary the number of policies keeping the anomaly size (i.e number of anomaly attribute values submitted by the detection engine) constant at 10. Note that the anomaly attribute values include the "Objs" attribute values. The size of the $\mathcal{PCL}$ is kept at 1000 implying that the system can support a maximum of 1000 policies. The results are shown in figure 4(a). The policy selection time is very low at approximately 20 ms. Moreover, it remains almost constant irrespective of the number of policies in the database. The reason is that the queries to $\mathcal{PG\_PCL}$ and $\mathcal{PG\_SOURCE\_PCL}$ tables are very efficient (due to indexing), while the bulk of the time of the policy selection algorithm is instead spent in obtaining the policy ids from the final $\mathcal{PCL}$ (step 4 of the algorithm). This is because we currently use PostgreSQL's built-in *bit-string* datatype for storing the $\mathcal{PCL}$s. We believe that the efficiency of the policy selection algorithm using $\mathcal{PCL}$s can be further improved by a more efficient encoding of the $\mathcal{PCL}$s.

Fig. 5. (a) ACLItem (b) ACLStateItem

In the *second experiment*, we observe the effect of an increase in the number of matching policies on the policy selection time. Note that varying the anomaly size is equivalent to fine-tuning the granularity of the detection engine. Also note that the number of policies that match an anomaly is dependent on the anomaly size. The graph for policy selection time vs number of matching policies is shown in Figure 4(b). As expected, the policy matching time increases as more policies match an anomaly. This shows that there is a trade-off between the granularity of detection mechanism and the overhead due to response policy selection. Overall, our experiments confirm the low overhead of the policy storage mechanism.

4.2 Privilege States

We now discuss the implementation scheme for maintaining privilege states in PostgreSQL's access control mechanism. In PostgreSQL, accesses to resources are controlled by using Access Control Lists (ACL) [1]. There is an ACL attached to every database object. An ACL is an array of *ACLItems* with an ACLItem for every user that has been granted privileges on that object. An ACLItem is a 32 bit unsigned integer (see figure 5(a)). The lower 16 bits are the privilege bits while the upper 16 bits are the grant option bits. If bit k is set to 1 ($0 <= k < 15$), privilege P_k is assigned to the user. If $(k + 16)^{th}$ bit is also set to 1, it means that the user has grant option on P_k. With this efficient design, the complexity of the access control check code is simply $O(n)$ where n is the size of the ACL array.

In practice, as our experiments show, the time spent in the access check code for a specific database object is few microseconds when the size of the ACL is equal to 50. Thus, we follow the same design strategy for storing the privilege

Table 7. Privilege states truth table

ACLItem k^{th} bit	ACLStateItem k^{th} bit	ACLStateItem $(k + 16)^{th}$ bit	Description
0	0	0	P_k is not assigned to user
0	0	1	Not Possible
0	1	0	Not Possible
0	1	1	Not Possible
1	0	0	State(P_k) : CLEAN
1	0	1	State(P_k) : SUSPENDED
1	1	0	State(P_k) : TAINTED
1	1	1	Not Possible

states as well. We attach an ACLState to each database object. An ACLState is an array of *ACLStateItems* with an ACLStateItem for every user that has been granted privileges on that object. Like an ACLItem, an ACLStateItem is also a 32 bit unsigned integer (see figure 5(b)). The lower 16 bits are the privilege TAINT bits, while the upper 16 bits are the privilege SUSPENSION bits. If the kth bit in an ACLStateItem is set to 1 ($0 <= k < 15$), and the $(k + 16)^{th}$ bit is set to 0, it means that P_k is TAINTED. The complete truth table for a privilege P_k's different states is then specified using the bits in ACLItem and ACLStateItem as shown in Table 7.

5   Related Work

Various commercial database monitoring and intrusion detection products are today available on the market [6]. We categorize them into two broad categories: *network-appliance-based* and *agent-based*. Network-appliance-based solutions consist of a dedicated hardware appliance that taps into an organization's network, and monitors network traffic to and from the data center. Agent-based solutions, on the other hand, have a software component installed on the database server that interacts with the DBMS in order to monitor accesses to the data. Each method has its own advantages and disadvantages. Network appliances, in general, are unable to monitor privileged users who can log into the database server directly [6]. Agent-based solutions, on the other hand, result in more overhead because of the additional software running on the database server and its usage of CPU and memory resources. Moreover, as mentioned earlier in Section 1, a common shortcoming of these products is their inability to issue a suitable response to an ongoing attack.

Peng Liu et al. have proposed architectures and algorithms for intrusion tolerant databases [10] and [3]. Their work focuses on techniques to restore the state of the DBMS to a 'correct' state after rolling back the effects of a malicious transaction. We instead focus on creating a framework for providing a real-time response to a malicious transaction so that the transaction is prevented from being executed.

A taxonomy and survey of intrusion response systems is presented in [18]. According to this taxonomy, our response mechanism may be termed as 'static' *by ability to adjust*, 'autonomous' *by cooperation ability*, 'dynamic mapping' *by response selection method* and both 'proactive' and 'delayed' *by time of response*. We direct the reader to [18] for further details on the taxonomy.

Foo et. al. [7] have also presented a survey of intrusion response systems. However, the survey is specific to distributed systems. Since the focus of our work is development of a response mechanism in context of a stand-alone database server, most of the techniques described in [7] are not applicable our scenario.

6   Conclusion and Future Work

In this paper, we have presented a framework for specifying response actions to anomalous database requests. We have extended the Event-Condition-Action language with *confirmation* and *alternate* actions semantics for supporting novel response mechanisms. We have also introduced the notion of *tainted* and *suspended* privilege states as more fine-grained ways to respond to database anomalies. We have implemented our methods in PostgreSQL and through experimental analysis shown the efficiency of our techniques.

The implementation currently does not support storing policies with predicates involving attributes with an infinite domain such as real numbers, and infinite regular expressions. We intend to investigate techniques for storing and indexing such predicates in a DBMS as part of our future work. Another direction for future work is to extend the privilege state mechanism to work with role and permission hierarchies.

References

1. Postgresql 8.3, http://www.postgresql.org/
2. The cyber enemy within.. countering the threat from malicious insiders. In: Proceedings of the 20th Annual Computer Security Applications Conference (ACSAC) (2004)
3. Ammann, P., Jajodia, S., Liu, P.: Recovery from malicious transactions. IEEE Transactions on Knowledge and Data Engineering (TKDE) 14(5), 1167–1185 (2002)
4. Bertino, E., Kamra, A., Early, J.: Profiling database application to detect sql injection attacks. In: IEEE International Performance, Computing, and Communications Conference (IPCCC), April 2007, pp. 449–458 (2007)
5. Bertino, E., Kamra, A., Terzi, E., Vakali, A.: Intrusion detection in rbac-administered databases. In: Proceedings of the 21st Annual Computer Security Applications Conference (ACSAC) (2005)
6. Conry-Murray, A.: The threat from within. Network Computing (August 2005), http://www.networkcomputing.com/showArticle.jhtml?articleID=166400792
7. Foo, B., Glause, M., Modelo-Howard, G., Wu, Y.-S., Bagchi, S., Spafford, E.H.: Information Assurance: Dependability and Security in Networked Systems. Morgan Kaufmann, San Francisco (2007)
8. Kamra, A., Bertino, E., Terzi, E.: Detecting anomalous access patterns in relational databases. The International Journal on Very Large Data Bases (VLDB) (2008)
9. Litchfield, D., Anley, C., Heasman, J., Grindlay, B.: The Database Hacker's Handbook: Defending Database Servers. Wiley, Chichester (2005)
10. Liu, P.: Architectures for intrusion tolerant database systems. In: Proceedings of the Annual Computer Security Applications Conference (ACSAC) (2002)
11. Mogull, R.: Top five steps to prevent data loss and information leaks. Gartner Research (July (2006), http://www.gartner.com
12. Natan, R.B.: Implementing Database Security and Auditing. Digital Press (2005)
13. Nicolett, M., Wheatman, J.: Dam technology provides monitoring and analytics with less overhead. Gartner Research (November 2007), http://www.gartner.com
14. S. S. B. Online. Database-level roles. 21.aspx (1891), http://msdn2.microsoft.com/en-us/library/ms
15. S. S. B. Online. Deny (transact-sql), http://msdn2.microsoft.com/en-us/library/ms188338.aspx

16. Ramaswamy, C., Sandhu, R.: Role-based access control features in commercial database management systems. In: Proceedings of the 21st NIST-NCSC National Information Systems Security Conference (1998)
17. Squicciarini, A.C., Bhargav-Spantzel, A., Bertino, E., Czeksis, A.B.: Auth-sl - a system for the specification and enforcement of quality-based authentication policies. In: Proceedings of 9th International Conference on Information and Communications Security (ICICS)
18. Stakhanova, N., Basu, S., Wong, J.: A taxonomy of intrusion response systems. International Journal of Information and Computer Security (IJICS) 1(2), 169–184 (2007)
19. Widom, J., Ceri, S.: Active Database Systems: Triggers and Rules for Advanced Database Processing. Morgan Kaufmann, San Francisco (1995)

Auditing Inference Based Disclosures in Dynamic Databases

Vikram Goyal[1], S.K. Gupta[1], Manish Singh[1], and Anand Gupta[2]

[1] Department of Computer Science and Engineering, IIT Delhi
Hauz Khas, New Delhi-16
{vkgoyal,skg,cs5040215}@cse.iitd.ernet.in
[2] Dept. of Comp. Sci. and Engg. N.S.I.T. Delhi, Sector-3, Dwarka,
New Delhi
anand@coe.nsit.ac.in

Abstract. A privacy violation in an information system could take place either through explicit access or inference over already revealed facts using domain knowledge. In a post violation scenario, an auditing framework should consider both these aspects to determine exact set of minimal suspicious queries set. Update operations in database systems add more complexity in case of auditing, as inference rule applications on different data versions may generate erroneous information in addition to the valid information. In this paper, we formalize the problem of auditing inference based disclosures in dynamic databases, and present a sound and complete algorithm to determine a suspicious query set for a given domain knowledge, a database, an audit query, updates in the database. Each element of the output set is a minimal set of past user queries made to the database system such that data revealed to these queries combined with domain knowledge can infer the valid data specified by the audit query.

1 Introduction

Privacy concerns have become prominent in e-commerce, e-governance and a host of services delivered through the Internet. Governments have also enacted regulatory laws balancing various needs to provide robust and acceptable privacy. Academic and commercial organizations have carried out research to achieve the holy grail of complete privacy. However despite considerable efforts [1,2,3,4], privacy intrusions [5,6,7,8,9] continue to rise and raise serious concerns. Providing robust privacy infrastructure remains an elusive and perhaps a Utopian goal.

Privacy intrusions do take place even in the presence of privacy and access control systems (which prevent direct privacy violation) due to inference channels or social engineering. Inference channels in relational databases are created by combining database constraints and non-sensitive data. The mechanisms [10,11,12,13,14] to prevent information disclosure through inference channels can be organized into two categories. The first category includes mechanisms that operate during database design by increasing the number of categories of information and users. The mechanisms in second category prevent violation during query processing time, where a current query result is analyzed with past answers to find out whether the current query discloses sensitive

W. Jonker and M. Petković (Eds.): SDM 2008, LNCS 5159, pp. 67–81, 2008.

information. However, by using either one of the above mentioned inference based prevention technique, the violations can be reduced. But the violations that occur due to social engineering are difficult to stop. For example, if an authorized user misuses the authorized information, none of IT technique can prevent a privacy violation. Therefore, privacy violations due to social engineering require the development of auditing solutions to determine the authorized users, who have accessed a particular information which led to a privacy violation. We focus in the paper on social engineering type of violation, and propose an auditing framework which audits violation by inference.

In an auditing system [15,16,17], during normal operation the text of every query processed by the database system is logged in User Accesses Log (UAL) along with annotations such as the execution time, the user submitting the query, and the purpose of the query. The data updates are stored in temporal database which make it possible to determine the actual set of objects accessed by a user query. For the audit, an administrator/ auditor specifies target data (data which lead to a privacy violation) and a suspicion notion in the form of an audit query. Suspicion notion defines the criteria to determine the suspiciousness of a query set. The criterion defines parameters like number of tuples/ columns from the target data which should have been accessed including information disclosure ways like explicit access or inference based access, single query or a set of queries etc., to decide suspicion label. The audit query is executed over the UAL and temporal database to output a exact set (with no false positives and negatives) of suspicious user queries from the UAL.

In this paper, we give an algorithm for determining suspicious query set for a given audit query, a query log UAL, a temporal / rollback / history database, and attack sophistication as 'inference'. Each element of the output set, is a minimal set of user queries whose result combined with the domain knowledge, infers the information that satisfy the suspicion notion of the input audit query. Our work is complementary to the work done for prevention of information disclosure through inferencing [13]. They determine whether the current query discloses a secure object for a given set of revealed facts, a database, updates in the database, and a domain knowledge. The following example shows a proper execution of the suspicious queries determination and different issues that need to be addressed.

Consider the relation Employee in Table 1, containing information about the name, rank, salary and department of employees. The relation satisfies the FD (a database constraint) *Rank → Salary*. Let us assume that the input audit query specifies target data as 'name and salary of John' information and suspicion notion as 'at least one tuple of the audit query identified target data tuples', attack sophistication as inference based disclosure.

Suppose there are following queries in the query log UAL for a user Lucy:
(*"Select Rank, Salary from Employee where Rank='Clerk' "*,t1;
"Select Name, Rank from Employee where Dept='CSE' ", t2;
*"Select * from Employee where Name='Robert' "*,t3)

Let us consider two different cases (a) Database with no updates, and (b) Database with updates. In case (a), Lucy would have following answers:

Query 1: {<*Clerk, 30000*>}
Query 2:{<*John, Clerk*>; <*Harry, Admin*>; <*Joe, Clerk*>}
Query 3:{<*Robert, Clerk, 30000, Electrical*>}

The following can be inferred on application of FD *Rank* → *Salary* on the result of these queries:

{(<*Clerk, 30000*>, *Q1*); (<*John, Clerk*>, *Q2*); (<*Harry, Admin*>, *Q2*); (<*Joe, Clerk*>, *Q2*); (<*John, Clerk, 30000*>, {*Q1, Q2*},{*Q2, Q3*}); (<*Joe, Clerk, 30000*>, {*Q1, Q2*}, {*Q2, Q3*}), (<*Robert, Clerk, 30000, Electrical*>, *Q3*)}

The audit query would select only one tuple out of the inferred tuples, i.e. <*John, Clerk, 30000*>, {*Q1,Q2*},{*Q2,Q3*}. Therefore, the resultant suspicious query set would be {{*Q1, Q2*},{*Q2,Q3*}}.

It may be noted from the above example that (i) a subset of the power set of set containing all candidate user queries is associated with each tuple, such that each member of that set can derive the tuple using inference rules, (ii) associated set does not contain two elements such that one element is the subset of other element, i.e. each element is a minimal subset, and (iii) this information of queries set is propagated and assigned to each new inferred partial tuple.

For the case (b), let us assume the following sequence of events.

Time 1: Lucy submits Query 1.
Time 2: Lucy submits Query 2.
Time 3: John is promoted to Admin and Harry is promoted to Manager.
Time 4: Salary of a Clerk is increased to 35000.
Time 5: Lucy submits Query 3.

The resultant updated Employee relation will be as given in Table 2. In this case the answers to the queries would be:

Query 1: {<*Clerk, 30000*>}
Query 2:{<*John, Clerk*>; <*Harry, Admin*>; <*Joe, Clerk*>}
Query 3:{<*Robert, Clerk, 35000, Electrical*>}

The following can be inferred based on application of the database constraint *Rank* → *Salary*:

{(<*Clerk, 30000*>, *Q1*); (<*John, Clerk*>, *Q2*); (<*Harry, Admin*>, *Q2*); (<*Joe, Clerk*>, Q2); (<John, Clerk, 30000>, {Q1, Q2}); (<Joe, Clerk, 30000>, {Q1, Q2});(<Robert, Clerk, 35000, Electrical>, Q3); (<John, Clerk, 35000>, {Q2, Q3}); (<Joe, Clerk, 35000>, {Q2, Q3});(<Robert, Clerk, 30000, Electrical>,{Q1,Q3})}

In this case, Lucy would infer two different values of Salary for both John and Joe. Hence, she may conclude that Salary of John and Joe was 30000 earlier and has been increased to 35000 now. If the audit query is applied over inferred relation, it would select $\{(<John, Clerk, 30000>, \{Q1, Q2\}), (<John, Clerk, 35000>, \{Q2, Q3\})\}$ tuples. It may be noted that Lucy did not know about database updates and hence infers wrong tuple *<John, Clerk, 35000>*; this tuple never existed in earlier versions of database from Time 1 to Time 5. Our algorithm does not consider wrong tuples as sensitive information and thus has to detect the wrong or invalid inferences. It outputs only $\{Q1, Q2\}$ in the output set for the given audit query, which makes our process a sound and complete, i.e., our process does not generate any false positives and negatives. Inclusion of invalid tuple like *<John, Clerk, 35000>* would violate the soundness property as this is not a sensitive information from the application perspective due to its non existence in any version of database from Time 1 to Time 5. Thus, it requires a mechanism to determine the validity of a inferred tuple. We solve this problem by first determining all the valid audit tuples and then checking for those audit tuples in the inferred relation.

Table 1. Employee Table

ID	NAME	RANK	SALARY	DEPT
1	John	Clerk	30000	CSE
2	Harry	Admin	45000	CSE
3	Robert	Clerk	30000	Elect.
4	Joe	Clerk	30000	CSE
5	Thomas	Manager	50000	Elect.

Table 2. Updated Employee Table

ID	NAME	RANK	SALARY	DEPT
1	John	Admin	45000	CSE
2	Harry	Manager	50000	CSE
3	Robert	Clerk	35000	Elect.
4	Joe	Clerk	35000	CSE
5	Thomas	Manager	50000	Elect.

In this paper, we propose a conceptual framework for auditing that determines a suspicious query set for a dynamic database in the presence of inference based information disclosure. To the authors' best knowledge this is the first work that considers inferences in database dependent auditing and is sound and complete. Our model addresses generalized database dependencies which are represented as Horn-clause constraints and formalizes the problem.

The paper is organized as follows. In the next section we present related work. Section 3 describes architecture and the proposed algorithm. Section 4 contains preliminaries, notations and proves correctness of proposed algorithm. Finally, we conclude in Section 5 and recommend future work.

2   Related Work

In this section, we describe earlier auditing and prevention work done by different authors.

2.1   Data Dependent Auditing of SQL Queries

In [15], Agrawal et al. explore the auditing problem of determining whether any single SQL query in the query log accessed a specific information specified by an audit expression. Their syntax for audit expressions (given below) closely resembles SQL queries.

```
AUDIT attribute list FROM table names WHERE conditional expression
```

An audit expression essentially identifies the tuples of interest via predicates in the *WHERE* clause from the cross-product of tables in the *FROM* clause. Any query which has accessed all the attributes in the audit list and the *WHERE* clause of which gets satisfied by any of the identified tuples is tagged as a suspicious query. We illustrate this with examples. Consider the audit expression:

```
AUDIT disease FROM Patients WHERE zipcode=120016
```

This expression tags all queries that returned disease information about any patient living in area 120016. Now consider the SQL query:

```
SELECT zipcode FROM Patients WHERE disease='cancer'
```

This SQL query will be considered suspicious with respect to the above audit expression if any patient who has cancer lives in area *120016*. It would not, however, be suspicious with respect to the following expression if no patient having both cancer and diabetes exists.

```
AUDIT zipcode FROM Patients WHERE disease='diabetes'
```

This is due to the fact that this audit expression checks only whether the zipcode of any patient with diabetes was disclosed. It may be noted here that the authors do not consider real life attacks sophistication such as multiple queries or inference based attacks.

Motwani et al. [18] extends this work for multiple queries and determines the suspiciousness of a query batch for a given audit query. The authors consider only current database instance and do not work for dynamic databases.

2.2 Data Independent Auditing of SQL Queries

This type of auditing is done independent of a database instance, i.e., a database is not accessed. Due to being independent from a database instance, this would be very fast as compared to database dependent auditing as accessing a database is a costly operation. But, unfortunately, it is computationally intractable to determine suspicion for many query types for a given audit expression and a notion of suspicion [18,19,20].

The authors in [19,20] have considered the problem of "perfect privacy" which determines whether a database system discloses *any information* at all about a secret view through various views revealed by it. Here secret view corresponds to the audit expression and the views that were revealed to answered queries.

The authors have also proved that deciding whether a conjunctive query q is secure w.r.t. a set of conjunctive secret views $A_1, \cdots A_k$ is π_2^p-complete [20]. Further in [19], the authors have shown this problem as tractable for different subclasses of conjunctive queries by establishing a connection between perfect privacy enforcement and the query containment problem [21,22].

In [18], Motwani et al. show that a subclass of conjunctive queries, i.e., queries with out inequalities, is NP-hard for the "semantically suspicious notion for a batch of queries". Therefore, they have given another notion of suspicion called "weak syntactic suspiciousness" which has stronger disclosure guarantee as compared to the notion of "semantic suspiciousness" given by Agrawal et al. [15] and show that this subclass of queries is tractable for their suspicion notion.

It may be noted that these work do not consider any inference type of disclosure for auditing and focus only on defining suspicion notions and determining the classes of SQL queries for which suspiciousness is decidable.

2.3 Data Dependent Prevention of Information Disclosure by Inference

Prevention techniques [10,11,12,13,14] detect and remove the inference channel either at the design time or during query processing time. Design time approaches are not flexible and may lead to over classification of data. This prevents even an authorized user to access an information. On the other hand, query processing approaches are flexible but take more time to answer a query, and hence increase a query response time.

We find the work done by Farkas et al. [13] in query processing category closely related to our work. They consider database updates while inference, and increase data availability for a user as they avoid inference of wrong tuples. Their work is different from ours as they decide for the current user query answer, i.e. whether the current query should be denied or allowed. Their algorithms for dependency application and disclosure are not applicable in our problem. We determine a suspicious queries set, each element of which contains a minimal set of past user queries that collectively combined with domain knowledge infer the information specified by an input audit query.

3 Auditing Architecture

Auditing process starts after a privacy violation is reported to the administrator. The auditor on the base of available information; such as malafide intention of the attacker, target data characteristics and attacking way etc.; forms an audit query [23]. The auditing system, consider Figure 1, returns a set of minimal set of suspicious queries which satisfy the constraints given in the audit query. The system works for static as well as dynamic databases. The audit query and domain knowledge are used by the *Candidate Queries Selector* module to determine the parameters to prune *non-candidate* queries. These parameters computation is done on the basis of input attack configuration. For example, in case of no inference based attack, this module does not apply domain knowledge to determine the parameters. A query is termed as a *non-candidate* query if its result can not be used to infer any target data tuple specified by the audit query.

The selected candidate queries are executed over temporal database by the *Queries Executer* module to determine the actual data objects revealed to these queries. The domain knowledge is applied over these query answers which returns all the disclosed information. The query tags are also propagated during this process such that every data object tag specifies the set of queries through which it can be obtained. The audit

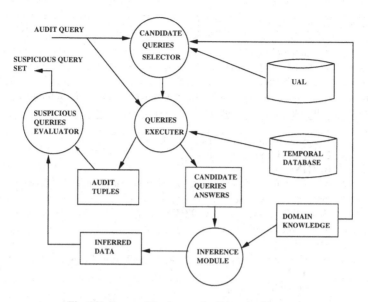

Fig. 1. Inference Disclosure Auditing Architecture

query data objects which are obtained through Query Executer module are searched in the inferred data. The suspicious query set is determined by taking the union of tags associated with the audit query tuples in the inferred data.

The algorithm for auditing inference disclosure is given in Figure 2.

4 Inference Disclosure Auditing

4.1 Preliminaries and Notations

To avoid dealing with the intricacies of relational data model, we assume database as a single "universal" relation consisting of Cartesian product of the base relations [11,24]. The relation is denoted as R, its instance as r and its attributes as $A_1, ..., A_n$. We denote projection of relation R on attributes $A_1, ..., A_k$ as $A_1, ..., A_k[R]$.

Definition 1. *(Data Fact)*
A data fact d_i in relation $R(A_1, ...A_n)$ is an expression of the form

$$d_i = R[A_1 = a_1^i, ..., A_n = a_n^i]$$

where R is a relation, $A_1, ..., A_n$ are the attributes in relation R and $a_1^i, ..., a_n^i$ are constants or null of the respective domains.

A database instance is viewed as a set of data facts such that each data fact has associated with it a unique tuple identifier *ID*.

As stated earlier, temporal database makes it possible to retrieve the actual contents accessed by a past user query. We assume its organization similar to the organization as discussed in [15].

Algorithm 1. Inference Disclosure Auditing
Input   1. a candidate queries set in UAL (Q, TS) 2. a domain knowledge D 3. a temporal Database TR 4. an audit Query A
Output   A suspicious queries set S such that each element $e \in S$ is a minimal set of user queries deriving target data tuple

Method
   1. Create an empty answer-query relation, i.e., $rq = \phi$
   2. **For** every candidate query (q, τ) in (Q, TS) do
   BEGIN
   —— Determine $Facts_{(q,\tau)}$ and extend each partial tuple $t_i \in Facts_{(q,\tau)}$
   to create an answer-query fact (d_i, qs_i).
   —— **IF** $(d_i \notin A_1, ..., A_n[rq])$ **THEN**
   ——add (d_i, qs_i) to relation rq
   —— **END IF**
   ——**IF** the data fact d_i is present as an answer-query fact $(d_i, qs_j) \in rq$
   ——**THEN**
   ——reset the value qs_j, s.t.
   ——$qs_j = \{x | (x \in qs_i$ or $x \in qs_j) \wedge \nexists y, (y \in qs_i$ or $y \in qs_j)$ s.t. $y \subset x\}$
   ——**END IF**
   END FOR
   3. Chase relation rq with inference rules D
   4. Determine audit tuples O_A for audit query A
   5. $S = \phi$
   6. Determine the answer-query facts $rq_i \in rq$ which have its attributes value
   equal to any of the audit tuple values.
   7. Set $S = \cup_i QS[rq_i]$
   8. return S

Fig. 2. Algorithm for Suspicious Queries Determination

Definition 2. *(Temporal Data Relation) A temporal data relation of relation $R(A_1, ...,$ $A_n)$ is defined to be relation $TR(A_1, ..., A_n, OP, TS)$ where $OP = \{ins, del\}$ is an operation and TS is a time stamp.*

Definition 3. *(Temporal Data Fact) A temporal data fact td_i, in relation $TR(A_1, ..., A_n,$ $OP, TS)$ is an expression of the form*

$$td_i = TR[A_1 = a_1^i, ..., A_n = a_n^i, OP = op_i, TS = ts_i]$$

where TR is a relation name, $A_1, ..., A_n, OP, TS$ are attributes in relation TR, $a_1^i, ..., a_n^i$ are constants, $op_i \in OP = \{ins, del\}$, and ts_i is a valid time stamp.

A temporal database is a sequence of temporal data facts $td_1, ..., td_n$ such that for all $1 \leq j \leq n - 1, ts_j \leq ts_{j+1}$.

Each data manipulation operation over current database instance is logged in temporal database with operation and time stamp annotations. In case a data fact d_i is inserted in current database R at time stamp ts_i, a temporal data tuple td_j is formed by extending

Table 3. Current Instance of Employee Database

ID	NAME	RANK	SALARY	DEPT
2	Harry	Admin	55000	CSE

Table 4. Temporal Employee Database

ID	NAME	RANK	SALARY	DEPT	OP	TS
1	John	Clerk	30000	CSE	ins	T_1
2	Harry	Admin	45000	CSE	ins	T_2
1	John	Clerk	30000	CSE	del	T_3
2	Harry	Admin	45000	CSE	del	T_4
2	Harry	Admin	55000	CSE	ins	T_4

the data tuple d_i with two attributes OP and TS and setting their values as $OP = ins$, $TS = ts_i$ respectively. This formed tuple is then inserted into temporal database TR. Similarly, when a deletion of a data fact d_i occurs in current database, a temporal data fact is formed by annotating d_i with operation value as del, time stamp as ts_i; and is inserted into relation TR. Update operation on data fact d_i is simulated by a sequence of two operations, i.e., insert operation followed by a delete operation. As an example consider the employee database *Employee(Name, Rank, Salary, Dept)* and its corresponding temporal database as *T-Employee(Name, Rank, Salary, Dept, OP, TS)*. Let us assume that the following sequence of operations takes place on relation Employee:

Time 1: Insert Employee [Name=John, Rank=Clerk, Salary=30000, Deptt=CSE]
Time 2: Insert Employee [Name=Harry, Rank=Admin, Salary=45000, Deptt=CSE]
Time 3: Delete Employee [Name=John, Rank=Clerk, Salary=30000, Deptt=CSE]
Time 4: Update [Name=Harry, Rank=Admin, Salary=45000, Deptt=CSE] to [Name= Harry, Rank=Admin, Salary=55000, Deptt=CSE]

The state of the relations Employee and T-Employee after the above operations will be as given in Table 3 and Table 4.

A user query Q in the query log UAL is a select-project query $(\pi_Y \sigma_C, ts)$ where π_Y denotes a projection on set of attributes Y, σ_C denotes selection operation of query and ts denotes the time stamp at which time the query was executed. Here, C is conjunction or disjunction of binary operations of the form (A op B) or (A op b) and $op \in \{=, <, >\}$, where A, B are attribute names and b is a constant. We denote by C_Q the attribute names that appear any where in query Q. We denote Q_{UAL} as the set of all past user queries (Q, τ) in UAL.

Data facts set $Facts_{(Q,TS)}$ revealed to a user query $(\pi_Y \sigma_C, \tau)$ in UAL are determined by executing the query over the temporal database as given below

$$Facts_{(\pi_Y \sigma_C, \tau)} = \pi_{C_Q}(\{t \mid t \in TR \land t.TS \leq \tau \land$$
$$t.OP \neq del \land \nexists r \in TR \text{ s.t. } t.id = r.id \land$$
$$r.TS \leq \tau \land r.TS > t.TS \land t \text{ satisfies } C\}).$$

We consider Horn clause constraints for specifying domain knowledge which forms the basis of data disclosures.

Definition 4. *(Horn-clause constraint) A Horn-clause constraint is an expression of the form* $\forall x_1,...,x_k(p_1 \wedge ... \wedge p_n \rightarrow h)$ *where* $x_1,...,x_k$ *are all the free variables in* $p_1 \wedge ... \wedge p_n \rightarrow h$, *each* p_i *is of the form*

$$R[A_1 = a_1,...,A_k = a_k]$$

each a_i *is either a variable or a constant, and each h is of the following form*

$$R[A_1 = a_1,...,A_n = a_n],$$

where $A_1,...,A_n$ *are all the attributes of database R and each* a_i *is either a constant or variable that must appear in* $p_1,...,p_n$.

We use $p_1,...,p_n \rightarrow h$ as shorthand for Horn-clause constraint and will refer $p_1,...,p_n$ as the body and h as the head. Horn-clause constraint can express variety of user defined knowledge including database constraints such as functional dependencies and multi valued dependencies [13,24].

For an example, let $R(A,B,C,D)$ is a relation, a functional dependency $A \rightarrow B$ based inference rule can be represented as:

$$R[A=a,B=b1,C=c1,D=d1] \wedge R[A=a, B=b2,C=c2,D=d2] \rightarrow R[A=a, B=b1, C=c2, D=d2]$$

This rule represents that if two data facts match in their attributes $A's$ value and differ in attribute $B's$ value then we can infer new tuple which is formed by using attribute $B's$ value of one tuple and all other attribute's value of other tuple.

The database constraints are applied recursively on the explicitly disclosed information by Chase algorithm (figure 3) to get all the disclosed data. During this process of domain knowledge applications we also propagate the queries through which the resultant data fact is inferred. We control the generation of new data fact by using tuple dominance.

Definition 5. *(Tuple Dominance) A data fact t is said to dominate data fact r if data fact r can be obtained through application of projection operation on data fact t. We denote tuple dominance relation by* $t \models r$.

For example, the data fact $R[Name=John, Rank=Clerk, Salary=30000]$ dominates data fact $R[Name=Null, Rank=Clerk, Salary=30000]$. But the data fact $R[Name=John, Rank=Clerk, Salary=30000]$ does not dominate $R[Name=John, Dept=CSE]$. It may be noted that we assume here that a constant value dominates *Null* value.

We determine the set of suspicious queries from the inferred information which requires us to associate queries related information with inferred tuples.

Definition 6. *(Answer-query fact) An answer-queries fact* $rq_i = (d_i, QS_i)$ *is a pair, where* d_i *is a data fact and* QS_i, *query label, is a set of sets of queries in* Q_{UAL}, *where* Q_{UAL} *is the set of queries in UAL.*

It may be noted that $QS_i \subset 2^{Q_{UAL}}$ as it is a subset of power set of queries in Q_{UAL}. Intuitively, an answer query fact $(< d_i >, QS_i)$ represents that the fact d_i can be derived from the facts revealed to queries in any element of QS_i by applying the domain knowledge D. For example, the answer-queries fact (<John, Clerk, 30000>, $\{Q1, Q2\}, \{Q2, Q3\}$) from the example given in section Introduction, represents that the fact <John, Clerk, 30000> can be derived by either queries set $\{Q_1, Q_2\}$ or queries set $\{Q_2, Q_3\}$ by applying domain knowledge $D = \{Rank \rightarrow Salary\}$.

In our case, we apply domain knowledge on the explicitly disclosed facts to a user (users) queries. It may be noted that these revealed data facts are partial data facts as they do not contain values for each attribute present in the relation R. Therefore, we extend these facts to Answer-queries fact form by (i) setting the value equal to *Null* for each attribute that is not present in the revealed fact, and (ii) setting query label QS_i equal to $\{\{Q\}\}$, where Q is the query through which that fact was disclosed to the user.

Definition 7. (*Answer-Query Relation*) *An answer-query relation $RQ(A_1, ..., A_n, QS)$ is a set of answer queries facts $(A_1 = a_1^i, ..., A_n = a_n^i, QS = qs_i)$.*

Definition 8. (*Atom Mapping of a Horn-clause Constraint*) *Given an answer-query relation rq, and a Horn-clause constraint $A_1, ..., A_n \rightarrow H$, an atom mapping is defined as a function*

$$f : A_1, ..., A_n \rightarrow rq$$

such that

1. *constants are preserved in mapping f; i.e., if $f(RQ[..., A_i = c, ...]) = c_1, ..., c_i, ..., c_n \in rq$ and c is a constant, then $c = c_i$, and*
2. *equalities are preserved in mapping f; i.e., if $P_i = RQ[..., A_i = a, ...], P_j = RQ[..., A_j = a, ...]$ and $f(P_i) = (..., c_i, ...), f(P_j) = (..., c_j, ...)$, then $c_i = c_j$.*

Definition 9. (*Query label generation*) *A query label generation function $QS = g(QS_1, ..., QS_m)$ is a function of type $g : 2^{Q_{UAL}}, 2^{Q_{UAL}, ...} \rightarrow 2^{Q_{UAL}}$ defined as follows*

$$QS' = \{ y_1 \cup ... \cup y_m \mid \forall y_1, ..., y_m, 1 \leq i \leq m : y_i \in QS_i \}$$
$$QS = \{ x \mid x \in QS', \nexists y \in QS' \text{ s.t. } y \subset x \}$$

Definition 10. (*Dependency Application*) *A dependency $P_1, ..., P_m \rightarrow RQ[A_1, ..A_n, QS]$ application on an answer-query relation rq by using atom mapping function f and query label generation function g, generates an answer-query fact (d_i, qs_i) if $\forall i, 1 \leq i \leq m$, no data fact $f(P_i)$ dominates the data fact d_i, i.e., $f(P_i) \nvDash d_i$, where $d_i = (f(A_1), ..., f(A_n))$ and $qs_i = g(QS[f(P_1)], ..., QS[f(P_m)])$. If the fact d_i is not present in $A_1, ..., A_n[rq]$ then*

$$add (d_i, qs_i) \text{ to } rq,$$

else if the data fact d_i is present as an answer-query fact (d_i, qs_j) then reset the value qs_j as follows:

$$qs_j = \{x \mid (x \in qs_i \text{ or } x \in qs_j) \wedge \nexists y, (y \in qs_i \text{ or } y \in qs_j) \text{ s.t. } y \subset x \}.$$

Algorithm Chase	
INPUT	1. A set of Horn-clause constraints D
	2. An answer-query relation rq, which may contain *null* values
OUTPUT	Inferred relation rq
Method	**begin**
	Apply dependencies in D on rq until no more changes to rq occur
	end

Fig. 3. Chase Algorithm

It may be noted that the $QS[f(P_1)]$ is QS attribute value of the mapped tuple $f(P_1)$, and $A_1, ..., A_n[rq]$ is projection of temporal relation instance rq on attributes $A_1, ..., A_n$. We use the *Dependency Application* definition to describe a *Chase* process which is different from chase defined in [13,24]. Algorithm for the chase process is given in Figure 3.

Definition 11. *(Audit tuples or Target Data) Let $A = \pi_Y \sigma_C$ be a audit query, the audit tuples O_A for time interval (t_1, t_n) are determined by executing audit query A over the temporal database TR as follows:*

$$O_A = \pi_Y(\{t | t \in TR \wedge t \text{ satisfies } C \wedge ((t.OP = ins \wedge t.TS \le t_n \wedge t > t_1) \vee (t \in O_1))\})$$

where

$$O_1 = (\{t | t \in TR \wedge t.TS \le t_1 \wedge t.OP \ne del \wedge \nexists r \in TR$$
$$s.t. \ t.id = r.id \wedge r.TS \le t_1 \wedge r.TS > t.TS\}).$$

We in the paper assume the indispensable tuple suspicion notion given by Agarwal et al. [15]. A data tuple is indispensable for a query if the data tuple presence or absence in the database effects its output. They label a query suspicious if the user query and the audit query has a common indispensable tuple.

Definition 12. *(Inference Disclosure Auditing) Let A be an audit query, TR be a temporal database, D be a set of inference rules, Q_{UAL} be a set of user queries in query log. Inference disclosure auditing determines a suspicious query set $S \subset 2^{Q_{UAL}}$ which contains all the elements e, where*

1. *$e \in S$ is a minimal set of user queries $Q_1, ..., Q_k$,*
2. *the queries $Q_1, ..., Q_k$ disclose a set of data facts such that application of inference rules $I \in D$ on this set of data facts infer a data tuple p, which dominates at least one tuple $t \in T$, where T is a set of audit tuples identified by audit query A.*

Theorem 1. *(Inference Disclosure Auditing Decidability) The following problem is decidable: Given a set D of inference rules, a temporal database TR, a query log Q_{UAL}, whether $S \subset 2^{Q_{UAL}}$ is a suspicious query set for a given audit query A.*

Theorem 1 is corollary to Theorems 2 and 3 which states correctness of the algorithm given in Figure 2

Theorem 2. *The Inference Disclosure Auditing algorithm (figure 2) is sound.*

Proof. We prove soundness by contradiction. Assume that a set $s = \{Q_1, ..., Q_k\}$ is returned by our algorithm, but it does not derive any target data tuple $t \in T$. Given the inferred relation ar, the set s must have been included in output suspicious query set due to an answer-query fact $aq_j \in ar$; which contains s as a element in attribute QS value, i.e., $s \in QS[aq_j]$, data fact $d_j = A_1, ..., A_n[aq_j] \vDash t$ and there does not exist any other answer-query tuple $aq_i \in ar$ with a query set p_i as a member in its QS attribute value such that $p_i \subset s$. These all the above conditions are checked while any user query set is included in the returned output. The tuple dominance $d_j \vDash t$ ensures that target data is inferred from the answer query tuple aq_j and non-existence of any other set p_i such that $p_i \subset s$ ensures that set s is minimal. These two conditions do not remove a candidate minimal suspicious query set that derives any target data tuple $t \in T$ from the output.

Further, an answer-query tuple is generated either due to application of some inference rule $I_k \in D$ or it is formed from an explicitly disclosed partial tuple for some user query Q by extending that tuple to data tuple and associating query Q. If the tuple aq_j is explicitly disclosed then it's attribute QS value necessarily derives the target data. On the other hand if it is generated by a sequence of inference rules $I_1, ..., I_k$ then its data tuple d_j can be inferred from the answer queries facts obtained from queries $Q_1, ..., Q_k$, as application of an inference rule generates a answer-query tuple only if its body clauses evaluate to already existing tuples. If the generated tuple is not present in the already inferred relation then the value of QS attribute is determined by taking cartesian union of respective query sets and removal of non-minimal sets. Otherwise, QS attribute value is defined by taking the union of generated query set and already associated query set by removing non-minimal query set. Hence the query set s must have been in the output query set only if it is minimal and derives any target data tuple $t \in T$. This contradicts the assumption, and therefore the proposed algorithm is sound.

Theorem 3. *The Inference Disclosure Auditing algorithm (figure 2) is complete.*

Proof. Assume that there is a minimal query set $s = Q_1, ..., Q_k$, which derives the target data tuple $t \in T$ and s is not a member of output query set S. A set p is a member of output query set only if it is a member of QS attribute value of some tuple ar_i, i.e., $p \in QS[ar_i]$, data tuple part of that answer query tuple dominates some $t \in T$ and p is minimal over all the sets $qs_j \in QS[ar_j]$ where ar_j are all the answer-query tuples in ar which dominates some $t \in T$. Clearly, these steps while determining members of output query set do not remove any candidate set.

During application of inference rules, the non minimal query sets are removed at the time of QS attribute value determination, i.e., when attribute QS value of either existing tuple or newly generated tuple is set during chasing. Hence, the algorithm do not remove any minimal query set that can derive some target data tuple $t \in T$ in any of the step of the algorithm. Therefore, if s is a minimal query set and derives the target data tuple t by using domain knowledge D, it would be a member of output set. This contradicts the assumption. Therefore, the algorithm is complete.

5   Conclusion and Future Work

In this paper, we formalize the problem of auditing privacy violation for inference based disclosure in presence of database updates. We give a sound and complete algorithm to return a suspicious query set, each element of the output set contains a set of past user queries which have revealed the information such that the revealed information either explicitly or if combined with domain knowledge infers the information that satisfy the input audit query. To the author's best knowledge this is the first effort which audit inference based disclosures in presence of updates.

We conclude with suggestions for further work. Currently, our solution can be treated as brute force solution. It generates all the invalid inferences and are used further in inference application process. The generation of invalid inferences increases computation time of algorithm. Therefore, it would be interesting to find out a solution which checks invalid inferences and generates only valid inferences and is still sound and complete.

Acknowledgments

The authors acknowledge with thanks support from the projects "Design and development of Malafide intention based Privacy Violation Detection" sponsored by Department of Information Technology, and "Advanced Information Systems Security Laboratory".

References

1. AT & T privacy bird, http://www.privacybird.com/
2. OASIS, eXtensible Access Control Markup Language (XACML) TC,
   http://www.oasis-open.org/committees/tc_home.php?wg_abbrev=xacml
3. Ashley, P., Hada, S., Karjoth, G., Powers, C., Schunter, M.: Enterprise Privacy Authorization Language (EPAL 1.1), IBM Research Report (2003),
   http://www.zurich.ibm.com/security/enterprise-privacy/epal
4. Bhattacharya, J., Gupta, S.K.: Privacy Broker for Enforcing Privacy Policies in Databases. In: Proceedings of Fifth international conference on knowledge based computer systems, Hyderabad, India (2004)
5. Rosencrance, L.: Toysrus.com faces online privacy inquiry,
   http://archives.cnn.com/2000/TECH/computing/12/14/toysrus.privacy.
   inquiry.idg/toysrus.privacy.inquiry.html
6. Associated Press: Fliers File Suit Against Jetblue (2003),
   http://www.wired.com/politics/security/news/2003/09/60551
7. Barse, E.L.: Logging For Intrusion And Fraud Detection. PhD Thesis, ISBN 91-7291-484-X Technical Report no.28D ISSN 1651-4971, School of Computer Science and Engineering, Chalmers University of Technology (2004)
8. Bruno, J.B.: Security Breach Could Expose 40M to Fraud (2005),
   http://www.freerepublic.com/focus/f-news/1425334/posts
9. Teasley, B.: Does Your Privacy Policy Mean Anything (2005),
   http://www.clickz.com/experts/crm/analyze_data/article.php
10. Broadsky, A., Farkas, C., Jajodia, S.: Secure Databases: Constraints, inference channels and monitoring disclosures. IEEE Transaction of Knowledge and Data Engineering 12(6), 900–919 (2000)
11. Marks, D.: Inference in MLS database systems. IEEE Transactions on Knowledge and Data Engineering 8, 46–55 (1996)

12. Dawson, S., de Capitani di Vimercati, S., Samarati, P.: Specification and enforcement of classification and inference constraints. In: Proceedings of the 1999 IEEE Symposium on Security and Privacy, pp. 181–195 (1999)
13. Farkas, C., Toland, T.S., Eastman, C.M.: The Inference Problem and Updates in Relational Databases. In: Das 2001: Proceedings of the fifteenth annual working conference on Database and application security, Norwell, MA, USA, pp. 181–194. Kluwer Academic Publishers, Dordrecht (2002)
14. Stachour, P., Thuraisingham, B.: Design of LDV: A Multilevel Secure Relational Database Management. IEEE Transactions on Knowledge and Data Engineering 02, 190–209 (1990)
15. Agrawal, R., Bayardo, R., Faloutsos, C., Kiernan, J., Rantzau, R., Srikant, R.: Auditing compliance with a Hippocratic database. In: VLDB 2004: Proceedings of the Thirtieth international conference on Very large data bases, VLDB Endowment, pp. 516–527 (2004)
16. Gupta, S.K., Goyal, V., Gupta, A.: Malafide Intension Based Detection of Violation in Privacy. In: Bagchi, A., Atluri, V. (eds.) ICISS 2006. LNCS, vol. 4332, pp. 365–368. Springer, Heidelberg (2006)
17. Böttcher, S., Steinmetz, R.: Detecting Privacy Violations in Sensitive XML Databases. In: Jonker, W., Petković, M. (eds.) SDM 2005. LNCS, vol. 3674, pp. 143–154. Springer, Heidelberg (2005)
18. Motwani, R., Nabar, S., Thomas, D.: Auditing a Batch of SQL Queries. In: IEEE 23rd International Conference on Data Engineering Workshop, pp. 186–191 (2007)
19. Machanavajjhala, A., Gehrke, J.: On the Efficiency of Checking Perfect Privacy. In: PODS 2006: Proceedings of the twenty-fifth ACM SIGMOD-SIGACT-SIGART symposium on Principles of database systems, pp. 163–172. ACM Press, New York (2006)
20. Miklau, G., Suciu, D.: A Formal Analysis of Information Disclosure in Data Exchange. J. Comput. Syst. Sci. 73(3), 507–534 (2007)
21. Aho, A., Sagiv, Y., Ullman, J.D.: Equivalence of relational expressions. SIAM Journal of Computing 8(2), 218–246 (1979)
22. Chandra, A.K., Merlin, P.M.: Optimal implementation of conjunctive queries in relational databases. In: Proceedings of the Ninth Annual ACM Symposium on Theory of Computing, pp. 77–90 (1977)
23. Goyal, V., Gupta, S.K., Gupta, A.: A Unified Audit Expression Model for Auditing SQL Queries. In: DAS 2008, London, UK. LNCS, vol. 5094, pp. 33–47. Springer, Heidelberg (2008)
24. Ullman, J.D.: Principles of Database and Knowledge-Base Systems, vol. I and II. Computer Science Press (1988,1990)

An Approach to Evaluate Data Trustworthiness Based on Data Provenance*

Chenyun Dai[1], Dan Lin[1], Elisa Bertino[1], and Murat Kantarcioglu[2]

[1] Department of Computer Science, Purdue University
{daic,lindan,bertino}@cs.purdue.edu
[2] Department of Computer Science, The University of Texas at Dallas
muratk@utdallas.edu

Abstract. Today, with the advances of information technology, individual people and organizations can obtain and process data from different sources. It is critical to ensure data integrity so that effective decisions can be made based on these data. An important component of any solution for assessing data integrity is represented by techniques and tools to evaluate the trustworthiness of data provenance. However, few efforts have been devoted to investigate approaches for assessing how trusted the data are, based in turn on an assessment of the data sources and intermediaries. To bridge this gap, we propose a data provenance trust model which takes into account various factors that may affect the trustworthiness and, based on these factors, assigns trust scores to both data and data providers. Such trust scores represent key information based on which data users may decide whether to use the data and for what purposes.

1 Introduction

With the advances of information technology, individual people, governmental organizations, financial corporations and medical hospitals nowadays can obtain and process data from different sources. The availability of comprehensive data makes it possible to extract more accurate and complete knowledge and thus support more informed decision making. However reliance on data for decision making processes requires data to be of good quality and trusted. We refer to such requirements as *high-assurance data integrity*. Without high-assurance integrity, information extracted from available data cannot be trusted.

While there have been some efforts to ensure data confidentiality, the problem of high-assurance data integrity has not been widely investigated. Previous approaches have either addressed the problem of protection from data tampering, through the use of digital signature techniques, or the problem of semantic integrity, that is, making sure that the data is consistent with respect to some

---

* The authors have been partially supported by AFOSR grant FA9550-07-1-0041 "Systematic Control and Management of Data Integrity, Quality and Provenance for Command and Control Applications".

W. Jonker and M. Petković (Eds.): SDM 2008, LNCS 5159, pp. 82–98, 2008.

semantic assertions. However, even though these techniques are important components of any comprehensive solution to high-assurance data integrity, they do not address the question on whether one can actually trust certain data. Those techniques, for example, do not protect against data deception, according to which a malicious party may provide on purpose some false data, or against the fact that a party is unable, for various reasons, to provide good data. Techniques, like those developed in the area of data quality (e.g. [1]), may help; however they often require the availability of good quality data sources against which one can compare the data at hand and correct them.

It is clear that in order to address the problem of high-assurance data integrity we need comprehensive solutions combining several different techniques. In particular, one important issue in determining data integrity is the trustworthiness of data provenance. For example, a malicious source provider may announce that a small company has successfully signed a big contract which is not true in reality. This information is then passed to a stock analysis agent, based on which the agent infers that the stock prize of that company will go up with high probability and send this information to end users. If the data users, based on this information, decide to acquire stocks of such company, they may end up with severe financial losses. In contrast, if the data users are aware that the source provider is very trustworthy, they will likely be more careful in making their decisions. Though a lot of research has been carried out on data provenance [10,4,8,6], these approaches mainly focus on the collection and semantic analysis of provenance information. Little work has been done with respect to the trustworthiness of data provenance.

To evaluate the trustworthiness of data provenance, we need to answer questions like "Where did the data come from? How trustworthy is the original data source? Who handled the data? Are the data managers trustworthy?" More specifically, for example, if data X is from source A, how do we determine the trustworthiness of source A. If X arrives at D via B and C, how to tell if the version that D received of X is accurate? Is X accurate at D? Also if an intermediate agent F merges data X received from D and data Y received from E, how do we determine the trustworthiness of the resulting data? To address these challenges, we propose a data provenance trust model which estimates the level of trustworthiness of both data and data providers by assigning trust scores to them. Based on the trust scores, users can make more informed decisions on whether to use the data or not.

To build such trust model, we take into account various aspects that may affect the trustworthiness of the data. In particular, these aspects are *data similarity, data conflict, path similarity* and *data deduction*. Similar data items are considered as support to one another, while conflicting data items compromise the trustworthiness of one another. Besides data similarity and data conflict, the way that the data is collected is also an important factor when determining the trustworthiness of the data. For example, if several independent sources provide the same data, such data is most likely to be true. Data deduction measures the effect of the process (e.g. data mining) on the data. Usually, the trustworthiness of the resulting data depends on the trustworthiness of input data and the on the parties that process the data.

We also observe that a data is likely to be true if it is provided by trustworthy data providers, and a data provider is trustworthy if most data it provides are true. Due to such inter-dependency between data and data providers, we develop an iterative procedure to compute the trust scores. To start the computation, each data provider is first assigned an initial trust score which can be obtained by querying available information about data providers. At each iteration, we compute the trustworthiness of the data based on the combined effects of the aforementioned four aspects, and recompute the trustworthiness of the data provider by using the trust scores of the data it provides. When a stable stage is reached, that is, when changes to the trust scores are negligible, the trust computation process stops. We summarize our contributions as follows.

- We formulate the problem of evaluating data provenance in order to determine the trustworthiness of data and data providers.
- We propose a data provenance trust model which defines the trustworthiness of data and data providers. We models four key factors that influence the trust scores.
- We develop algorithms to compute trust scores; our experimental results demonstrate its efficiency.

The rest of the paper is organized as follows. Section 2 introduces preliminary definitions. Section 3 presents the proposed data provenance trust model including the algorithms for trust score computation. Section 4 reports the experimental results. Section 5 reviews related work. Finally, Section 6 concludes the paper and outlines future research directions.

2   Preliminary Definitions

In this section, we first describe a scenario illustrating the problem of data provenance, and then introduce several definitions used in our trust model.

Data provenance includes information about the process through which data has been generated and the input and output data of this process. In this paper, we consider a common scenario (see Figure 1) in which there are multiple parties characterized as data source providers, intermediate agents and data users. Each party is identified by a unique identifier. Data source providers could be sensor nodes or agents that continuously produce large volumes of *data items*. Those data items describe the properties of certain entities or events. Intermediate agents could simply pass the data items obtained from data source providers to data users, or make use of the data items to generate *knowledge items* consumed by data users or other intermediate agents. Data users are the final information consumers who expect to receive trustworthy data. For presentation simplicity, we will refer to a data item or a knowledge item as an item when the context is clear.

In this paper, we model an item (denoted as r) as a row in a relational table; each item has k attributes A_1, ..., A_k. For an item r, its value for attribute A_i

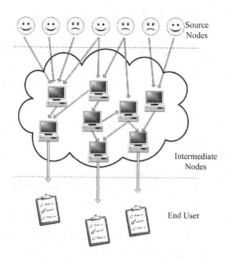

Fig. 1. Example scenario

Table 1. Data Representation

RID	SSN	Name	Gender	Age	Location	Date
1	479065188	Chris	Male	45	West Lafayette	4pm 08/18/2007
2	47906518	Chris	Male	45	West Lafayette	4pm 08/18/2007
3	479065188	John	Male	45	Los Angels	7pm 08/18/2007
4	4790651887	Chris	Male	45	Chicago	4pm 08/18/2007
5	479065188	Chris	Male	45	Purdue University	4pm 08/18/2007

$(1 \leq i \leq k)$ is denoted as $r(A_i)$. Table 1 gives an example of location reports that will be used throughout the paper. As shown in the table, there are five items, each of which has seven attributes $\langle$RID, SSN, Name, Gender, Age, Location, Date$\rangle$. RID is the identifier of each item.

Due to the possible presence of malicious source providers and inaccurate knowledge generated by intermediate agents, the information provided to the data users could be wrong or misleading. Therefore, it would be very helpful that each item received by data users be rated by a trust score indicating the trustworthiness level of the item. By using the trust score, data users can determine whether they want to directly use the received information or need to further verify the information. Moreover, each data source provider (intermediate agent) is also assigned a trust score based on the amount of correct information it has provided. In the following, we present formal definitions of the level of trustworthiness for data items, knowledge items, data source providers and intermediate agents.

Definition 1. *Trustworthiness of data items and knowledge items.* *The trustworthiness of a data item f (or a knowledge item k), denoted as $t(f)$ (or $t(k)$), is the probability of f (or k) being correct.*

Knowledge items are derived from data items according to some inference techniques.

Definition 2. *Trustworthiness of source providers and intermediate agents. The trustworthiness of a source provider s (or an intermediate agent a), denoted as $t(s)$ (or $t(a)$), is the average trustworthiness of the data items provided by s (or a).*

Different items about the same entity or event may be either supportive or conflicting. For example, one item in Table 1 claims that a person named "Chris" was in Lafayette at 4pm on 08/18/2007, while another item claims that he was in Chicago at that time. Obviously, at least one of the items is false. In another case, there is another item claiming that "Chris" was at Purdue University at 4pm on 08/18/2007, this item is more likely to report some true information provided that the first item is true. This is because Purdue University is located at West Lafayette, and the two items support each other. In order to represent such relationships, we introduce the notions of *data similarity* and *data conflict*. Specifically, data similarity models how the trust scores of similar items affect each other, while data conflict models how the trust scores of conflicting items affect each other.

In addition to data similarity and conflict, the source providers and routing paths also affect the trustworthiness of data items and knowledge items. Suppose that each source provider (or intermediate agent) has associated a probability quantifying the likelihood of reporting wrong information. The probability of multiple source providers (or intermediate agents) reporting the same wrong information is lower than that of a single source provider. Therefore, the less correlation among source providers and routing paths of the same information, the more one can trust this information. For example, the first two items in Table 1 report location information about the same person "Chris", both of which claimed that "Chris" was in West Lafayette at 4:00pm on 08/18/2007. If these two items are from different source providers and have been routed to the data user through different paths, they can be considered as valuable supports to each other. If the two reports are from the same source providers or shared very similar routing paths, the importance of considering these two reports as supportive of each other is reduced. Based on these observations, we introduce the notion of *path similarity*, which is the similarity between two *item generation paths* as defined below.

Definition 3. *Item Generation Path. For an item r, let S be its source provider, and let $I_1, \ldots, I_m$ be m intermediate agents that processed r. The item generation path of r is a sequence of "$S \rightarrow I_1 \rightarrow \ldots \rightarrow I_m$".*

In a network system, an item generation path (path for short) is corresponding to a sequence of IP addresses of source providers and intermediate agents. In information processing organizations, a path corresponds to a sequence of department names. Consider the first item in Table 1. Suppose that the item was generated by a source provider named "airport" and passed by intermediate agents *"police station1"* and *"police station2"*, the path of this item is represented as "*airport* → *policestation1* → *policestation2*". In this paper, we assume that every source provider and intermediate agent has a unique identifier.

Items can be merged or processed by intermediate agents. As an example, consider the first and fourth items in Table 1. The first item states that "Chris" was in West Lafayette at 4:00pm 08/18/2007 and the fourth one states that "Chris" was in Los Angeles at 7:00pm 08/18/2007. Given these two inputs, an intermediate agent produces the knowledge that from 4:00pm to 7:00pm 08/18/2007 "Chris" was on an airplane from West Lafayette to Los Angeles. The trustworthiness of such generated knowledge items largely depends on the trustworthiness of input data and the agent. To model this scenario, we introduce another concept, namely *data deduction* (details will be presented in Section 3.4).

3   A Trust Model for Data Provenance

In this section, we present the data provenance trust model that we use for assigning trust scores to items (i.e., data items or knowledge items), source providers and intermediate agents. Trust scores range from 0 to 1; higher scores indicate higher trust levels. The trust score of an item is computed by taking into account four factors: (i) data similarity; (ii) path similarity; (iii) data conflict; and (iv) data deduction. In what follows, we present the details on the evaluation of these factors.

3.1   Data Similarity

Data similarity refers to the likeness of different items. Similar items are considered as supportive to each other. The challenge here is how to determine whether two items are similar. Consider the example in Table 1. We can observe that the first two items are very similar since they both report the same locations of Chris at the same date. The only difference between these two items is a possible typo error in the person's SSN. In contrast, the third item is different from the first two because the third one reports a totally different location. Based on these observations, we propose to employ a clustering algorithm to group items describing the same event. The purpose of clustering is to eliminate minor errors like typos in the example and hence we adopt a strict threshold σ. After clustering, we obtain sets of items and each set represents a single event.

For each item r, the effect of data similarity on its trust score, denoted as $sim(r)$, is determined by the number of items in the same cluster and the size of the cluster. The formal definition of $sim(r)$ is as follows.

$$sim(r) = e^{-\frac{\phi_C}{N_C}} \tag{1}$$

In equation (1), N_C is the number of items in cluster C and ϕ_C is the diameter of cluster C. Here we define ϕ_C as the maximum distance between two records in the cluster. It is worth noting that items in the same cluster have the same data similarity score. Equation (1) captures the effects of both the number of items and the diameter of the cluster. When N_C is very small, $sim(r)$ is also small. When N_C is a very large number, $sim(r)$ is close to 1. ϕ_C has the contrary effect on $sim(r)$. The value of $sim(r)$ ranges from 0 to 1.

We now proceed to elaborate the clustering procedure. The key of a clustering algorithm is the distance function that measures the dissimilarities among data items and the cost function which the clustering algorithm tries to minimize. The distance functions are usually determined by the type of data being clustered, while the cost function is defined by the specific objective of the clustering problem.

The data we consider in our problem contains different types of attributes. In this paper, we focus on three commonly used types of attributes, namely numerical, categorical and string. Note that it is very easy to extend our clustering method to all kinds of attributes.

Distance between two numerical values. The numerical attribute values are of integer, real, or date/time data types. The distance between two numerical values v_1 and v_2 is defined based on their difference as shown in equation 2, where $v_1, v_2 \in \mathcal{D}$. $|\mathcal{D}|$ is the domain size, which is measured by the difference between the maximum and minimum values in $\mathcal{D}$ defined by the system.

$$\delta_N(v_1, v_2) = |v_1 - v_2|/|\mathcal{D}| \tag{2}$$

Distance between two categorical values. For the categorical values, we not only consider the exact match of two values, but also consider their semantics similarity. Let $\mathcal{D}$ be a categorical domain and $\mathcal{T}_\mathcal{D}$ be a taxonomy tree defined for $\mathcal{D}$. Then distance between two categorical values v_1 and v_2 $(v_1, v_2 \in \mathcal{D})$[5] is defined as follows.

$$\delta_c(v_1, v_2) = H(R(v_1, v_2))/H(\mathcal{T}_\mathcal{D}) \tag{3}$$

where $R(v_1, v_2)$ is the subtree rooted at the lowest common ancestor of v_1 and v_2, and $H(\mathcal{T}_\mathcal{D})$ represents the height of tree $\mathcal{T}_\mathcal{D}$.

Distance between two string values. The distance between two string values is defined based on edit distance [12]. The edit distance between two strings of characters is the number of operations (i.e., *change, insert, delete*) required to transform one of them into the other. Given two string values v_1 and v_2, their distance is defined as follows.

$$\delta_S(v_1, v_2) = E(v_1, v_2)/|\mathcal{L}| \tag{4}$$

where $|v_1|$ and $|v_2|$ are the number of characters in v_1 and v_2 respectively, $\mathcal{L}$ is $\max\{|v_1|, |v_2|\}$, and $E(v_1, v_2)$ is the edit distance between v_1 and v_2. The edit distance between two string values can be computed in $O(|v_1| \cdot |v_2|)$ time using a dynamic programming algorithm. If v_1 and v_2 have a 'similar' length, about 'n', this complexity is $O(n^2)$.

Combining the distance functions of numerical, categorical and string values, we are now able to define the *distance between two items* from a table T. Let $\mathcal{A}_T = \{A_{N_1}, \ldots, A_{N_m}, A_{C_1}, \ldots, A_{C_n}, A_{S_1}, \ldots, A_{S_j}\}$ be the attributes of table

T, where $A_{N_i}(i = 1, \ldots, m)$ is a numerical attribute, $A_{C_i}(i = 1, \ldots, n)$ is a categorical attribute and $A_{S_i}(i = 1, \ldots, j)$ is a string attribute. The distance between two items $r_1, r_2 \in T$ (denoted as $\triangle(r_1, r_2)$) is defined as follows.

$$\triangle(r_1, r_2) = \sum_{i=1,\ldots,m} \delta_N(r_1[A_{N_i}], r_2[A_{N_i}]) + \sum_{i=1,\ldots,n} \delta_C(r_1[A_{C_i}], r_2[A_{C_i}])$$
$$+ \sum_{i=1,\ldots,j} \delta_S(r_1[A_{S_i}], r_2[A_{S_i}]) \tag{5}$$

Thus, the diameter of a cluster ϕ_C is computed as follows.

$$\phi_c = max_{r_1 \in C, r_2 \in C} \triangle(r_1, r_2) \tag{6}$$

Next, we present how to cluster items by using our defined distance functions. The clustering problem has been well studied in the past [7]. Our clustering algorithm cluster the items incrementally. First, we make the first item a cluster and the representative of that cluster. Second, for each unvisited item, we compare it with representatives of existing clusters. If we find a representative such that the distance between the item and this representative is within the threshold σ and is the least distance, we add this item to the cluster the representative belongs to. If we cannot find such a representative, we generate a new cluster of which this time is the representative. This procedure continues until all the items have been visited. Finally, we obtain a set of clusters such that the distance between the representative and the members of the cluster is within threshold σ. Note that the value of σ is very small as the goal of the clustering process is to find most similar items. This makes it possible to randomly select an item as the representative of each cluster. Note that we can also adopt other clustering algorithms using our defined distance functions.

Updating the clustering result can be executed according to two strategies. The first strategy is based on storing all the newly arrived data items in a buffer. After a period of time, items in the buffer will be merged with previous received items and a reclustering procedure will be performed. The frequency of the reclustering procedure can be specified by the users, depending on the quality of the cluster and the performance of the system they want. Another strategy is based on our clustering algorithm. Each time an item arrives, it will be compared with the representatives of all clusters. The new item will either be absorbed by a cluster or form a new cluster.

3.2 Path Similarity

As we already mentioned, we know that a larger number of similar data cannot guarantee a higher trust level of this set of data since path similarity affects the importance of supports obtained from similar data. In what follows, we show how to compute path similarity and how to integrate the impact of path similarity to the computation of the overall trust score.

Given two items r_1 and r_2, suppose that their paths are P_1 and P_2 respectively. The path similarity between P_1 and P_2 is defined as follows.

$$pathsim(r_1, r_2) = \frac{max\{|P_1|, |P_2|\} - Idist}{max\{|P_1|, |P_2|\}} \quad (7)$$

where $max\{|P_1|, |P_2|\}$ is the maximum number of identifiers in the two sequences, and $Idist$ is the edit distance between two sequences. Note that unlike edit distance of two strings which is based on the difference of characters, $Idist$ is based on the difference of identifiers. An example of path similarity computation is given below.

Example 1. Suppose $P_1 =$ "*purdueairport* $\rightarrow$ *policestation1* $\rightarrow$ *policestation2*" and $P_2=$ "*LosAngelesairport* $\rightarrow$*policestation1* $\rightarrow$*policestation2*". $max\{|P_1|, |P_2|\} = max\{3,3\} = 3$. $Idist$ is 1, since only one difference exists between P_1 and P_2 which is the first identifier, the airport name. Finally, $pathsim$ is (3-1)/3=0.67.

Next, we modify equation (1) by taking into account the effect of path similarity. The new $sim(r)$ denoted as $sim^*(r)$ is defined as follows, where ω_c is the *path similarity factor* ranging from $\frac{1}{N_c}$ to 1.

$$sim^*(r) = e^{-\frac{\phi_c}{N_c \cdot \omega_c}} \quad (8)$$

The *path similarity factor* ω_c summarizes the effect of path similarity on the items in the same cluster. To obtain ω_c, we first randomly select an item from cluster C, denoted as r. We mark r and assign it a weighted value 1. Second, we randomly select an unmarked item from C, denoted as r'. We compute $pathsim$ between r' and all marked items, among which we keep the maximum $pathsim(r', r_i)$. Then we mark r' and assign it a weighted value $1 - pathsim(r', r_i)$, which means the more similar paths the two items have, the lower weight value will be assigned. We repeatedly execute such steps until all items are marked. Finally, we compute the average of the weighted values of all items in cluster C as ω_c.

3.3 Data Conflicts

Data conflict refers to inconsistent descriptions or information about the same entity or event. A simple example of a data conflict is that the same person appears at different locations during the same time period. It is obvious that data conflict has a negative impact on the trustworthiness of items, and hence in the following we discuss how to quantify its effect on the trust score computation.

There are various reasons for data conflicts, such as typos, false data items generated by malicious source providers, or misleading knowledge items generated by intermediate agents. Data conflict largely depends on the knowledge domain of the specific application. Therefore, our trust model allows users to define their own data conflict functions according to their application-dependent requirements.

To determine if two items conflict with each other, data users first need to define the exact meaning of conflict, which we call *data consistency rules*. Consider the example in Table 1 again. The attribute value of "SSN" in the first item is the same as that in the third item, but the attribute value of "Name" in the first item is different from that in the third one. This implies a data conflict, since we know that each single SSN should correspond to only one individual. We can further infer that there should be something wrong with either source providers (airports) or intermediate agents (police stations) whichever handled these two items. The data consistency rule we use here is that $if\, r_1("SSN") = r_2("SSN")$ then $r_1("Name") = r_2("Name")$. If two items cannot satisfy the condition stated by such data consistency rule, these two items are considered conflicting with each other. To facilitate automatic conflict detection, we propose a simple language (see definition 4) for data users to define data consistency rules.

Definition 4. Data Consistency Rule. *Let $\mathcal{A}$ be a set of attribute names in the database and let $condition_1$ and $condition_2$ be Boolean expressions on $\mathcal{A} \times \mathcal{A}$. A data consistency rule has the form: $condition_1 \implies condition_2$. For any two tuples r_1 and r_2 containing attributes in $\mathcal{A}$, we say that r_1 and r_2 satisfy this rule iff when $condition_1$ is evaluated true on the attribute values of r_1 and r_2, then $condition_2$ is also evaluated true on the attribute values of r_1 and r_2.*

Based on data consistency rules, we define the notion of data conflict between two items.

Definition 5. Conflicting Items. *Let r_1 and r_2 be two items, and $Rule_1$, ..., $Rule_m$ be data consistency rules. We say that r_1 conflicts with r_2 iff $\exists Rule_i, (1 \leq i \leq m)$, such that r_1 and r_2 cannot satisfy $Rule_i$.*

We next discuss how to automatically detect data conflicts according to the above definitions. Recall that items are clustered by using a strict threshold for the purpose of ruling out possible typos and hence items in the same cluster are considered almost the same. By leveraging this property, we do not need to compare all items to find out the conflicting pairs. Instead, we only check a representative of each cluster which has the minimum sum of distance to all the other items in the same cluster. Suppose that the representatives of two clusters C_1 and C_2 conflict with each other. The data conflict score of one cluster against another cluster is determined by the distance between the two clusters and the number of items in the second cluster by taking into account path similarity. In particular, we have the following equation of data conflict.

$$con_{c_1}(C_1, C_2) = e^{-\frac{1}{d(C_1, C_2) \cdot N_{c_2} \cdot \omega_{c_2}}} \tag{9}$$

where N_{c_2} is the number of items in cluster C_2, $d(C_1, C_2)$ is the distance between the two clusters and ω_{c_2} is the path similarity factor.

3.4   Data Deduction

The trustworthiness of a knowledge item also depends on the trustworthiness of information used to generate it and the trustworthiness of parties that handle it.

Generally speaking, if the source information or the responsible party is highly trusted, the resulting data will also be highly trusted. We define the function of data deduction as follows.

Definition 6. *Data Deduction*. *Let a be an intermediate agent, and let k be a knowledge item generated by a based on items r_1, ..., r_n. The data deduction of k, represented as a function $Ded_k(t(a), t(r_1), ..., t(r_n))$, indicates the impact of the trustworthiness of r_1,..., r_n, and a on the trustworthiness of k.*

We compute the effect of trustworthiness of a source provider or an agent on its resulting data by taking into account the actions it took on this data. Types of actions may differ in different applications. In this paper, we consider two typical actions, "PASS" and "INFER". "PASS" means merely passing data to another agent or data user, and "INFER" means that the agent produces a knowledge item based on the input information and possibly some local knowledge. Different actions may have different impact on the *trustworthiness* of the output information. For example, the "PASS" action simply passes the input items to successive parties. Since such action does not change the content of the information, the trustworthiness of the output should be the same as that of the input if no error is introduced during the transmission. By contrast, "INFER" generates new knowledge based on the input information.

Given a set of items and an intermediate agent, we employ a weighted function to compute the trust score of the output information.

$$t(k) = \frac{w_i \cdot t(a) + \frac{\sum_{j=1}^{n} t(r_j)}{n}}{2} \tag{10}$$

Here, w_i is a parameter based on the operation the intermediate agent executes and its impact on the trustworthiness of knowledge item k.

3.5 Computing Trust Scores

So far, we are clear how the four aspects influence the trustworthiness of items. In this subsection, we show how to combine the effects of these four aspects to obtain an overall trust score for data items, knowledge items, source providers and intermediate agents.

The computation of the overall trust scores is an iterative procedure. Initially, we assign each source provider and intermediate agent an initial trust score by querying the information that the end users already know. The initial *trustworthiness* of each data item and knowledge item is then set to the *trustworthiness* of its source providers and intermediate agent, denoted as $t(f)$ and $t(k)$ respectively. Then, we start the iteration. At each iteration, there are four main steps.

First, we update current trust score of each data item and knowledge item by using the $sim^*(r)$ function. For a data item f in cluster C with $sim^*(f)$, its updated trustworthiness is defined by equation 11, where r is an item in cluster C.

$$t(f) = 1 - \prod_{r \in C} (1 - t(r) \cdot sim^*(f)) \tag{11}$$

The reason why we use this equation to combine the trust scores of items within a cluster is based on the following observation. For items within a cluster, we consider them to represent the same event in the real world. In such as a case, the probability of the event being true equals to one minus the multiplication of the probability of every item in that cluster being false. To take the similarity between two items into account, we multiply $t(r)$ by $sim^*(f)$ in the equation. In another word, the more similar of two items, the more likely they represent the same event. The above equation can be rewritten as follows.

$$1 - t(f) = \prod_{r \in C} (1 - t(r) \cdot sim^*(f)) \tag{12}$$

After taking the logarithm on both sides, we have

$$\ln(1 - t(f)) = \sum_{r \in C} \ln(1 - t(r) \cdot sim^*(f)) \tag{13}$$

Let $\tau(f) = -\ln(1 - t(f))$, and $\varphi(r) = -\ln(1 - t(r) \cdot sim^*(f))$. Equation 13 is rewritten as follows.

$$\tau(f) = \sum_{r \in C} \varphi(r) \tag{14}$$

Second, we integrate the effect of data conflict into the current trust score. For a f in cluster C_1, if C_1 conflicts with C_2, we update $\tau(f)$ to $\tau^*(f)$ as follows.

$$\tau^*(f) = \tau(f) + \tau(r_{c_2}) \cdot conc_{c_1}(C_1, C_2) \tag{15}$$

where r_{c_2} is the representative of C_2 and $\tau(r_{c_2})$ is its trust score. Then, we rewrite $t(f)$ as follows.

$$t(f) = 1 - e^{-\tau^*(f)} \tag{16}$$

Similarly, we can compute $t(k)$ for each knowledge item.

Third, we consider the data deduction for the knowledge item and update $t(k)$. Finally, we compute the trust scores for source providers S and intermediate agents I, denoted as $t(S)$ and $t(I)$ respectively. $t(S)$ is computed as the average trustworthiness of data items provided by S. $t(I)$) is computed as the average trustworthiness of data items and knowledge items provided by I.

$$t(S) = \frac{\sum_{f \in F(S)} t(f)}{|F(S)|} \tag{17}$$

$$t(I) = \frac{\sum_{f \in F(I)} t(f) + \sum_{k \in K(I)} t(k)}{|F(I)| + |K(I)|} \tag{18}$$

where $F(S)$ ($F(I)$) is the set of data items provided by S (I), and $K(I)$ is the set of knowledge items generated by I. The iteration stops when the changes to trust scores become negligible. The complexity of our algorithm is dominated by the cost of computing the data similarity, path similarity and data conflict, which are all $O(n^2)$ and only need to be computed once.

An overview of the algorithm is shown in Figure 2.

Procedure Turst_Score_Computation
1. cluster data item and knowledge items
2. **for** each cluster
3.   compute data similarity
4.   compute path similarity
5. compute data conflict
6. assign initial trust scores to all the source providers
      intermediate agents
7. **repeat**
8.   **for** each data item and knowledge item
9.   compute its trust score
10.   **for** each knowledge item
11.   compute data deduction
12.   recompute trust score of the knowledge item
           by combining the effect of data deduction
13.   compute trust scores for all the source providers
      and intermediate agents
14. **until** the change of trust scores is ignorable

Fig. 2. Trust Score Computation

4   Performance Study

The goal of our experiments is to evaluate efficiency of our approach, i.e., running time. We plan to carry out human studies in the future to evaluate the effectiveness of our approach.

Our experiments are conducted on a 2.6-GHz Pentium 4 machine with 1 Gbyte of main memory. We generate synthetic datasets according to the scenario given in Table 1. We first generate a set of seeds which are tuples with seven attributes as shown in Table 1. Each seed represents a unique event. To generate items in the dataset, we randomly select a seed and slightly modify a randomly chosen attribute of this seed. In order to simulate data conflicts, we use a data consistency rule stating that items with same SSN and similar name must be in the same location at the same time. Then we modify the location information in

Table 2. Parameters and Their Settings

Parameter	Setting
Number of source providers	100
Number of intermediate agents	1000
Number of seeds	100, 500, **1000**, 5000, 10000
Percentage of conflicting items	10%
Average length of path	**5**, 6, 7, 8, 9, 10
Dataset Size	10k, 20k, **30k**, 40k, 50k

the same set of seeds to generate conflicting items. The percentage of conflicting items is set to 10%. In this way, we ensure that a dataset contains both similar items and conflicting items.

To generate the item generation path, we construct a network containing 100 source providers and 1000 intermediate agents. For each item, its generation path is then generated by randomly selecting a source provider and multiple agents. We have tested the cases when the average length of item generation path varies from 5 to 10. Table 2 offers an overview of the parameters used in the ensuing experiments, where values in bold are default values.

Effect of Varying Data Sizes. We first study the efficiency of our approach when varying the size of datasets from 10K to 50K. The trust score computation consists of two main phases: the initialization phase (the first two steps which compute data similarity, conflict and path similarity) and the iteration phase. We plot running time of the two phases in Figure 3(a) and (d) respectively.

As shown in Figure 3(a), the running time of initialization phase increases quickly when the dataset size becomes large. The reason is that in the worst case the complexity of the clustering algorithm, the computation of data similarity, path similarity and data conflict is $O(n^2)$. Although the initialization phase looks costly, it takes less than two minutes for a dataset of 50K items, which is still practical for off-line applications. Also, we need to note that this phase needs to be executed only once as long as the items remain the same. That is, the results obtained from this phase can be reused when trust scores of source providers or agents are changed. Further, an insertion or a deletion of an item only affects several clusters containing or close to this item, which means a large portion of previously computed results are still valid.

Compared to the initialization phase, the iteration phase is much faster (see Figure 3(d)). It needs less than one second to compute trust scores for 50K items. This is because the iteration phase simply computes score functions based on the results obtained from initialization phase and trust scores converge to stable values in a short time using our algorithm.

Effect of Varying the Number of Seeds. Next, we study the performance when varying the number of seeds to generate a dataset of 30K items. As shown in Figure 3(b), the running time of the initialization phase first decreases and then increases as the number of seeds increases. The reason of such behavior is the following. The number of seeds is proportional to the number of clusters. When there are few clusters, the computation of data conflict among clusters is very fast and most time is spent on computing data similarity and path similarity within the same cluster. In contrast, when the number of clusters is large, most time is spent on computing data conflict among clusters.

As for the iteration phase, the running time (see Figure 3(e)) is not affected by the change of the number of seeds. This is because the performance of the iteration phase is determined by the number of items and the network structure that affects data deduction computation. As long as these two factors remain unchanged, the performance is constant.

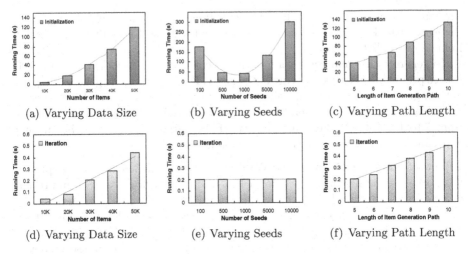

Fig. 3. Experimental Results

Effect of Varying the Length of Item Generation Path. In this experiment, we examine the effect of varying the average length of item generation path. As shown in Figure 3(c) and (f), the running time of both phases increases with the length of item generation path. This is because the longer the path is, the more time is needed to compare the similarity between two paths in initialization phase and the more time to compute the data deduction in the iteration phase.

5   Related Work

The related work to our approach falls into two categories: reputation-based trust management and data provenance management.

Several reputation systems and mechanisms have been proposed for online environments and agent systems. The most popular trust management technique in such systems, for example in p2p systems [13,11], is to compute the trust score for each peer based on user feedback, e.g. the number of satisfactory transactions. Though our system seems similar to existing reputation systems in that we also need to compute certain types of trust scores, the fundamental idea of our approach is much different. First, our focus is on evaluating trustworthiness of data while reputation systems mainly care about the reputation of participating parties. Second, we evaluate data based not only on trustworthiness (i.e. reputation) of a single data provider, but also on many other factors like the process for the data collection and generation, data similarity and conflict, which have not been analyzed in reputation systems.

As for data provenance management, a large number of approaches have been proposed [10,4,6,8,2,3], but none of them deals with evaluating trust of data sources and provenance paths. In the context of the Trio project [2,3], Benjelloun et al. propose a novel database management system which considers data uncertainty and lineage. Their approach computes the confidence of query results based on the confidence on the base tuples in the database. A major difference between their approach and ours is that they assume that the confidence of each base tuple be known, whereas we actually compute the trust score for each base tuple.

Another related work is PGP (Pretty Good Privacy) proposed by Zimmermann [15], in which a user evaluates the trustworthiness of a public-key certificate based on the trust he places on the signers (also called introducers) of the certificate. The amount of trust placed on any introducer is up to the user. Our work is different from PGP with respect to the following aspects. First, PGP deals with the evaluation of the trustworthiness of PKI (Public Key Infrastructure), while we assume that a trustworthy PKI exists. In other words, we assume that the identity of the sender can be verified and the routing path of a data item cannot be cheated. Therefore, PGP can be considered as a building block of our method. Second, PGP itself still cannot prevent malicious sources sending wrong data item, on which we focus in this paper.

The most relevant work is by Yin et al. [14], which aims at discovering true facts from conflicting information provided by different web sites. Compared to our trust model, they do not show how to compute the implication between two items, whereas we introduce the notions of data similarity and data conflicts and propose an approach to quantify them. Moreover, they assume that an identifier exists able to link different items corresponding to the same object. Without a correct identifier, their approach does not work. Such an assumption is however too strong and may not be realistic. In contrast, our approach does not require such an assumption.

6   Conclusions

In this paper, we introduce and formulate the problem of determining the trustworthiness of data and data providers in the context of a data provenance framework. To address this problem, we propose a trust model which assigns trust scores to both data and data providers. We have considered four important factors that influence trustworthiness, and our trust model effectively combines these factors during the trust score computation. We have evaluated the efficiency of our approach and the experimental results indicate the feasibility of our approach.

Our proposed method can deal with both unintentional errors and malicious attacks without collusion. If a data item is neither similar nor conflicting to any other items from other source providers, then regardless of its trust score, it will be labeled as "newly arrived" and stored in a separate database. The reason for doing so is to prevent a malicious source provider that obtains high trust score by reporting a large amount of correct data items, from injecting wrong data items to the system. No matter how high the trust score of its source provider is, a data item will not be used if it is labeled "newly arrived" until a different source reports a similar data item.

If users need to use an item labeled as "newly arrived", two possible approaches can be adopted. For a data item, users can use the privacy-preserving linkage technique [9] to verify the data item by asking other source nodes. For a knowledge item, the situation is more complex since inference techniques used by intermediate agents may involve personal opinions. We need to track the routing path of the knowledge item and record the inference techniques adopted by the intermediate agents on its path. After that, users can verify the process by asking other agents to perform the same procedure.

In the near future, we plan to develop an approach to estimate the confidence results of a query and develop a policy language to specify which is the minimum confidence level that a query result must have for use by users in certain roles. We will also investigate how to dynamically adjust our trust model when information keeps streaming into the system and how to certify data provenance so as to achieve a *certified data lineage*. We also plan to relax the assumption of the trustworthy PKI and integrate the PGP approach to our system.

References

1. Batini, C., Scannapieco, M.: Data quality: Concepts, methodologies and techniques. Springer, Heidelberg (2006)
2. Benjelloun, O., Sarma, A.D., Halevy, A.Y., Theobald, M., Widom, J.: Databases with uncertainty and lineage. VLDB Journal 17(2), 243–264 (2008)
3. Benjelloun, O., Sarma, A.D., Hayworth, C., Widom, J.: An introduction to uldbs and the trio system. IEEE Data Eng. Bull. 29(1), 5–16 (2006)
4. Buneman, P., Khanna, S., Tan, W.C.: Why and where: A characterization of data provenance. In: ICDT, pp. 316–330 (2001)
5. Byun, J.-W., Kamra, A., Bertino, E., Li, N.: Efficient k-anonymization using clustering techniques. In: International Conference on Database Systems for Advanced Applications, pp. 188–200 (2007)
6. Greenwood, M., Goble, C., Stevens, R., Zhao, J., Addis, M., Marvin, D., Moreau, L., Oinn, T.: Provenance of e-science experiments - experience from bioinformatics. In: UK OST e-Science second All Hands Meeting (2003)
7. Han, J., Kamber, M.: Data mining: Concepts and techniques. Morgan Kaufmann, San Francisco (2001)
8. Lanter, D.P.: Design of a lineage-based meta-data base for gis. Cartography and Geographic Information Systems 18, 255–261 (1991)
9. Scannapieco, M., Figotin, I., Bertino, E., Elmagarmid, A.K.: Privacy preserving schema and data matching. In: SIGMOD Conference, pp. 653–664 (2007)
10. Simmhan, Y.L., Plale, B., Gannon, D.: A survey of data provenance techniques. Technical Report (2007)
11. Song, S., Hwang, K., Zhou, R., Kwok, Y.-K.: Trusted p2p transactions with fuzzy reputation aggregation. IEEE Internet Computing 9(6), 24–34 (2005)
12. Wagner, R.A., Fischer, M.J.: The string-to-string correction problem. J. ACM 21(1), 168–173 (1974)
13. Xiong, L., Liu, L.: Peertrust: Supporting reputation-based trust for peer-to-peer electronic communities. IEEE Trans. Knowl. Data Eng. 16(7), 843–857 (2004)
14. Yin, X., Han, J., Yu, P.S.: Truth discovery with multiple conflicting information providers on the web. In: ACM SIGKDD, pp. 1048–1052 (2007)
15. Zimmermann, P.: Pretty Good Privacy Users Guide. Distributed with the PGP software, vol. I & II (June 14, 1993)

Exploiting Preferences for Minimal Credential Disclosure in Policy-Driven Trust Negotiations

Philipp Kärger, Daniel Olmedilla, and Wolf-Tilo Balke

L3S Research Center and Leibniz University of Hannover, Hannover, Germany
{kaerger,olmedilla,balke}@L3S.de

Abstract. Business processes in open distributed environments such as the Web force users to interact with other parties be it users or companies even if they have never had any common transaction in the past. Policy-driven trust negotiations emerged in order to address these situations. But although many policy languages and protocols have been defined, the problem of deciding which credential disclosure set to choose from those that possibly make a negotiation succeed is still subject of research. This paper explores the use of qualitative preferences in order to solve the problem and exploits the recently introduced notions of amalgamated and incremented preferences in order to allow for automated decisions which negotiations are preferred by the user. Our solution eases the task for the user of selection among all possible negotiations by removing irrelevant alternatives and it may even automatize negotiations that otherwise would require manual intervention.

1 Introduction

Open distributed environments such as the Web allow users to interact even if they have never had any common transaction in the past. However, in this situation, traditional access control mechanisms do not apply anymore. Identity-based solutions are of no use when deciding whether to interact or to disclose information to a stranger. In order to address this situation, so-called attribute-based access control mechanisms have emerged and among them, trust negotiation [22] has emerged as a flexible yet powerful solution. Trust negotiation permits both parties willing to interact to specify statements (aka. policies) with requirements to be satisfied by the other party and establishes an iterative process in which this information is disclosed. Typically, each step in the negotiation may include the disclosure of a requested credential and therefore increases the level of trust between the parties towards the success of the negotiation.

Many languages to specify access control policies for trust negotiation have been lately created, e.g., [14,4,16], focusing on different application scenarios and providing different expressivity. However, although they are able to find successful negotiations if they exist, they do not provide the user with means to decide in advance which one to choose in case there are several alternatives.

In this paper we address the problem from a user perspective: our approach provides the user with control over the negotiations her trust agent performs

W. Jonker and M. Petković (Eds.): SDM 2008, LNCS 5159, pp. 99–118, 2008.
© Springer-Verlag Berlin Heidelberg 2008

by exploiting preferences among credential disclosures such as "I prefer to disclose my e-mail address before I disclose my telephone number". By doing this a personalized view to the negotiation process is given, and, further, we improve security since nothing is disclosed which is not preferred by the user, i.e., which would have been of higher sensitivity to the user. We build on new theoretical research results from preference handling which is a very promising field in database retrieval. We further extend these results in order to provide a theoretical basis of how to use preference constructs in order to personalize the negotiation process.

The rest of the paper is organized as follows: Section 2 introduces a running example and motivates the need for a user-based selection among the different alternatives a negotiation may raise. Section 3 compares our approach to existing related work. An introduction to preference theory is provided in Section 4. Section 5 extends current state of the art in preference handling to address disclosure set selection and demonstrates our approach using our running scenario as an example. Section 6 presents our implementation and experiments. Finally, Section 7 concludes the paper and outlines further work to be performed.

2   Credential-Disclosure Selection during a Negotiation

In a trust negotiation two entities specify policies stating the requirements the other party must satisfy to get access to a resource. Without loosing generality in the following we will assume these requirements to be specific signed attributes which we also call credentials throughout the paper. The two policies must be matched in order to find out whether a negotiation exists that satisfies both parties' policies and leads to the provision of the initially desired resource. In this paper we assume that at least one party's policies are public. Considering both parties' policies private increases the complexity of the problem and is left for future work since it creates new problems such as suboptimal decisions allowing for malicious entities to exploit this situation (see Section 7).

2.1   Alice Negotiates with a Book Store

This section presents a running example scenario to highlight some of the problems to be addressed during a negotiation and will be used throughout the paper to illustrate our work.

A user named Alice wants to buy a book in an on-line book store. For committing the transaction the store requires the user to register and also to specify the payment information in order to be charged with the price of the book. The store accepts several registration possibilities involving the disclosure of several different credentials. See Figure 1 for the policies of the book store.[1] Registration can

---

[1] For our policy examples depicted in Figure 1 and 2 we use similar notation as in [24] and include the properties of the language there defined such as monotonicity and use of propositional symbols to represent credentials. In order to improve readability of the policy, we have abused notation by creating the symbols $p_{registration}$ and $p_{payment}$ which must be understood as a placeholder for the right side of the clause.

$$purchase \leftarrow p_{register} \wedge p_{payment}$$
$$p_{register} \leftarrow (c_{name} \wedge c_{bdate} \wedge (c_{email} \vee c_{pcode})) \vee$$
$$c_{id} \vee$$
$$c_{passport} \vee$$
$$(c_{name} \vee c_{email}) \wedge c_{id}$$
$$p_{payment} \leftarrow (c_{bank\_name} \wedge c_{bank\_account}) \vee$$
$$(c_{credit\_card} \wedge c_{pin})$$
$$c_{bbb} \leftarrow true$$
$$c_{osc} \leftarrow true$$

$$c_{name} \leftarrow true$$
$$c_{birthdate} \leftarrow c_{bbb}$$
$$c_{telephone} \leftarrow c_{bbb}$$
$$c_{email} \leftarrow c_{bbb}$$
$$c_{post\_code} \leftarrow c_{bbb}$$
$$c_{id} \leftarrow c_{bbb}$$
$$c_{passport} \leftarrow c_{bbb}$$
$$c_{bank\_name} \leftarrow c_{bbb} \wedge c_{osc}$$
$$c_{bank\_account} \leftarrow c_{bbb} \wedge c_{osc}$$
$$c_{credit\_card} \leftarrow c_{bbb} \wedge c_{osc}$$
$$c_{pin} \leftarrow c_{bbb} \wedge c_{osc}$$

Fig. 1. The book store's policies   **Fig. 2.** Alice's policies

be achieved by some sort of identification of the user; this is possible by specifying the name, the date of birth[2] and the user's country code or her e-mail address (from which the country of registration can be extracted). Identification can also be achieved via the personal ID card number or the passport number. In addition, registration is automatically performed, if either name or e-mail address, and an ID card number are provided[3]. Regarding payment, the book store offers two options: either bank account information together with the bank's name or a credit card number together with a PIN must be provided. As stated before, we assume that these policies are public for any requester asking to buy a book.

Alice does not mind to share her name with anyone, but she specifies some conditions before other information about her is disclosed (see Figure 2). She is willing to provide her general personal information to any entity that is certified by the Better Business Bureau (BBB) seal program that guarantees that its members will not misuse or redistribute disclosed information. However, in order to disclose her bank account or credit card, an additional Online Security Certificate (OSC) must be disclosed, ensuring that the store website is secured and no-one else will be able to retrieve her information during the transaction.

2.2   Selecting among Possible Alternative Negotiation Paths

By matching the policies of both, the book store and Alice, one can find all possible negotiation paths, that is, all the credential disclosure sets that will make the negotiation succeed. How to extract such a negotiation path is described in [24,7]. The matching of our two policies return several possible negotiation

---

[2] Note that in some cases it is possible to apply zero-knowledge proofs (e.g., [15]) in order to avoid disclosure of information (e.g., whether a user is older than 18). This is orthogonal to our approach since we deal with situations where the actual value *must* be retrieved (e.g., name).

[3] Although in this simple example it may be evident that this last possibility of registration overlaps with other policies, it may not be so evident for more complex policies or policy languages, or when the whole policy is specified by more than one single administrator.

Table 1. Disclosure sets for a successful negotiation between the book store and Alice

	1 name	2 bdate	3 telephone	4 e-mail	5 postcode	6 id	7 passport	8 bank name	9 bank account	10 credit card	11 pin
S_1	×	×	×					×	×		
S_2	×	×	×							×	×
S_3	×	×		×				×	×		
S_4	×	×		×						×	×
S_5						×		×	×		
S_6						×				×	×
S_7							×	×	×		
S_8							×			×	×
S_9	×					×		×	×		
S_{10}	×					×				×	×
S_{11}				×		×		×	×		
S_{12}				×		×				×	×

paths and there exist 12 different credential disclosure sets (see Table 1) leading to a successful negotiation. Therefore, Alice has to select among 12 different possibilities that would all make the negotiation succeed. However, not all of them may be necessarily equally desirable to her. In fact, Alice may have several preferences concerning the disclosure of her credentials: she might for example prefer to disclose her ID card number instead of her passport number and she may prefer to provide her bank account instead of paying via credit card. This information is not given by her policies. In fact, the policies specify that access to resources is granted if certain conditions are satisfied but not how to decide which credential to disclose in case only k out of n conditions are required. Alice's trust agent would have to ask Alice to decide which of all the 12 alternatives she prefers to disclose. And as soon as complex policies come into play, she may be easily overloaded with too many options. Furthermore, many of these options are already overruled by other ones so the user does not even need to consider them. Therefore, Alice's preferences shall be exploited in order to rule out suboptimal negotiations. The following requirements sum up what we consider necessary to be taken into account when providing a solution to Alice:

Total vs. partial orders. It may be difficult for Alice to define a total order preference for all her credentials. First, it is time consuming, and second it may be impossible to say whether a frequent flyer card is more or less sensitive than a video club card. Moreover, it is useless to specify such a preference since it is unlikely that they will be given as an alternative to each other. Therefore, it should be possible to reason over Alice's preferences even if only a partial ordering among her credentials is available.

Preferences among more than one credential. Generally, preferences among disclosure sets of credentials (and not only among single credentials) should be allowed, too. For instance, it could be preferred to disclose the e-mail address instead of the date of birth together with the postal code (since postal code and date of birth are considered a quasi-identifier [21]).

Conditional Preferences. Contrarily to this preference, in case the date of birth is not disclosed, Alice may strongly prefer to disclose her postal code instead of her e-mail address. However, if she also has to disclose her date of birth, she would switch her preference and prefer to disclose her e-mail instead of her post code because the latter together with her date of birth is a quasi-identifier. Even more general, preferences may depend on other situational attributes such as the party the user is negotiating with. Therefore, a preference-based approach should allow for conditional preferences such as "This preference only holds if my date of birth is disclosed, too. In all other cases, I have the opposite preference.".

Quantitative vs. qualitative preferences. It may be clear that Alice considers her ID card number less sensitive than her passport number. However, quantifying the sensitivity of a credential is difficult (e.g., $s_{id} = 10, s_{passport} = 11$ or $s_{id} = 10, s_{passport} = 51$), especially when having a large number of credentials. Furthermore, the aggregation of this quantification to sets of credentials is even more difficult: calculating the cost of disclosing *two* (or more) credentials using arbitrary quantitative aggregation methods (as they are used in [7]) is difficult to understand by users (assigning sensitivity 11 or 51 to $s_{passport}$ may have a great difference later on). Therefore, *qualitative* preferences among credentials should be allowed.

Dynamic generation of preferences. It may be impossible for Alice to provide in advance all preferences required to automatically choose a single negotiation path. In case more than one disclosure set that fulfills the negotiation remains, it is straightforward to ask Alice to deliver more preferences. However, if it is required to ask Alice, a set of possible preferences to additionally decide upon should be shown to her and her answer should be (optionally) recorded in order to avoid the same request for future negotiations. Therewith, the system should incrementally build up a knowledge base about her preferences.

Selecting the Optimum. Finally, any solution provided to Alice has to meet a trivial but very important requirement, i.e., to reduce the number of negotiations by strictly following the users preferences: any procedure should ensure that no preferred alternative is ruled out and no suboptimal disclosure set should be contained in the selected alternatives.

3   Related Work

The work in [24] introduces generic strategies, giving the user the possibility to generally specify a negotiation's behaviour, such as termination criteria or when to disclose an unlocked credential (speeding up the negotiation with less or more cautious strategies). However, the problem of personalization in terms of which successful negotiation path to choose among several alternatives has not been addressed.

Defining preferences in the context of trust negotiation has been described in [7] by attaching weights to credentials and comparing accumulated costs of a negotiation path. However, using numbers to express preferences has several drawbacks (as described in the previous section). In particular, assigning numbers to all credentials is complex and unintuitive for users [11] and assuming the linear aggregation of weights as a measurement for composition of objects is in our opinion undesirable; for cases like the quasi-identifier example it may even yield a lack of security. Furthermore, assigning weights implies the preference order to be a total order which is too restrictive since it may not be possible to express a preference between every two credentials (cf. for instance [9]). The same drawbacks apply to the approach of [23] where a point-based trust management model is introduced enabling the users to quantitatively distinguish the sensitivity of their credentials by assigning a certain amount of points to each credential.

A similar approach is presented in [17] where preference elicitation for negotiating agents is discussed. Case studies concerning how to acquire knowledge about the user's preferences are described. However, similar to [7], preferences are quantitatively defined, utilizing satisfaction degrees to be defined by a user.

In [5], preferences are applied in the context of policy-driven network control. The authors introduce the policy language PPDL allowing for preference definitions between possible actions preventing a hazardous network situation that may be generated by a policy. Although this approach does not tackle trust negotiation, it is related to our work since it integrates the concept of preference orders into a policy-driven behavior control. However, PPDL restricts to preferences on which action to block and it further focuses solely on total orders. It provides a leveling approach for partial orders but this leveling does not work with all sets of partial order preferences (such as the one described in our running scenario and depicted in Figure 3 later in the paper—do post code and telephone or post code and date of birth belong to the same level?).

4   Specification of Preference Relations

In order to model Alice's preference for the disclosure of certain credentials, we will now introduce the notion of qualitative preferences. As we have motivated in the scenario, the selection of a suitable negotiation path according to a user's preferences is needed for a secure and satisfactory negotiation. Picking the 'right' negotiation path is basically similar to personalization techniques used in today's database research, like for instance retrieving the best object out of a database or a digital product catalog. The notion of retrieval preferences in the context of databases and information systems has been formalized, e.g., by Kießling [12] and Chomicki [8]. To describe users' preferences in a way exploitable for selecting optimal objects, in the following we will rely on the preference query formalization proposed by Chomicki in [8]. In this extension to relational algebra, preferences are expressed on object level as binary relations over a set of objects O with certain attributes. In our case, the objects are the sets of possible negotiations and their attributes will be the different credentials that either have to be disclosed or not.

Definition 1 (Object-Level Preference). *Let $A = \{A_1, \ldots, A_n\}$ be the set of available attributes of the elements in O, and U_i, $1 \leq i \leq n$ the respective domain of possible values of A_i. Then any binary relation $\succ$ which is a subset of $(U_1 \times \ldots \times U_n) \times (U_1 \times \ldots \times U_n)$ is a qualitative preference relation over the object set O.*

Typically, preference relations are not directly defined on object level. In the area of database retrieval, users usually need to explicitly provide their preferences on the attribute values of each object attribute. For example, for the attribute "model of the car" a user needs to explicitly state that she prefers a Volkswagen to a Nissan. Therefore, preferences are rather stated with respect to the attribute values of each single attribute. Certain values are preferred over others, thus forming a partial order of attribute values:

Definition 2 (Attribute-Level Preference). *Let A be the set of available attributes of the elements in O and $A_i \in A$ an attribute in such set with U_i its respective domain of possible values. The attribute level relation $\succ_i$, which is a subset of $U_i \times U_i$, is a qualitative preference relation over the value set of A_i.*

The extension of an attribute level preference to respective object level preferences generally follows the well-known ceteris paribus semantics [18] ("all other things being equal"). The ceteris paribus condition states that a domination relationship between two objects can only be applied, if one object dominates the other in one attribute and the remaining attributes of both object show exactly the same values. That is, if $x_i \succ_i y_i$ and $x_j = y_j (\forall j \neq i)$ then x is preferred to y.

After defining preferences with respect to each attribute, objects have to be compared considering all attributes. Therefore it is needed to combine the attribute preferences and build up an object level preference. For such a composed preference, the combined attribute level preference relations are called *dimensions* of the resulting preference relation. Two multidimensional compositions are common [8]: *lexicographic composition* combines any two dimensions by strictly considering one as more important than the other. *Pareto composition* allows to combine two preference relations without imposing a hierarchy on the dimensions: all dimensions are considered as being of equal importance.

A lexicographic composition $\succ_L$ is based on the assumption that one relation can be considered more important than the other, i.e., there is a total ordering between all attributes. Thus, objects are generally ranked according to the more important attribute and only in case of ties the less important attribute is used for ranking.

Definition 3 (Lexicographic Composition). *Given the preference relations* $\succ_1, \ldots, \succ_n$ *over the attributes* $A_1, \ldots, A_n$ *and assuming a total order among* $A_1, \ldots, A_n$, *the lexicographic composition* $\succ_L$ *is defined as:* $x \succ_L y \Leftrightarrow x \succ_1 y \vee (x_1 = y_1 \wedge x \succ_2 y) \vee (x_1 = y_1 \wedge x_2 = y_2 \wedge x \succ_3 y) \vee \ldots \vee (x_1 = y_1 \wedge \ldots \wedge x_{n-1} = y_{n-1} \wedge x \succ_n y)$.

In contrast, Pareto composition yields a new preference relation following the fair principle of Pareto domination: an object X is said to *Pareto-dominate* another object Y iff X shows better or equal values than Y with respect to all attributes preferences and is strictly better with respect to at least one attribute preference.

Definition 4 (Pareto Composition). *Given the preference relations* $\succ_1, \ldots,$ $\succ_n$ *over the attributes* $A_1, \ldots, A_n$, *the Pareto composition* $\succ_P$ *is defined as:* $x \succ_P y \Leftrightarrow (\forall i : x \succ_i y \vee x =_i y) \wedge \exists j : x \succ_j y$.

The evaluation of Pareto composition for database retrieval is often referred to as "skyline queries" and is a direct application of the maximum vector problem [13]. Like for the preference modeling recently a lot of research has been invested to find efficient skylining algorithms, as e.g., [6,20,2]. The two composition paradigms form the extreme cases of possible compositions: whereas a lexicographic order adheres to a strict ranking between the preferences, the Pareto composition assumes no order at all. However, for the application in trust negotiation both paradigms are problematic: by focusing on the highly preferred attributes the lexicographic order biases towards negotiations that will *not* disclose a very sensitive credential, even if they disclose all other credentials. Given the fact that the set of credentials disclosed should be kept rather small this is definitely not a desirable behavior. The Pareto composition on the other hand is too careful: by considering the disclosure of each credentials as equally problematic a lot of incomparability between different negotiations is introduced and the user has to choose between lots of possible negotiations. In fact, the result sets of Pareto compositions are known to grow exponentially with the number of dimensions (here: the number of possible credentials) [3]. Our solution to reduce the amount of incomparable disclosure sets is described in the next section: we will allow users to specify a preference order over the attributes themselves and thus distinguish between more or less preferred (i.e., sensitive) credentials.

4.1   Amalgamating Preference Relations

Specifying preferences for each single attribute yields the challenge to combine them on the object level: what if an object is better than another in terms of one attribute but worse in terms of another? In the application for negotiations this is problematic, too: a disclosure set can be more or less preferred depending on *which* credentials are contained in this disclosure set (and not only *whether* one credential is disclosed or not which is considered in the comparison following the Pareto composition). To overcome this problem, recently the concept of preference amalgamations (or trade-offs) has been proposed [1] forming a useful extension of the Pareto composition. It does not only consider all attributes equally desirable, it additionally allows the user to specify a connection between two or more attributes. This is especially helpful, because in many practical applications, users are willing to perform trade-offs, i.e., relax their preferences in one (or a set of) attributes in favor of an object's better performance in another (set of) attributes.

Example 1. Alice may state that a negotiation where she has to disclose her credit card and not her bank account is less preferred than a negotiation where she does not disclose her credit card but her bank account. Mind that these two disclosure sets are incomparable from the Pareto composition point of view because in the bank account dimension the first is better (it does not include the disclosure of the bank account and the other does) but in the credit card dimension the second is better (the second set does not contain the credit card). Hence, Alice relaxed her preference for not disclosing her bank account instead of disclosing it in favor of the fact that the credit card is not disclosed.

Definition 5 (Amalgamated Preference). *Given the preference relations* $\succ_1, \ldots, \succ_n$ *over the set of attributes* $A_1, \ldots, A_n$, *a set* $\mu \subseteq \{1, \ldots, n\}$ *with cardinality* k, *as well as two* $k-$*dimensional tuples* X_μ, Y_μ *restricted to attributes with indices in* μ, *then (with* π *as the projection in the sense of relational algebra) the function* $AmalPref(X_\mu, Y_\mu)$ *is defined as:* $AmalPref(X_\mu, Y_\mu) :=$ $\{(x, y) \mid \forall i \in \mu : (\pi_{A_i}(x) = \pi_{A_i}(X_\mu) \wedge \pi_{A_i}(y) = \pi_{A_i}(Y_\mu)) \wedge \forall j \in \{1, \ldots, n\} \backslash \mu :$ $(\pi_{A_j}(x) = \pi_{A_j}(y) \vee \pi_{A_j}(x) \succ_j \pi_{A_j}(y))\}$. *An amalgamated preference is a relation denoted by* $\succ_\mu^{X_\mu, Y_\mu}$ *such that* $x \succ_\mu^{X_\mu, Y_\mu}$ $y \Leftrightarrow (x, y) \in AmalPref(X_\mu, Y_\mu)$.

In order to better understand this definition we provide a formalization of Example 1 after introducing some notation in the next section (see Example 3). In general, this definition means: given two tuples X_μ, Y_μ from the same amalgamated dimensions given in μ, the relation $\succ_\mu^{X,Y}$ is a set of pairs of the form (o_1, o_2) where the attributes of o_1 projected on the amalgamated attributes equal those of X_μ, the attributes of o_2 projected on the amalgamated dimensions equal those of Y_μ, and furthermore all other attributes (which are not within the amalgamated dimensions defined in μ) are identical in o_1 and o_2. The last requirement again denotes the ceteris paribus condition [18], i.e., the dominated object has to show equal values with respect to all non-amalgamated attributes.

5   Preference-Based Selection of Credential Disclosure Sets

In this section we extend the preference theory from the previous section in order to handle credential disclosure sets and to find the most preferred negotiations out of the set of all possible negotiations. This process is based on qualitative preferences defined over single credentials[4] (such as "I prefer to give my bank

---

[4] "Credentials" and "signed attributes" are used interchangeably throughout the paper.

account information. My credit card number would be the second choice.") or over sets of credentials (such as "giving my e-mail is preferred to disclosing my postal code together with my date of birth").

5.1 Modeling Credential Disclosure Sets

Let $C = \{c_1, \ldots, c_n\}$ be the set of credentials a party of a negotiation owns. The set of credentials a party has to disclose during the whole negotiation in order to succeed is a subset of C. Following the representation in Table 1, we represent a set of credentials as a bit vector with n dimensions comprising one dimension for each single credential such that setting a bit i to 1 means that during the negotiation the credential c_1 is disclosed.

Definition 6 (Credential Disclosure Vector). *Let S be a credential disclosure set over the set of credentials C. The Credential Disclosure Vector representing S is the bit vector $X = (x_1, \ldots, x_n)$ ($n = |C|$) such that $x_i = 1$ iff $c_i \in S$ and $x_i = 0$ otherwise.*

Example 2. In our scenario, the set of credentials Alice owns is $C = \{c_{name}, c_{bdate}, c_{phone}, c_{email}, c_{pcode}, c_{id}, c_{passp}, c_{bname}, c_{bacc}, c_{cc}, c_{pin}\}$. Mapping this set into a vector allows us to easily represent the disclosure set S_1 from Table 1 as $(1, 1, 0, 1, 0, 0, 0, 1, 1, 0, 0)$. In the following, we will assume this order as it is depicted in Table 1 for the rest of our examples.

These bit vectors represent objects (credential disclosure sets) for which each attribute dimension is the credential name and only two possible values exist: either 0 (a certain credential is not disclosed) or 1 (a credential is disclosed). In the following, we will refer to a credential disclosure set and its bit representation interchangeably.

5.2 Modeling Preferences

As we have seen so far, preference relations act on two different levels: on the object level and on the attribute level.

Object Level Preferences. Preference relations on the object level act among disclosure sets or, more precisely, on their bit vectors. These preferences are computed out of attribute level preferences given by the user. Since object level preferences cannot be easily defined by the user, preferences on the attribute level are used to build up preferences on object level.

Attribute Level Preferences. Privacy plays a main role in trust negotiations and therefore it may be assumed that a user always prefers "not to disclose" a credential in a negotiation. Therefore, for our running scenario we assume the attribute level preference $0 \succ_i 1$ for each credential c_i. However, a user may want to specify the opposite preference for some credentials in order to force the negotiation to select a negotiation path in which a specific credential is

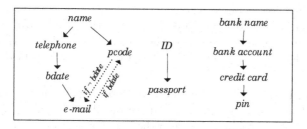

Fig. 3. Alice's preferences for the disclosure of her credentials

disclosed.[5] Therefore, our theory allows for attribute level preferences in both directions.

The Pareto composition of the attribute level preferences allows us to compare on the object level. However, as it is described in the previous section, in our scenario we exploit amalgamated preferences, i.e., preferences crossing the border of one single attribute dimension.

Amalgamated Preferences. Amalgamated Preferences in our scenario connect two credentials with a preference relation. In Figure 3, Alice's amalgamated preferences are represented in a graphical manner.

Example 3. Returning to Example 1 and following Definition 5, we may now define the preference that the bank account is preferred to the credit card as an amalgamated preference. For defining the numbers of the different dimensions in μ we rely on the order in Table 1 (as it is done for the vectors representing the credential disclosure sets) starting with 1. Hence, the bank account's dimension is 9 and the credit card's dimension is 10: $\succ_{\{9,10\}}^{(1,0),(0,1)}$. This relation amalgamates the two dimensions 9 and 10 and allows to decide between two negotiations where in one the credit card is disclosed but the bank account is not and in the other the bank account is disclosed but the credit card is not; according to the ceteris paribus condition all dimensions except the amalgamated ones 9 and 10 have to show equal values in both negotiations.

Conditional Preferences. The notion of amalgamated preferences allows for conditional preferences. In Figure 3, conditional preferences are depicted as dotted arrows with a condition attached. Alice's preference concerning post code and email depends on whether the date of birth is additionally disclosed or not. For each value of the condition, we introduce a new amalgamated preference: for the case where date of birth is disclosed we introduce $\succ_{\{2,4,5\}}^{(1,1,0),(1,0,1)}$ and for the other case we introduce $\succ_{\{2,4,5\}}^{(0,0,1),(0,1,0)}$. This example solves the quasi-identifier problem presented in Section 2.2. However, conditions may be even more complex: they may be situational [10] and therefore include the external context

---

[5] This may be the case for vouchers or discount credentials that may allow the user to receive a discount or even a free purchase when performing a transaction.

of a negotiation. For example whom one is negotiating with may play a role (e.g., one prefers to disclose the bank account to the credit card number if the requester is the bank and vice versa otherwise). These kinds of conditions can easily be modeled by our framework as additional dimensions in the vectors to be compared.

Possible Conflicts. As soon as one considers more than one preference in order to build up a concise knowledge base of all the user's preferences, one has to resolve possible conflicts between the given preferences. This is because a contradicting preference relation may lead to cycles in the object level preference and therefore does not allow for concise comparison anymore: finding the optimal object in a given set of objects becomes non-deterministic.

Example 4. One example could be that two amalgamations given by the user directly contradict, such as $\succ_{\{2,3\}}^{(1,0),(0,1)}$ and $\succ_{\{2,3\}}^{(0,1),(1,0)}$.

But although amalgamated preferences do not directly contradict, they may also conflict as soon as one considers a transitive chain as in the following example:

Example 5. Assume there already exists one amalgamated preference $\succ_{\{2,3\}}^{(1,0),(0,1)}$. Adding the amalgamation $\succ_{\{1,2,3\}}^{(1,0,1),(0,1,0)}$ would lead to an indirect contradiction: $(0,1,0) \succ_{\{2,3\}}^{(1,0),(0,1)} (0,0,1) \succ_1 (1,0,1)$ holds but this directly contradicts the amalgamation to be added which states the opposite: $(1,0,1) \succ_{\{1,2,3\}}^{(1,0,1),(0,1,0)} (0,1,0)$.

In order to avoid possible conflicts in a set of preferences, a preference to be added to this set has to meet certain conditions:

Definition 7 (Consistent Preferences). *Let O be a set of objects and $P \subseteq O^2$ a preference relation on these objects. Let further P^{conv} be the converse relation wrt. to P such that $(x,y) \in P \leftrightarrow (y,x) \in P^{conv}$. We call a preference relation $S \subseteq O^2$ consistent wrt. P iff*
1. $\forall x,y \in O : (x,y) \in S \rightarrow (y,x) \notin S$ and
2. $S \cap (P \cup P^{conv}) = \emptyset$.
(We will see later (in Remark 2) that the first condition in this definition takes care of cases like the one in Example 4 and the second condition corresponds to Example 5).

Combining Preferences Transitively. Based on this condition, we are now able to consistently add preferences to our knowledge base and incrementally build up one single preference relation which we call Incremented Preference Relation. This relation includes the transitive closure of the preferences incrementally added:

Definition 8 (Incremented Preference Relation). *Let O be a set of objects, $P \subseteq O^2$ a relation on these objects, and $S \subseteq O^2$ the set of object pairs representing the preference to be added to P. Let further be S consistent wrt. P. We define T as the transitive closure $T := (P \cup S)^+$. Then we define the Incremented Preference Relation of P incremented by S as $P^* := \{(x,y) \in T | (y,x) \notin T\}$.*

5.3   Filtering out Non-preferred Disclosure Sets

In this section, we present how the theoretical basis such as Pareto composition, amalgamated preferences, and incremented preferences is used to select the non-dominated objects, i.e., the most preferred disclosure sets according to the given preferences. At the end of this section we will develop the preference relation $\succ\succ$ which allows us to compare any two disclosure sets according to a set of preferences given by a user. Based on this relation, we will provide a formal definition of the set of optimal disclosure sets.

The following example shows how Pareto dominance helps to rule out non-preferred disclosure sets in our running scenario:

Example 6. Given the two disclosure sets S_6 and S_{10} from Table 1, $S_6 = (0,0,0,0,0,1,0,0,0,1,1)$ and $S_{10} = (1,0,0,0,0,1,0,0,0,1,1)$, and the set of attribute level preference relations over c_i $\{0 \succ_{c_{name}} 1, \ldots, 0 \succ_{c_{pin}} 1\}$ it is obvious to infer that $S_6 \succ S_{10}$ holds since $S_6 \succ_1 S_{10}$ and $S_6 =_i S_{10}$ for $(2 \leq i \leq 11)$. In any case, it is possible to automatically infer that a user always prefers to disclose only a subset of credentials, i.e., only ID card number and bank account.

Remark 1. We want to point out that this holds since we are considering the preferences $\neg c_i \succ_i c_i$ on attribute level. Given these preferences over the binary value space for attributes, computation of Pareto domination is reduced to simple set containment checking.

The following example shows how taking the amalgamated preferences into account prunes out additional dominated objects:

Example 7. Given the sets (from Table 1) $S_5 = (0,0,0,0,0,1,0,1,1,0,0)$ and $S_7 = (0,0,0,0,0,0,1,1,1,0,0)$, and the amalgamated preference $\succ_{\{6,7\}}^{(1,0),(0,1)}$ (that is, it is preferred to disclose the ID card number to the passport number) it is possible to infer that $S_5 \succ S_7$. Therefore, it is possible to automatically infer that the user would prefer to disclose her ID number *and* bank information instead of disclosing her passport number *and* bank information.

Pareto composition (in Example 6) and preference amalgamation (in Example 7) applied in isolation to filter out dominated disclosure sets is not sufficient in some cases—as it is shown in the following example:

Example 8. S_5 and S_6 cannot be compared with the mechanisms given so far: there is no way to combine Alice's amalgamated preference concerning bank name and credit card and her amalgamated preference concerning bank account and pin.

This example motivates the exploitation of incremented preferences (see Definition 8) in order to further reduce the number of disclosure sets. According to Definition 5, only one amalgamated preference is applied at a time; for the remaining dimensions the ceteris paribus condition fires. However, it may be possible that several preferences—be it simple attribute level preferences or amalgamated ones—need to be applied over the same two disclosure sets in order to compare them. Therefore, we exploit the transitive combination of preferences as it is delivered by the concept of the incremented preference relation. The following example shows how an incremented preference relation enables us to compare the two disclosure sets from Example 8.

Example 9. In order to compare S_5 and S_6 we need to combine two of Alice's preferences; for example her preference saying that bank name is preferred to credit card ($p_1 = \succ_{\{8,10\}}^{(1,0),(0,1)}$) and her preference saying that bank account is preferred to pin ($p_2 = \succ_{\{9,11\}}^{(1,0),(0,1)}$). To achieve this combination we apply the definition of an incremental preference relation (see Definition 8) in the following way. To an initially empty incremented preference P_0^* we first add p_1. From the definition of amalgamated preferences (Definition 5) and from the fact that P_0^* is empty, it is obvious that p_1 is consistent wrt. P_0^*. Adding p_1 yields the incremented preference $P_1^* = p_1$. In the second step, we add p_2 to P_1^* in order to construct the incremental preference P_2^*. Similarly to the first step, p_2 is consistent wrt. P_1^*. This is due to the ceteris paribus condition in the definition of amalgamated preference: for any pair in p_1 the dimensions 9 and 10 are equal where for any pair in p_2 they are different. Therefore, no pair in p_1 contradicts a pair in p_2. By applying the transitive closure in order to construct P_2^* the pair (S_5, S_6) is introduced as an element of P_2^*. This is due to the transitive chain built from the following two pairs: in p_1 we have $(S_5, (0,0,0,0,0,1,0,0,1,1,0))$ and p_2 states $((0,0,0,0,0,1,0,0,1,1,0), S_6)$. By transitively combining p_1 and p_2 to P_2^* we get $(S_5, S_6) \in P_2^*$.

This example forms a base case and provides evidences that the extension of an isolated application of the Pareto domination and the amalgamated preferences given by the user is needed. In order to provide *all possible combinations* of all given preferences, we need to build up an incremented preference relation which we call Complete Preference Relation $\succ\!\succ$:

Definition 9 (Complete Preference Relation). *Let $\succ_P$ be the Pareto composition of attribute level preferences $\succ_1, \ldots, \succ_n$. Let further be $P = \{p_1, \ldots, p_m\}$ a set of amalgamated preferences. The Complete Preference Relation $\succ\!\succ$ is defined as the incremented preference relation of $\succ_P$ incremented by $(\bigcup P)$.*

Remark 2. Because of the conditions in Definitions 7 and 8, this includes two implicit requirements:

1) each amalgamated preferences must not contradict another, i.e., $p_n \cap p_m^{conv} = \emptyset$ holds for each n, m. This case matches Example 4 and condition 1 in Definition 7; it implies that our framework requires user-given amalgamated preferences not to directly contradict each other.

2) the union of the amalgamated preferences has to be consistent wrt. the Pareto composition. This restriction ensures that the incremented preference relation does not contain any cycles [1]. Instantiated for our scenario, this restriction requires that no amalgamated preference stated by the user contradicts the Pareto domination (i.e., each amalgamated preference has to be consistent wrt. the

Pareto composition of the attribute level preferences). This requirement corresponds to Example 5 and to condition 2 in Definition 7.

Further, these two requirements imply that adding new preferences to the incremented preference relation is a monotonic process [1]: adding new preferences will never make former comparisons invalid, it will always add comparable pairs and never remove some. This is in particular helpful for the preference elicitation process as is allowed for in our implementation (see Section 6): after adding new elicited preferences it is not needed to recompute the whole set of optimal disclosure sets but to simply remove the new dominated objects from the set.

Remark 3. In the theory developed in this paper we do not consider equivalence preferences such as "disclosing my ID card number is as equally preferred as disclosing my passport number". They can easily be introduced according to [1]; due to space conditions we left them out in this paper.

The incremented preference relation forms the basis for our object level preference relation. It is clear from its definition, that it comprises the Pareto dominance relation as well all single amalgamated preference relations given by the user. It additionally contains all combinations of these base preferences. Therefore, it enables us to filter out all the disclosure sets which are not preferred:

Definition 10 (Optimal Disclosure Sets). *Let O be a set of disclosure sets and $\succ\!\succ$ a complete preference relation. We define the set of optimal disclosure sets $O_{\succ\!\succ}$ as follows: $O_{\succ\!\succ} := \{o \in O \mid \nexists o' \in O : o' \succ\!\succ o\}$.*

5.4 Revisiting the Scenario

In this section we show on our running scenario how the techniques and concepts defined in previous sections may be used to find out the optimal negotiations for Alice given the disclosure sets $S_1, \ldots, S_{12}$ yielding a successful negotiation. As we have shown above, the incremented preference relation contains the Pareto composed attribute level preferences as well as the amalgamated preference. However, in order to see the improvement of each preference concept introduced in the paper, we will divide the process of ruling out dominated disclosure sets into three steps: we show (A) how objects are ruled out by simple Pareto composition, (B) how objects are ruled out by single amalgamated preferences, and (C) how the transitive combination in the incremented preference relation rules out the remaining dominated objects.

Pareto Composition. Using the attribute level preferences $0 \succ_i 1$ (as described in Section 5.2), we can apply Pareto composition to remove dominated sets. From Pareto domination we conclude that disclosure set S_{10} can be removed since it is dominated by the set S_6 (all dimensions are equally good in S_6 and in S_{10} except dimension 1 (c_{name}) in which S_6 is preferred to S_{10}). This may be considered straightforward since S_{10} additionally requires Alice to disclose c_{name} which is an unnecessary disclosure. In addition, also S_9 can be removed since it is dominated by S_5. Furthermore, S_6 Pareto dominates S_{12} and S_5 Pareto dominates S_{11}. Hence, simple Pareto composition is able to filter out already four dominated disclosure sets, namely, S_9, S_{10}, S_{11}, and S_{12}.

Amalgamated Preferences. In addition to Pareto composition, we may exploit the amalgamated preferences specified by Alice to further reduce the number of disclosure sets. From Alice's preference for disclosing her ID card number instead of her passport number (amalgamated preference $\succ_{\{6,7\}}^{(1,0),(0,1)}$), we can conclude that S_7 is dominated by S_5 and that S_8 is dominated by S_6. Furthermore, Alice has an amalgamated preference over three dimensions because of her fear of being quasi-identified: $\succ_{\{2,4,5\}}^{(1,1,0),(1,0,1)}$. From this preference we may infer that S_2 dominates S_4 and S_1 dominates S_3. This way it is possible to remove yet another four dominated disclosure sets, namely S_3, S_4, S_7, and S_8.

Transitive Combination of Preferences. After having performed the previous steps, the remaining disclosure sets are S_1, S_2, S_5, and S_6. Among the inferred preferences, there is the preference transitively combined out of the preferences 'bank name is preferred to credit card' ($\succ_{\{8,10\}}^{(1,0),(0,1)}$) and 'bank account is preferred to pin' ($\succ_{\{9,11\}}^{(1,0),(0,1)}$). Applying both preferences transitively enables us to rule out S_2 because it is dominated by S_1 and S_6 because it is dominated by S_5. (as it is shown in Example 9).

The procedure described in this section is able to filter out ten non-preferred credential disclosure sets based on qualitative preferences, therefore facilitating Alice's interaction with her negotiation agent. However, two disclosure sets are still remaining: S_1 and S_5. Both are not comparable according to the specified preferences. In the next section we give an idea of how a system could elicit which disclosure set she prefers.

6   Implementation and Experiments

We implemented a prototype computing preferred credential disclosure sets given a set of successful negotiation paths and a set of preferences specifying which credential's disclosure is preferred to another's. The user interface is web-based and the logical core of our approach is implemented in Prolog. Given a set of credentials a connected policy engine provides all disclosure sets yielding a successful negotiation. From this set the Prolog engine computes the non-dominated and therefore preferred disclosure sets. In case there exists one single non-dominated disclosure set, this one will be used automatically. Otherwise, the user can either choose one disclosure set or go for an iterative preference elicitation process. If the elicitation process is selected, the preference information the user provides after selecting one of the shown options is exploited to further reduce the set of non-dominated disclosure sets (see Remark 2 about monotonicity). Depending on the new result, the user has again the possibility to either choose one set of credentials to be disclosed or to perform another elicitation process. This process continues iteratively until the user either directly selects the disclosure set to use or until any set but one is filtered out.

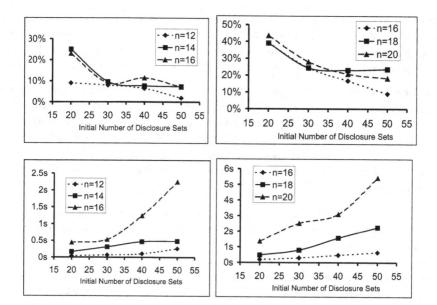

Fig. 4. Optimal Disclosure Sets (top) and Computation Time (bottom) for $k = 5$ (left) and $k = 7$ (right). n is the number of credentials and k is the maximal number of credentials that can be disclosed during a negotiation.

We tested the efficiency of our approach in terms of how many disclosure sets are ruled out. This amount is crucial since our approach is only effective if a considerable set of suboptimal negotiations is actually ruled out. Since there is no trust negotiation benchmark available which may serve for our experiments, nor any available real data about disclosure sets (due to high sensitivity even if anonymized), we used generated data as follows:

In a trust negotiation, typically only one client credential of a certain type is needed. E.g., it is either required to disclose the passport number or the ID card number, rather than both. Therefore we partition the set of client credentials C into k disjoint subsets T called *credential types*. Further, we assume that for the success of a negotiation exactly one credential for each credential type has to be disclosed. Following this, it is obvious that each type should at least contain two credentials—otherwise this single credential will be contained in each disclosure set and will be disregarded in the comparison process. Further, for each credential type we assume a totally ordered preference on the client side. Therefore, for each run of the experiment we performed the following steps: **1)** randomly create k credential types $T_1, \dots, T_k$ for the n credentials. **2)** create a set of amalgamations such that for each type T_i we add $\succ_{j,j+1}^{(1,0),(0,1)}$ for all $c_j, c_{j+1} \in T_i$. **3)** create a set O of n disclosure sets such that each disclosure set contains one randomly chosen credential for each credential type. **4)** rule out all dominated disclosure sets following the definition of $\succ\succ$. In this setting the following parameters varied:

Number of Credentials n. The higher the number of credentials the higher the number of dimensions of the vectors to be compared. Increasing this value yields an increasing of incomparable pairs in the set of disclosure sets. For our experiments we assume a number of credentials between 12 and 20.

Number of Credential Types k. This number actually determines how many credentials are definitely disclosed in each negotiation. Increasing this value also decreases the amount of suboptimal objects because the probability an object is 'bad' in one credential type but 'good' in another becomes higher which leads to more incomparable pairs. We selected 5 and 7 credential types to cover negotiations where exactly 5 or 7 credentials *have* to be exchanged in each negotiation which we consider realistic.

Number of Disclosure Sets. Represents how many different negotiation paths exist and would have been shown to the user for selection, if no preference filtering was applied.

We made several experiments with varying values. For each setting we did 20 runs; see the upper graphs in Figure 4 for the results of some representative settings. It turned out that the average percentage of optimal disclosure sets is 18.3%. Hence, on average 81,7% of the alternatives a user has to chose from are ruled out. This is a huge improvement: instead of, e.g., 30 disclosure sets with obviously suboptimal alternatives only 6 sets are shown to the user. Moreover, removing the 24 dominated possibilities is needed from a privacy point of view: if the user selected one of the suboptimal negotiations, she would definitely disclose more sensitive information which she would not have to disclose to make the negotiation succeed. These results show that for a relatively big number of possible disclosure sets (a higher number will rarely occur in reality), our approach filters out a considerable subset of suboptimal alternatives and therefore reduces the work load for the user. Furthermore, it turned out that for our experimental setting the average computation time was about 2.3 seconds (see Figure 4). Our implementation does not consider any of the numerous optimization strategies available for skyline computation (e.g., [20]) which would make the computation even faster.

The modeling of trust negotiation in our experiments has several simplifications compared to a real scenario. We do not consider redundant policies, hence, Pareto domination was never applied in our scenario which would even lead to a higher number of suboptimal disclosure sets. Furthermore, in our experiment no preferences among different credential types are given which one can assume in a realistic setting and therefore more objects would be ruled out according to these preferences.

7   Conclusions and Further Work

Selection of credential disclosure sets in trust negotiations is a difficult task. Only allowing for total orders over the set of owned credentials or linear aggregation is undesirable. In this paper we have presented an approach based on qualitative partial order preferences including preference composition, amalgamated preferences, and conditional preferences and demonstrated with the help of an example how this approach can be used to solve the problem of finding optimal disclosure sets. Furthermore, an iterative process in order to allow the user to specify new preferences has been sketched and a web-based implementation of the whole system has been developed in order to test the results. Our solution eases the task of selecting among possibly many alternatives in a trust negotiation by exploiting the user's preferences. Although we applied our preference framework in the realm of trust negotiation, this preference scheme can be used in any other domain where objects need to be compared or selected based on preferences specified on the objects' attributes. The principle of preference based selection (or skylining) is one of the most promising current research fields in database retrieval.

The paper focuses on negotiations in which one party's policies are public and therefore the whole set of credentials to be disclosed may be precomputed. It is required to further study the implications of using qualitative preferences on negotiations with *private* policies, therefore assuming that possibly suboptimal decisions can be taken in different steps. This may even be exploited by malicious entities forcing the other party to disclose more credentials than needed for a successful negotiation (known as "need-to-know attacks" [19]). We are currently investigating the extensions and restrictions required to extend the contribution of this paper to such a scenario. We are also planning to further evaluate our approach. This will also include a a user study using our current implementation.

References

1. Balke, W.-T., Güntzer, U., Lofi, C.: Incremental trade-off management for preference based queries. International Journal of Computer Science and Applications (IJCSA) 4(1) (2007)
2. Balke, W.-T., Zheng, J., Güntzer, U.: Efficient distributed skylining for web information systems. In: Bertino, E., Christodoulakis, S., Plexousakis, D., Christophides, V., Koubarakis, M., Böhm, K., Ferrari, E. (eds.) EDBT 2004. LNCS, vol. 2992. Springer, Heidelberg (2004)
3. Bentley, J., Kung, H., Schkolnick, M., Thompson, C.: On the average number of maxima in a set of vectors and applications. Journal of the ACM (JACM) 25(4) (1978)
4. Bertino, E., Ferrari, E., Squicciarini, A.C.: Trust-x: A peer-to-peer framework for trust establishment. IEEE Trans. Knowl. Data Eng. 16(7) (2004)
5. Bertino, E., Mileo, A., Provetti, A.: PDL with preferences. In: POLICY 2005. IEEE Computer Society, Los Alamitos (2005)
6. Borzsonyi, S., Kossmann, D., Stocker, K.: The skyline operator. In: International Conference on Data Engineering, Heidelberg, Germany (2001)
7. Chen, W., Clarke, L., Kurose, J., Towsley, D.: Optimizing costsensitive trust-negotiation protocols. In: Annual Joint Conference of the IEEE Computer and Communications Societies (2005)
8. Chomicki, J.: Preference formulas in relational queries. ACM Trans. Database Syst. 28(4), 427–466 (2003)

9. Fishburn, P.: Preference structures and their numerical representations. Theoretical Computer Science 217, 359–383 (1999)
10. Holland, S., Kießling, W.: Situated preferences and preference repositories for personalized database applications. In: Atzeni, P., Chu, W., Lu, H., Zhou, S., Ling, T.-W. (eds.) ER 2004. LNCS, vol. 3288, pp. 511–523. Springer, Heidelberg (2004)
11. Keeney, R., Raiffa, H.: Decisions with Multiple Objectives: Preferences and Value Tradeoffs. Wiley, Chichester (1976)
12. Kießling, W.: Foundations of preferences in database systems. In: International Conference on Very Large Data Bases, Hong Kong, China (2002)
13. Kung, H., Luccio, F., Preparata, F.: On finding the maxima of a set of vectors. Journal of the ACM (JACM) 22(4) (1975)
14. Lee, A.J., Winslett, M., Basney, J., Welch, V.: Traust: a trust negotiation-based authorization service for open systems. In: SACMAT, ACM Press, New York (2006)
15. Li, J., Li, N.: Oacerts: Oblivious attribute certificates. IEEE Trans. Dependable Sec. Comput. 3(4) (2006)
16. Li, N., Mitchell, J.C.: Rt: A role-based trust-management framework. In: DISCEX (April 2003)
17. Luo, X., Jennings, N.R., Shadbolt, N.: Knowledge-based acquisition of tradeoff preferences for negotiating agents. In: International Conference on Electronic Commerce. ACM Press, New York (2003)
18. McGeachie, M., Doyle, J.: Efficient utility functions for ceteris paribus preferences. In: Conference on Artificial Intelligence and Conference on Innovative Applications of Artificial Intelligence, Edmonton, Canada (2002)
19. Olson, L.E., Rosulek, M.J., Winslett, M.: Harvesting credentials in trust negotiation as an honest-but-curious adversary. In: Workshop on Privacy in electronic society. ACM Press, New York (2007)
20. Papadias, D., Tao, Y., Fu, G., Seeger, B.: An optimal and progressive algorithm for skyline queries. In: ACM SIGMOD, San Diego, CA, USA (2003)
21. Sweeney, L.: Guaranteeing anonymity when sharing medical data, the datafly system. Journal of the American Medical Informatics Association (1997)
22. Winsborough, W.H., Seamons, K.E., Jones, V.E.: Automated trust negotiation. In: DARPA Information Survivability Conference and Exposition. IEEE Press, Los Alamitos (2000)
23. Yao, D., Frikken, K., Atallah, M., Tamassia, R.: Point-based trust: Define how much privacy is worth. In: Ning, P., Qing, S., Li, N. (eds.) ICICS 2006. LNCS, vol. 4307, Springer, Heidelberg (2006)
24. Yu, T., Winslett, M., Seamons, K.E.: Interoperable strategies in automated trust negotiation. In: CCS (2001)

A Trusted Approach to E-Commerce

Giannakis Antoniou[1], Lynn Batten[2], and Udaya Parampalli[1]

[1] The University of Melbourne
Department of Computer Science and Software Engineering
{gant,udaya}@csse.unimelb.edu.au
[2] Deakin University
School of Information Technology
lmbatten@deakin.edu.au

Abstract. It has been well documented that lack of trust between commercial entities and purchasers can restrict the potential of e-commerce. This may be because the purchaser is required to provide sensitive information to the commercial entity or because the purchaser may be suspicious that after payment has been processed, the goods purchased will not arrive. The challenge for the researcher is to determine the e-commerce model which maximizes the trust relationship. In this paper, we introduce a measure of the trust based on the information distributed to the parties in the transaction and isolate the instances which maximize trust for the purchaser. This leads us to propose four new models for e-commerce which would improve consumer trust and therefore likely lead to an increase in on-line commerce. We demonstrate that no new technologies are needed in order to implement these new models.

Keywords: Trust, E-Commerce, Privacy.

1 Introduction and Background

The convenience to consumers of remote twenty-four hour access to products online has driven e-commerce popularity [5, 15, 18]. However, many writers have argued that this same 'remoteness' has restricted the full potential of e-commerce because the purchaser may be asked to provide sensitive information to an unknown entity over the Internet and does not know how their information will be treated [7]. These studies underline the important role of trust in e-commerce [12, 13] and argue that some purchasers do not trust sellers because of a number of risks derived from the very nature of e-commerce.

A purchaser who wants to buy a product online searches for a seller of the product and is restricted to making a purchase only from a seller who can provide the needed product. Given a choice of sellers, the purchaser will normally choose one with whom the purchaser has completed a successful transaction in the past [4]. If this is not an option, the purchaser must make a decision based on other factors. In making this decision, the purchaser may consider such issues as how much of his personal information (full name, age, sex, address and email) will be distributed to other entities and whether or not his payment details (credit card information, amount of purchase) will be misused. He may also wonder how and where his information will be stored – will it be in a secured environment or vulnerable to attackers, will it be made available to

W. Jonker and M. Petković (Eds.): SDM 2008, LNCS 5159, pp. 119–132, 2008.

spammers. Moreover, the purchaser may worry about receiving the product once it is paid for. The reputation and credit-worthiness of the company may be a factor, or the range of products and services offered for potential future transactions.

Several models [3, 19] have been formulated to assist in attaining a sufficient trust level on the part of the purchaser. For example, several payment systems have been proposed which allow the purchaser to pay anonymously [8, 16]. It has also been argued that the attractiveness of an online shop is a factor in increasing trust. This has led to such inventions as virtual reality e-commerce [11]. While the key focus in all approaches has been on the relationship between the purchaser and seller, we point out that the financial organization and the deliverer of the goods need to be considered.

In [10] the definition of trust is "a trustor's expectations about the motives and be-haviours of a trustee". We adopt this definition in the e-commerce setting where a purchaser has a number of expectations of several parties. We argue that the financial organization (the bank supplying the credit card) involved in an online transaction is chosen well in advance by the purchaser, has a well established relationship with him and so is expected to act 'as usual' in completing the financial transaction component of a purchase. The purchaser has a good understanding of the motives and behaviours of the financial company. We also argue that the deliverer of the goods purchased may be chosen by the purchaser and can therefore be an organization with which the purchaser has a long-standing or trusted relationship. In many cases, the deliver would be the national postal service which has delivered goods to the purchaser for many years.

In this paper, we consider all three of these players (*seller, financial organization* and *deliverer*) from the point of view of the purchaser and examine the aspects of trust associated with each. We use only that information necessarily disclosed by the purchaser, which is essential to the transaction. We use this analysis to develop a model which optimizes the trust, from the perspective of a purchaser, in an e-commerce transaction. We also describe the technologies used in existing models and demonstrate that these same technologies are sufficient for the proposed models.

In section 2, we discuss the various kinds of information a purchaser is required to disclose in an e-commerce transaction. In section 3, we present an abstracted model for the e-commerce transaction situation. In section 4, we introduce a method of measuring the privacy concerns of a purchaser. Section 5 analyzes the traditional e-commerce models and compares these with the proposed models from the point of view of the theory of section 4. In section 6, we propose an implementation of the new models and demonstrate that no additional technologies are required. Section 7 concludes the paper.

2 Purchaser Information

The information that a purchaser is likely to reveal to a party in an e-commerce trans-action, but wants to protect from others, can be divided into the following categories:

Order Information: Information related to the characteristics of the product which can identify the product.

Delivery Information: Information which identifies the source and the destination of a delivered product (address or box number).

Payment Information: Information such as credit card number or social security number.

Personal Information: This includes name, age, email address and sex.

We assume that this information is sufficient to conclude a transaction and that the purchaser wishes all of the information to be kept confidential or private.

We argue that the level of trust expected in an e-commerce relationship is directly related to the purchaser's expectation of how the above information will be used or misused. Therefore, the abstract models we build in the following section are based on the transfer of the above information from the purchaser to the parties mentioned in the previous section.

Usually, a purchaser reveals personal information when registering with a seller. The seller also receives the order information and often, also the financial and delivery instructions [21]. Separately, these pieces of information may not be useful to a malicious entity, but combined, they reveal the identity of the purchaser along with credit card information and possibly his desires, habits, financial and health condition. This information may be used for the purposes of impersonation, theft, bribery or blackmail.

Our goal is therefore to introduce a measure of the value of combinations of the purchaser's information and a set of transactions between the parties which minimizes this value. We do this in the next section.

3 Abstract E-Commerce Models

In the models described in this paper, we assume that a transaction is electronic but that the product purchased requires physical delivery by a deliverer. We treat the deliverer as an entity distinct from the seller as often an e-shop will use the national postal service for delivery of goods. We also assume that the purchaser uses an e-payment system to pay and that payment is made by credit/debit card issued by a financial company. In any such e-commerce transaction the minimum information which a purchaser needs to reveal is:

1- Order Information
2- Delivery Information
3- Payment Information

Here we argue that the *Personal Information* of the purchaser identified in section 2 is not needed in order to successfully complete an online transaction. The three pieces of information listed above are sufficient.

Before turning to the abstract model, we point out also that some realizations of electronic consumer to business transactions involve proxies for the seller or deliverer (but usually not the financial organization). Our initial aim is to identify all possible models under the above assumptions based on the flow of information. We assume additionally that the seller knows at least the Order Information (1), the deliverer knows at least the Delivery Information (2) and the financial company knows at least the Payment Information (3). For every entity there are thus precisely 4 combinations yielding a total of 64 combinations of models as illustrated in Table 1.

For example, a seller may know:

Order information - 1
Order and Delivery information - 1, 2
Order and Payment information - 1, 3
Order, Delivery and Payment information - 1, 2, 3

Table 1. The 64 abstract e-commerce models

Entities	Models	Mi
Seller		1 ? ?
Deliverer		2 ? ?
Financial Organization		3 ? ?

In narrowing the set of models further, we again consider the perspective of the purchaser who, if paying by credit or debit card, already has an established relationship with a financial organization. We can assume that the relationship between the purchaser and this financial organization is a trusted one relative to payment information. Additionally, in considering the deliverer, we assume that the seller will use a well established organization such as a national postal service or that the purchaser may choose the deliverer. In either case, we assume that the purchaser is able to rely on a trusted delivery service.

On the other hand, in selecting the seller, the purchaser is restricted to choosing a seller from the set of sellers who own the object which the purchaser wishes to purchase. It is the object for purchase which is the key factor; the choice of seller is based on this object. Hence, the purchaser does not have unrestricted choice of seller. Thus, the seller may be a company not known to the purchaser and whose reputation is unavailable. The seller may in fact be located in a country where rules concerning the distribution of the private information about clients do not exist. For example, the lack of privacy recognition in India [14] may discourage potential purchasers worldwide to buy from that country. For these reasons, we argue that the relationship between the seller and purchaser is in most cases the least trust-worthy. It follows that the best possible model with regard to preserving the privacy of the purchaser is one in which the seller only has access to the order information.

We would also argue that a financial institution would not want the encumbrance of information about purchases other than the ones necessary to execute the financial component of the transaction. Nor do they need extraneous information. Hence, we will assume that the financial organization only has access to the payment information of the purchase.

We have thus established two hypotheses:

1) The seller should know only the order information
2) The financial organization should know only the payment information.

Based on the above hypotheses this reduces us to four e-commerce models, eliminating 60 models.

Table 2. Four e-commerce models under hypotheses 1 and 2

Entities \ Models	M1	M2	M3	M4
Seller	1	1	1	1
Deliverer	2	1,2	2,3	1,2,3
Financial Organization	3	3	3	3

We refer to these four models as the *'trust-enhanced'* models. It remains to examine the practicality of implementing these four cases.

The M1 model is most appropriate for an e-commerce environment in which a purchaser does not trust any entity. For instance, this model may be useful in communities where corruption is very high. Nevertheless, the necessary communications between the seller and financial organization, to authorize the transaction, and between the seller and deliverer, to pass on the product, may be untrustworthy from the purchaser's point of view.

Each of the models M2, M3 and M4 is appropriate where a purchaser trusts the deliverer to some extent. If the payment information is held to be more 'valuable' by the purchaser than the order information (or vice-versa), this will impact on which of these models to choose. The M3 model is appropriate where a purchaser buys goods which reveal sensitive information about the purchaser, such as sexual preferences or medical problems. The M4 model is appropriate where, for instance, the purchaser's community requires a level of transparency for security reasons in order to prevent the purchaser from buying illegal goods from outside of the community. We therefore introduce measurements by which we can better analyse these four situations. This measurement system can be applied to all sixty-four models in Table 1.

4 Measuring the Privacy Concern of Purchasers

As we have indicated in the Introduction, the level of privacy concern of purchasers for an e-commerce model is a major factor in the success of that model. Therefore, it is important to have a mechanism measuring the level of privacy retained by each of our models. From the point of view of the purchaser, a violation of privacy may occur where there is little trust between the purchaser and another entity in the transaction (in this case, the seller, deliverer or financial organization). In addition, the more sensitive the information disclosed, the greater the impact on privacy loss. We therefore use these two significant items as the basis of our measurement of an expected privacy violation [1], [17]. We refer to the level of mistrust between the purchaser and the other entities as *Level of Mistrust* [17], indicated by T, and use W to indicate the level or *Weight of Sensitivity* [1] of information disclosed. T can be indexed by the three entities and W by the three types of information, as indicated in Table 3. The actual values of these parameters can be taken from any set of non-negative ordered numbers. Obviously, different scales may be used for each of T and W.

Table 3. The notation used for measuring the privacy concern of a purchaser

Notation	
T	Level of Mistrust
W	Weight of Sensitivity
x	(seller, deliverer or financial company)
i	(order, delivery or payment information)

We now define **P to be the expected privacy violation** associated with a model from the perspective of the purchaser.

Let $P_x = T_x \sum^x (W_i)$ be the level of mistrust a purchaser has in an entity x multiplied by the sum of only those pieces of information W_i provided to entity x in a particular model as in Table 1. This measures the expected privacy violation between the purchaser and entity x. The total expected privacy violation in a transaction represented by this model is then the sum over all P_x or $\mathbf{P} = \sum P_x$.

A low value for **P** indicates a low level of violation of privacy, whereas a high level indicates a high privacy violation. If a value of 0 is assigned to any T_x, then the value of the sum of the weights is eliminated whether this is high or low. In order to maintain the impact of the sensitivity, we suggest taking 1 as the smallest value for T_x.

In computing the expected privacy violation for the four models of Table 2, we note that value for M1 will always be lower than the values for M2, M3 and M4, and that the value for M4 will always be the largest. However, the value for M2 may be smaller or larger than the value for M3.

We present a case example demonstrating how the expected privacy violation for the four models of Table 2 can be computed. The scale for weight of sensitivity and level of mistrust has been chosen by the purchaser to be the discrete set {1, 2, 3, 4, 5} where the values 1 and 5 correspond to the minimum and maximum levels respectively of mistrust or sensitivity. In order to demonstrate the affects of the interactions between the purchaser and the other entities, we keep the sensitivity weights W_i constant.

Case Study: Alice has just received a credit card from her new bank. It is a large, well-recognized bank with a good reputation, so despite the fact that she has not used it before, she is fairly confident that she will have no problems. She wishes to purchase a new television from an online company which she does not know. It offers the brand, size, features and colour she wants at the best price. The seller will ship it using Australia Post. Although she has never before had a large, breakable object shipped to her by Australia post, she has successfully received many items through them in the past.

As she does not want possible burglars to know about her purchase, she assigns a common sensitivity of 2 to the weights of each of the order, delivery and payment information. Because she has no experience with the seller and does not know anything about it, she attaches a (highest) weight of 5 to the level of mistrust; to each of the deliverer and financial organization, she allocates a weight of 2.

The four models of Table 2 can then be analysed from her point of view in the expected privacy violation, **P**, and she can see which of these models is best.

$T_{seller}=5$ $W_{order}=2$
$T_{deliverer}=2$ $W_{delivery}=2$
$T_{financial}=2$ $W_{payment}=2$

Models	M1	M2	M3	M4
Score	18	22	22	26

Clearly, the most attractive model for Alice is M1 followed equally by M2 and M3. In weighing comparative differences in models with respect to the value of **P**, a purchaser faced with a choice should consider the variation in values between M1 and M4. If this variation is large, M4 should be avoided. If it is small, then any one of the four models may be acceptable.

5   Existing E-Commerce Models

In this Section we describe and analyse two e-commerce models currently in use on the Internet. These models are not trust-enhanced as, in each, information other than order information is revealed to the seller. From the perspective of the purchaser, the two models are indistinguishable. However, the flow of the purchaser's private information differs in the models. The first model we refer to as the 'no proxy model' in which a purchaser deals only with entities he can identify. The second we call the 'proxy model', in which additional entities play a role not known to the purchaser. We may refer to both simultaneously as the 'traditional e-commerce model'.

5.1   The No Proxy E-Commerce Model

The participating entities in what we refer to as the no proxy e-commerce model are a purchaser, a seller, a financial organization and a deliverer. The process of the e-commerce model (Figure 1) is described below:

A purchaser requests information about a product (step 1). The seller replies with the related information, including the price of that product (step 2). If the purchaser is satisfied with the price, he requests delivery options and their costs (step 3). After the delivery options and their costs are provided (step 4) by the seller, the purchaser decides whether to buy the product or not. If the decision is yes, he sends the payment details (e.g. credit card information), the selected delivery option and his personal information, such as the telephone number, e-mail address, and the full name of the purchaser (step 5). Hence the seller obtains all order, delivery, financial and personal information from the purchaser and stores it in a database in order to use it for marketing purposes [6]. After the seller ensures that the payment information is valid (step 6) and obtains payment (step 7), it prepares the product for delivery by the deliverer. The seller gives the product to the deliverer, including the full delivery address (step 8). The seller also pays the deliverer based on the selected delivery option of the purchaser. Finally the deliverer delivers the product to the purchaser (step 9). Examples of this e-commerce model are Amazon (www.amazon.com) and Mayer (www.mayer.com).

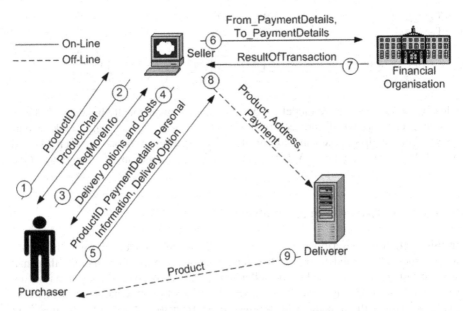

Fig. 1. The no proxy e-commerce model

The no proxy e-commerce model falls into the following model type.

	Model	No Proxy Model
Entities		
Seller		1,2,3
Deliverer		2
Financial Company		3

In this model, the distribution of the purchaser's personal information (steps 3 and 5) raises a number of privacy and security issues. The purchaser's information is stored in a database for a period of time the length of which is decided by the seller. A database which contains vast amounts of personal information and credit card details is a target for attackers [9]. An additional factor for consideration is what happens to the data that sellers hold when they close down or are sold to another company. If the head office moves from one country to another, what impact does the changing legal scene have on the way this data is held and managed? In such a situation, one should expect the mistrust level by the purchaser to be high.

According to [2, 20], sellers can increase their customer base by increasing the appearance of trust; therefore, it is desirable to have a trustworthy system which is responsible for data handling including confidentiality of personal information and accountability of sellers' actions. The traditional e-commerce model demands a high level of trust because of the high level of risk that purchasers and sellers face. Taking into consideration the dissemination of the personal information, the flow of information is as in Table 4 below.

Table 4. Information each entity has about the purchaser in the no proxy model

	Seller	Deliverer	Financial Organisation
Personal Information	√	×	√
Payment Information	√	×	√
Order Information	√	Limited	Limited
Delivery Information	√	√	×

5.2 The Proxy E-Commerce Model

Companies, especially small companies, who want to sell their products on-line, sometimes transfer a portion of the responsibility to a provider of online services which we call a proxy. For example, a small business supplier of honey may wish to sell its products through a large online supermarket. To a purchaser, the seller appears to be a trustworthy online seller, but in fact, the small business receives payment and delivers the product. We refer to a company which sells its products via another organization as 'product-oriented' (POC). Essentially, the transaction steps of the no proxy model are followed but an extra party is involved in some of the steps. The supermarket company (SC) may act as a direct seller of goods obtained from wholesalers, along with goods from a number of POCs. The SC is responsible for the website and the online purchasing. Each POC makes available the information about their products on the SC's web site. A purchaser visits the SC's web site (without seeing identification of the POCs), finds the desired product and pays the SC who then informs the relevant POC and the POC arranges for delivery of the item. The POC has no access to the financial and personal information of the purchaser

As an additional, somewhat different, example, Yahoo! operates as a proxy on behalf of a number of POCs and is responsible for handling the payment system, hosting the web site and the database, informing the POCs of the orders and generally taking on the technical responsibilities such as web development, web hosting, and e-payment. The POCs are responsible for updating the content of the web sites (such as product pricing, available offers etc) and arranging for the delivery of the products. Yahoo! itself does not sell its own products in this system. While in this case, a POC does not have access to the payment information of a purchaser, it has access to the personal, order and delivery information.

Thus, in the proxy model, a purchaser may not know who has access to his sensitive information and so has no way of determining with any accuracy the trust level required in the transaction.

In the tables below we represent the flow of information. The model type is the same as that for the no proxy case, so we do not give the table. The first chart gives the general proxy situation. Note the very small difference between Tables 5 and 6.

Table 5. Illustrates the type of information each entity has in the Yahoo! proxy e-commerce model

	Yahoo!	Small Business	Post Office	Financial Company
Personal Information	√	√	×	√
Payment Information	√	×	×	√
Order Information	√	√	Limited	Limited
Delivery Information	√	√	√	×

Table 6. Illustrates the type of information each entity has in the e-Supermarket model

	Supermarket	Small Business	Post Office	Financial Company
Personal Information	√	×	×	√
Payment Information	√	×	×	√
Order Information	√	√	Limited	Limited
Delivery Information	√	√	√	×

5.3 Comparison of the Trust-Enhanced and Traditional E-Commerce Models

In the case of the no proxy model, it is possible to apply the measurements of section 4 with precision. In the case of the proxy model, we can only determine the best case expected privacy violation figure, as the values assigned to unknown entities are not computable.

Clearly, a good e-commerce model should be transparent to the purchaser, indicating all the parties involved and allowing the purchaser to determine with accuracy the level of privacy violation which may occur.

To compare the trust-enhanced model with the proxy and no proxy models, we recall the case study of section 3. The table below shows these same values for T_i and W_i as were used in the study (Case 1) and gives the values for a possible second case.

Models Cases	Proxy & No Proxy	M1	M2	M3	M4
Case 1: $T_{seller}=5$, $T_{deliverer}=2$, $T_{financial}=2$, $W_i=2$	38	18	22	22	26
Case 2: $T_{seller}= W_{order}=5$, $T_{deliverer}=T_{financial}=W_{deliverer}= W_{payment}=2$	59	33	43	37	47

Observe that if the seller and deliverer are assigned the same weighting, then if all other values are preserved across the two situations, the expected privacy violation will be the same. Thus, the critical difference in the results above arises from our first hypothesis that, because the seller is the least likely entity to incur trust, the seller should know only the order information. In the next section, we describe the technologies needed for implementing the trust-enhanced models compared to those required for the traditional models.

6 Technology

In this section, we describe the technologies currently used to implement the proxy and no proxy models described earlier in this section and demonstrate that the proposed models can be implemented with the same technologies as the traditional models. These are:

Web Browser: A platform or application enabling a user to access and interact with web pages.

Web Server: A computer or application responsible for serving requests of a web browser.

Http: A request/response protocol between a web browser and a web server. Messages exchanged are in clear text and therefore vulnerable to eavesdroppers.

Digital Certificate: An electronic document which incorporates a digital signature to bind together a public key with an identity (information such as the name or address of a person or an organization).

Certificate Authority (CA): A trusted party responsible for issuing and signing digital certificates and for verifying their integrity.

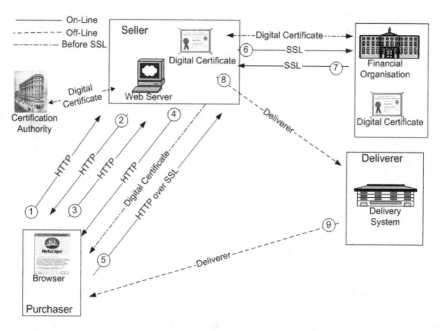

Fig. 2. Technologies used with the traditional protocol

Secure Socket Layer (SSL): A communication protocol which allows both participants to authenticate each other, while their communication is protected against eaves dropping.

Figure 2 illustrates the applications of the above technologies in the traditional model. Where proxies are used, for the sake of simplicity we identify them as appropriate with the associated entity (seller, deliverer or financial organization).

In considering the technologies needed for implementation of the trust-enhanced models proposed in section 3, we focus on model M4 as this is most similar to the traditional model because a single entity receives all personal information sent by the purchaser. Figure 3 below applies the same technologies in the M4 model, but in different ways. In Figure 3, the use of SSL between the web server and browser is the one critical addition enabling the privacy of information desired by the purchaser.

Figures 2 and 3 suggest that, in implementing M4, there need be no additional cost to the overall system, but that some cost is transferred from the seller to the deliverer. This is an acceptable cost, as the deliverer now has more opportunities for sales. On the other hand, the seller is in an improved situation, as there is no impact on their business, while their costs are, at the same time, reduced.

In an extended version of this paper, we give a detailed protocol implementing each of the four trust-enhanced models.

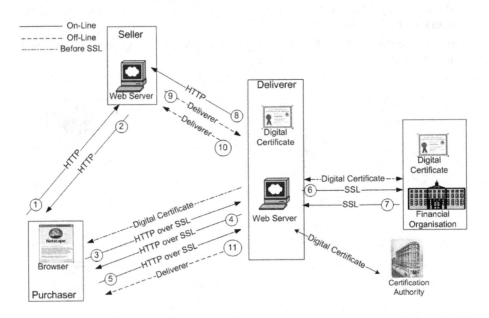

Fig. 3. Technologies used with the M4 model

7 Conclusions

In this paper, we introduce a measure of the trust based on the information distributed to the parties in an e-commerce transaction. Based on this precise method of measurement, we are able to isolate the instances which maximize trust for the purchaser, leading us to propose four new models for e-commerce which improve consumer trust. Implementation of these new models in the e-commerce market place would therefore likely lead to an increase in on-line commerce. We describe in detail the technologies used to implement existing models and demonstrate that no new technologies are needed in order to implement the new models. The overall cost to the e-commerce system would remain the same while, internally, costs would be moved from the seller to the deliverer. An extended version of this paper, to be submitted elsewhere, will give detailed protocols for implementation of all four trust-enhanced models, along with proofs of security.

References

1. Al-Fedaghi, S.: How sensitive is your personal information? In: Proceedings of the 2007 ACM symposium on Applied computing, pp. 165–169 (2007)
2. Anderson, B.B., Hansen, J.V., Lowry, P.B., Summers, S.L.: The application of model checking for securing e-commerce transactions. Communications of the ACM 49, 97–101 (2006)
3. Barnard, L., Wesson, J.: A trust model for e-commerce in South Africa. In: Proceedings of the 2004 annual research conference of the South African institute of computer scientists and information technologists on IT research in developing countries, pp. 23–32 (2004)
4. Bhargav-Spantzel, A., Woo, J., Bertino, E.: Receipt management- Transaction history based trust establishment. In: Proceedings of the 2007 ACM workshop on Digital identity management, pp. 82–91 (2007)
5. Burns, S.: Unique characteristics of e-commerce technologies and their effects upon payment systems. GSEC (GIAC Security Essentials Certification)–Version 1 (2002)
6. Camenisch, J., Shelat, A., Sommer, D., Fischer-Hubner, S., Hansen, M., Krasemann, H., Lacoste, G., Leenes, R., Tseng, J.: Privacy and identity management for everyone. In: DIM 2005, pp. 20–27. ACM, Virginia (2005)
7. Chau, P.Y.K., Hu, P.J.H., Lee, B.L.P., Au, A.K.K.: Examining customers' trust in online vendors and their dropout decisions: An empirical study. Electronic Commerce Research and Applications 6, 171–182 (2007)
8. Claessens, J., Preneel, B., Vandewalle, J.: Anonymity controlled electronic payment systems. In: Proceedings of the 20th Symposium on Information Theory in the Benelux, pp. 109–116 (1999)
9. Doherty, S.: Keeping data private. Network Computing 12, 83–91 (2001)
10. Doney, P.M., Cannon, J.P.: An examination of the nature of trust in buyer–seller relationships. Journal of Marketing 61, 35–51 (1997)
11. Fomenko, V.: Generating virtual reality shops for e-commerce. Dissertation, Vrije Universiteit Brussel (2006)
12. Jarvenpaa, S.L., Tractinsky, N., Vitale, M.: Consumer trust in an Internet store. Information Technology and Management 1, 45–71 (2000)
13. Katsikas, S.K., Lopez, J., Pernul, G.: Trust, privacy and security in e-business: Requirements and solutions. In: Bozanis, P., Houstis, E.N. (eds.) PCI 2005. LNCS, vol. 3746, pp. 548–558. Springer, Heidelberg (2005)
14. Kumaraguru, P., Cranor, L.: Privacy in India: Attitudes and Awareness. In: Danezis, G., Martin, D. (eds.) PET 2005. LNCS, vol. 3856, pp. 243–258. Springer, Heidelberg (2006)

15. Moores, T.: Do consumers understand the role of privacy seals in e-commerce? Communications of the ACM 48, 86–91 (2005)
16. Seigneur, J.M., Jensen, C.D.: Trust enhanced ubiquitous payment without too much privacy loss. In: Proceedings of the 2004 ACM symposium on Applied computing, pp. 1593–1599 (2004)
17. Sillence, E., Briggs, P., Harris, P., Fishwick, L.: A framework for understanding trust factors in web-based health advice. International Journal of Human-Computer Studies 64, 697–713 (2006)
18. Smith, L.M., Smith, J.L.: Cyber Crimes Aimed at Publicly Traded Companies: Is Stock Price Affected?: American Accounting Association Southwest Region, Oklahoma City (2006)
19. Tan, H., Guo, J.: Some methods to depress the risks of the online transactions. In: Proceedings of the 7th international conference on Electronic commerce, pp. 217–220 (2005)
20. Teo, T.S.H., Liu, J.: Consumer trust in e-commerce in the United States, Singapore and China. Omega 35, 22–38 (2007)
21. Tsiounis, Y.: A Security Framework for Card-Based Systems. In: Proceedings of the 5th International Conference on Financial Cryptography, pp. 210–231 (2002)

A Game-Theoretical Approach to Data-Privacy Protection from Context-Based Inference Attacks: A Location-Privacy Protection Case Study

Gabriele Gianini and Ernesto Damiani

Università degli Studi di Milano, Dipartimento di Tecnologie dell'Informazione
via Bramante 65, 26013, Crema - Italy
{gianini,damiani}@dti.unimi.it

Abstract. One of the approaches to the problem of data-privacy protection is given by the application of obfuscation techniques; in many situations, however, context information can help an attacker to perform inference over obfuscated data and to refine the estimate of the sensitive data up to a violation of the original privacy requirements. We consider the problem in a location privacy protection set-up where the sensitive attribute to be protected is the position of a Location Based Service user, and where the location anonymization technique is cloaking, whereas the context, supporting inference attacks, consists in some landscape-related information, namely positional constraints. In this work we adopt the assumption that the anonymizer and the attacker are two rational agents and frame the problem in a game theoretical approach by modeling the contest as a two-player, zero-sum, signaling game, then we point to the corresponding equilibrium solution and show that, when the anonymizer plays the equilibrium strategies, the advantage provided to the attacker by a non-neutral landscape gets canceled. We suggest that the game theoretical solution could be used as a reference solution for inter-technique comparisons.

1 Introduction

One of the approaches to data-privacy protection is given by the application of obfuscation techniques actuated by a trusted agent before the data are communicated to third parties. In many situations, however, context information can help a third party to perform inference over those data and to refine the estimate of the sensitive data up to a violation of the original privacy requirements. We stage the problem in a location privacy protection set-up where the sensitive attribute to be protected is the position of a Location Based Service (LBS) user.

LBS applications, while on one side hold the promise of new business opportunities and a wide range of life enhancing services, on the other open door new threats to location privacy: in fact instance service providers could pass location information to unknown parties. For instance an employer could learn

W. Jonker and M. Petković (Eds.): SDM 2008, LNCS 5159, pp. 133–150, 2008.
© Springer-Verlag Berlin Heidelberg 2008

about the employee's medical conditions, alternative lifestyles or unpopular political views, by obtaining information such as visits to clinics, doctor offices,
entertainment districts, or political events. In extreme cases, public location information can lead to physical harm, for example in stalking or domestic abuse
scenarios. Preventing location privacy from being invaded is thus an issue of
utmost importance [3,10,8].

Location-privacy refers to the ability to prevent other unauthorized parties
from learning one's current or past location. One of the ways to achieve this
goal is to anonymize the location data: a trusted middle-ware called location
anonymizer, transforms the location information before sending it to the LBS's
provider, so as to reduce – to some degree specified by a service level agreement
with the user – the degree of association of the user with some location. The
most common location anonymization technique applied by the anonymizer is
k-anonymity – a well established technique in data privacy protection [13] – that
here consists in collecting location data of several users and to provide the LBS
provider the set of locations, or a cloak wide enough to cover the corresponding
locations: here the user specifies the degree of anonymization by setting the
minimum number of users's locations to be encompassed by the cloak [8].

The work [2] – arguing that strong positive correlations among users can
render k-anonimity ineffective (by resulting in a relatively small cloak even tough
the number of users relatively encompassed by the cloak is large) whereas strong
negative correlations (which produces a wide cloak) or lack of users, can make
the application impractical or impossible – proposes an anonymization technique,
which works independently of the presence of extra users, and specifies directly
the size of the cloak and a randomization procedure for the cloak location: here
the degree of anonymization is chosen by the user by setting the maximum
probability with which she could be associated to any given unit areas.

An example scenario of the application of any of the two techniques could
be the following: the user has subscribed to a LBS which provides a list of
interest points available in any given area according to her personal profile;
she does not contact the LBS provider directly, but sends her position to the
location anonymizer, along with the service request; the anonymizer obfuscates
the location by a suitably sized cloak and passes the request to the LBS, who in
turn provides the list of all the interest points, relative to that user, contained in
the larger obfuscated area; at this point the anonymizer filters out some interest
points and passes to the user only those closer to her actual position.

Inference Attacks. The main problem with both location anonymization techniques is that they rely on the tacit, simplifying assumption of a neutral (flat)
landscape (and of a general neutral context) that doesn't lend any help in refin-
ing the location estimates.

A first issue to consider is that landscape is not neutral in those real-world
environments, where, for instance, the movement of the user is bound by natural or men-made barriers, which confine the user in a reduced area, or constrain
her movement along specific paths. In most real situations, landscape/map (or in
general context related) information – not excluded the user's propensity to stay

closer to some reference point (or to avoid it) – can help a third party to perform inference over the data obfuscated by the trusted party and to refine the location estimate up to a violation of the user's location-privacy requirements.

A second issue to consider is that – even in a non-constraining landscape – the violation of location privacy can be less or more harmful to the user depending on the sensitivity of the location points from the user's perspective: furthermore, for completeness, one has to consider both the damage received by the service's user if she is found at a sensitive location and the payoff obtained by an hypothetical attacker from his attacks (although for sake of simplicity and with little loss of generality we can assume the two payoffs are proportional to the sensitivity of the place as perceived by the user).

Hence in general, an anonymizer needs, to operate an obfuscation procedure which is aware of possible subsequent landscape-based attacks considering both non-uniform location probability and non- uniform location sensitivity (i.e. user's and attacker's utility) since they play together in the economy of an attack. We can assume that the goal of the trusted party is to minimize the loss of the user, whereas the goal of the attacker is maximizing his own payoff. In this work we will adopt the assumption that the anonymizer and the attacker are two fully rational agents, and will frame the problem in a game-theoretical approach, modeling the obfuscation problem as a non-collaborative game.

Goals and Outline of the Paper. The goal of the present paper is to address the location-privacy protection issue in the general case of a non-neutral context, and in the specific case of a non-flat landscape. In other words, our problem is to find the key elements of a *landscape-aware/map-dependent* obfuscation procedure that enables the release of the maximum possible information about the user location that does not lead to a violation of the user's location-privacy preferences, even when refined through *map-based* inference. We approach the problem from a game-theoretical point of view, by modeling the contest between a data-obfuscator and a data-attacker (Section 2) as a two-player, zero-sum, (incomplete information) signaling game, then we point to the corresponding equilibrium solution, a refinement of the Bayes-Nash equilibrium known as Perfect Bayes Equilibrium (Section 3), which can be computed in practical cases by solving a linear system. To clarify the rationale of the equilibrium solution we provide some illustrative examples (Section 4). We conclude by discussing the relation with the relevant works (Section 5).

We point out that although the attribute to be protected in this case study is location, the proposed approach can easily be extended to other attributes.

2   Location Privacy Protection Set-Up

We briefly introduce the basic concepts and assumptions used in our work. We consider a privacy-aware location-based set-up involving three agents: the user, called *Alice*, in short A, who wanders within some (city/natural) landscape and carries a mobile device; the trusted agent *Bob*, in short B, who mediates the communication between the user and the third party and is responsible for the release of obfuscated location information to the latter; the third party, that is, the location-based service provider *Charlie*, in short C, which could try to de-obfuscate the location information he receives, by performing some inference with the help of the available map information (if the landscape is not flat).

We assume that the landscape map is common knowledge. The players of the game are Bob and Charlie: Bob's goal is to minimize the expected damage to Alice coming from Charlie's inference attacks, Charlie's goal is to maximize his own profit: we will adopt the assumption that Alice damage and Charlie's profit upon a successful attack are proportional, so that, adopting convenient units of measure, the game can be modeled as a zero-sum game (to each of the payoffs to Charlie for a successful attack will correspond an equivalent loss to Alice). We will shortly introduce the concept of game between rational players and the definition of game equilibrium, later, we will specify a procedure for the two players – Bob and Charlie – to compute the equilibrium strategy. To the equilibrium corresponds an expected loss for Alice and an opposite expected gain for Charlie, known as the *value* of the game; knowing this value in advance, the defendant can tune the size of the cloak so as to fulfill the threshold required by the service level agreement with the user. In this paper we disregard the somewhat secondary issue of the cloak size determination and focus on the mechanics of the game between Bob and Charlie.

3   Game-Theoretical View of Cloaking in Positioning

Game theory looks at rational behavior when each decision maker's well-being depends on the decisions of others as well as her own. Game theory attempts to find equilibria in these games: sets of strategies where individuals are unlikely to unilaterally change their behavior. Hereafter we will see that the above described obfuscation scenario can be modeled as a zero-sum sequential game with incomplete information from the side of the second mover: we will characterize it as a signaling game with prior information and will show that it admits an optimal solution for the two rational players, which represents an equilibrium, known as Perfect Bayesian Equilibrium, a refinement of the Bayes-Nash equilibrium referring to sequential games.

The games all share the common feature of interdependence between players: the outcome for each participant depends upon the choices of the other players. This introduces a circular reasoning which can be brought to a conclusion using a concept of equilibrium developed by John Nash: the equilibrium corresponds to a set of choices, one for each player, such that each person's strategy is best for him when all others are playing their stipulated best strategies. Strategies can be pure or mixed. Pure strategies correspond to deterministic choices, e.g. always giving the same response to a given move. Some games have no equilibria in pure strategies. In this case one has to resort to non-deterministic strategies, i.e. to mixed strategies: a mixed strategy is a probability distribution over pure strategies. Nash proved that if a player has a finite number of pure strategies, then there exist at least one equilibrium in (possibly) mixed strategies.

Borel, von Neumann and Morgenstern [4,14] had all discussed a specific rational way to play zero-sum games – games where one person's gain always is another's loss – called the min-max solution. They argue that each player should look at each of his available options and ask: "what is the *worst* that could happen to me if I choose this option?". Then he should pick the option that has the *best* what's-the-worst-that-could-happen outcome. In zero-sum games Nash equilibria and min-max equilibria coincide.

3.1   The Cloaking Game and Its Equilibria

Cloaking belongs to the class of the sequential games of incomplete information. Indeed the first mover, Bob, who knows perfectly the location of Alice, does not tell Charlie where Alice is exactly: he provides some information, telling where Alice is not (Alice is not outside the cloak). Furthermore, due to the fact that the first player has to decide what information to send to the second, this game belongs to the subclass of signaling games. The game would have a trivial solution for both players if there were no hints from the landscape (uniform probability of Alice position) or no variability in utility (uniform sensitivity/utility associated to locations): Bob would include randomly a neighborhood under a conveniently sized cloak, and Charlie would attack randomly over the cloak.

However we are assuming there are hints from the context, that allow (Bayesian) inference attacks: Alice is located (by "Nature") non-uniformly over the landscape; furthermore we are assuming the (negative) utility for Alice to be associated to the different locations is not uniform, i.e. that some locations are more sensitive than others, and that Charlie's utility for finding Alice at different locations is not uniform either. In this scenario we shall see that in order to maximize each player's utility we have to resort to a form of equilibrium know as Perfect Bayes Equilibrium.

Rules of the Game. In signaling games (see for instance [7]), such as the cloaking game, there are two players: B - the sender (a.k.a the leader) and C - the receiver (a.k.a the follower). In the cloaking game setting C has a prior believe $a(x)$ (the landscape prior) about the possible Alice's location, and this prior believe is common knowledge (is known also to B), furthermore

- A is located at some specific coordinate x in some space X
- B has *private* information about A's location $x \in X$ and – conditionally to this information – chooses a message $y \in Y$ (chooses which neighborhood to include under the cloak), here every y characterizes one of the possible neighborhoods of x i.e. one of the possible cloaks, and Y is the set of all the possible cloaks;
- C observes the message y and combines this information with the landscape prior, by obtaining a posterior believe $a^*(x)$ (the landscape posterior), and conditionally to this information chooses a coordinate $z \in Z$ to possibly attack; here Z is the set of all the possible points worth an attack, typically it corresponds to the set of coordinates encompassed by the cloak; notice that we are assuming that C can attack on a single coordinate only;

then

- a pure strategy for player B prescribes an action $y \in Y$ for each of A's locations $x' \in X$, and can be indicated by $(y|x')$;
- a pure strategy for player C prescribes an action $z \in Z$ for each of B's signals $y' \in Y$, and can be indicated by $(z|y')$;

and

- a mixed strategy for player B prescribes a probability distribution $\underline{b}(\cdot|x')$ over actions y for a given observed location x', which corresponds to an array $\underline{b}(\cdot|x') = (..., b(y|x'), ...)$ with the normalization condition $\sum_y b(y|x') = 1$;
- a mixed strategy for player C prescribes a probability distribution $\underline{c}(\cdot|y')$ over actions z for a B's received message y', which corresponds to an array $\underline{c}(\cdot|y') = (..., c(z|y'), ...)$ with the normalization condition $\sum_z c(z|y') = 1$.

The full set of mixed conditional strategies for a player, encompassing the strategies for all conditions is called a *strategy profile* and consists in a matrix of probabilities:

- a *strategy profile* for player B consists in a matrix $\underline{b}$ of probabilities with elements $b(y|x)$ (thanks to the normalization conditions can be characterized through a reduced array of parameters $\underline{p}$);
- a *strategy profile* for player C consists in a matrix $\underline{c}$ of probabilities with elements $c(z|y)$ (characterized through a reduced array of parameters $\underline{q}$ thanks to the normalization conditions and the limited extension of the cloaks);

Players'payoffs. Each triplet, consisting in a position x of A, a message choice y by B and an action z by C, determines a payoff for the players B and C: player B's payoff is denoted by $u(x, y, z)$ whereas player C's payoff is denoted $v(x, y, z)$.

Assume the two players adopt the choice of their strategy profiles simultaneously, at epoch zero, i.e. before the beginning of the game, and that each one's strategy profile is unknown to the other. Let us assume that we do not know Alice's position x', but we know that B adopts the strategy profile $\underline{b}$ and that C adopts the strategy profile $\underline{c}$.

At epoch one, Bob observes Alice's location x's; knowing that he will adopt the mixed strategy $\underline{b}(\cdot|x')$: we can compute the conditional or *ex-post expected payoff* to B for adopting this mixed strategy while player C plays the strategy profile $\underline{c}(\cdot|\cdot)$ as

$$\bar{u}(x = x', \underline{b}(\cdot|x'), \underline{c}) = \sum_y b(y|x') \sum_z c(z|y) \cdot u(x', y, z)$$

At epoch two, player Bob sends a message, which we indicate by y', randomly determined according to strategy $\underline{b}(\cdot|x')$. Upon reception of the message Charlie – were he not missing the knowledge of $\underline{b}$ – would be able to update his believes about x, thanks to Bayes' Theorem, obtaining the posterior distribution

$$a^*(x|y') = \frac{b(y'|x)a(x)}{\sum_{x'} b(y'|x')a(x')}$$

We can exploit the knowledge that C will adopt the mixed strategy $\underline{c}(\cdot|y')$ to compute the conditional, or *ex-post expected payoff to C*

$$\bar{v}(\underline{a}^*(\cdot|y'), y = y', c(\cdot|y')) = \sum_x a^*(x|y') \sum_z c(z|y') \cdot v(x, y', z)$$

We have, this far, focused on a pair of strategy profiles: the strategy profile $\underline{b}$ for B and the strategy profile $\underline{c}$ for C; however to every choice of the pair $(\underline{b}, \underline{c})$ will correspond a value for the *ex-post expected payoff to B* and to a value for the *ex-post expected payoff to C*.

Perfect Bayesian Equilibrium. Some specific strategy profile pair $(\underline{b}, \underline{c})$ – producing a value pair for the *ex-post expected payoffs* – will be such that no player would unilaterally move away from it, because the pair maximizes the player's expected payoffs conditional to the player's believes: this pair of strategy profiles will represent an *equilibrium* in the game theoretical sense. This is the core of the so called Perfect Bayesian Equilibrium (PBE) [7], more formally defined in the following, which refines the Bayes Nash equilibrium – which applies to the case of games with imperfect information – to sequential games. The notation used in the definition is summarized in Table 1.

Definition 1 (PBE). *A Perfect Bayesian Equilibrium (PBE) of a signaling game [7] consists in a strategy profile $\underline{\hat{c}}$ and posterior believes $\underline{a}^*(\cdot|y)$, such that*

$$\forall x \in X \ \underline{\hat{b}}(\cdot|x) \in arg \max_{\underline{b}(\cdot|x)} \bar{u}(x, \underline{b}(\cdot|x), \underline{\hat{c}}) \tag{1}$$

$$\forall y \in Y \ \underline{\hat{c}}(\cdot|y) \in arg \max_{\underline{c}(\cdot|y)} \sum_x a^*(x|y)\bar{v}(x, y, \underline{c}(\cdot|y)) \tag{2}$$

where $\underline{a}^*(\cdot|y)$ is obtained through the Bayes' theorem

$$\forall y \in Y \ a^*(x|y) = \frac{\hat{b}(y|x)a(x)}{\sum_{x'} \hat{b}(y|x')a(x')} \tag{3}$$

in the hypothesis that $\sum_{x' \in X} \hat{b}(y'|x')a(x') > 0$.

Conditions (1) and (2) are called the perfection conditions: (1) says that player B takes into account the effect of y on player C's action, (2) states that player C reacts optimally to player B's action, given his posterior believes about x, whereas (3) corresponds to the application of Bayes'Theorem. The PBE equilibrium is simply a set of strategies and believes such that at any stage of the game, strategies are optimal given the believes, and the believes are obtained from equilibrium strategies and observed actions using Bayes' Theorem: the believes are consistent with strategies, which in turn are optimal given the believes.

Table 1. Summary of the notation

A or Alice	the user whose location has to be protected		
B or Bob	the anonymizer, is the first player of the sequential game and plays the role of the *sender*		
C or Charlie	the attacker, is the second player in the sequential game and plays the role of the *receiver*		
$x \in X$	true Alice's location, it is know by Bob		
$y \in Y$	message sent by Bob to Charlie; within the Cloaking Game it univocally identifies a cloak; within the simplified 3-coordinate game it represents the leftmost coordinate of a two-unit wide cloak		
$z \in Z$	action taken by Charlie; within the Cloaking Game z corresponds to the coordinate of Charlie's attack		
$s(x)$	sensitivity of location x		
$a(x)$	a priori probability of Alice being located at x, it is known to Charlie, in turn Charlie's knowledge is known to Bob		
$a^*(x|y')$	a posteriori probability of Alice being located at x, as estimated by Charlie, based on the cloak y' indicated by Bob		
$(y|x')$	a pure (conditional) strategy for Bob, prescribing a message $y \in Y$ for Alice's location $x' \in X$	$(z|y')$	a pure (conditional) strategy for Charlie, prescribing an action $z \in Z$ in response to Bob's signal $y' \in Y$
$\underline{b}(\cdot|x')$	a mixed strategy for Bob prescribing a probability distribution over actions y for a given observed location x'; it corresponds to a normalized array $\underline{b}(\cdot|x') = (..., b(y|x'), ...)$	$\underline{c}(\cdot|y')$	a mixed strategy for Charlie prescribes a probability distribution over actions z in response to Bob's message y'; it corresponds to a normalized array $\underline{c}(\cdot|y') = (..., c(z|y'), ...)$
$\underline{b}(\cdot|\cdot)$	a *strategy profile* for Bob, represents the collection of all Bob's conditional mixed strategies; thanks to the normalization conditions can be characterized through a smaller set of parameters collected in the array $\underline{p}$	$\underline{c}(\cdot|\cdot)$	a *strategy profile* for Charlie, represents the collection of all Charlie's conditional mixed strategies; thanks to the normalization conditions can be characterized through a smaller set of parameters collected in the array $\underline{q}$
$\underline{\hat{b}}(\cdot|x')$	the equilibrium mixed strategy for Bob conditional to the Alice's position x'	$\underline{\hat{c}}(\cdot|y')$	the equilibrium mixed strategy for Charlie conditional to Bob's signal y'
$\underline{\hat{b}}$	the equilibrium *strategy profile* for Bob	$\underline{\hat{c}}$	the equilibrium *strategy profile* for Charlie

4 Zero-Sum Obfuscation Games

We introduce now the assumption that Alice's damage and Charlie's profit upon a successful attack are proportional and opposite in sign, so that, adopting convenient units of measure, the game can be modeled as a zero-sum game; furthermore we assume that the utilities are non-zero only when Charlie's attack coordinate is the same as Alice's position.

We can write $v(x, y, z) = -u(x, y, z) = s(x)\delta(z - x)$ where $\delta(z - x)$ equals 1 only if $z = x$ and is null otherwise, and where $s(x)$ is the payoff to Charlie associated to the attack being successful at a specific location; under our assumptions this quantity can be interpreted as the sensitivity of location x to Alice.

It will be straightforward to show that in the case we are considering there is no equilibrium in pure strategies and that one has to resort to mixed strategy equilibria, i.e. indifference equilibria: such equilibria correspond to values of the mixing parameters which induce in the opponent the indifference among the different pure strategy choices. This can be easily translated into a set of linear equations. Therefore finding the equilibrium of any zero sum obfuscation game results in a straightforward procedure, based on solving a linear system of equations.

4.1 A 2-Coordinate Cloak, Zero-Sum Toy Model

The class of zero-sum obfuscation games as a special subclass the one where $s(x) = 1\ \forall x$: $v(x, y, z) = -u(x, y, z) = \delta(z - x)$, which means that every point has the same sensitivity for Alice and in case of successful attack yields the same utility to Charlie.

We will now give the definition and find the equilibrium of a of a uniform sensitivity simplified obfuscation game, based on a space of three coordinates and with a cloak width of two units, as shown in Fig.1.

Rules of the Game. In this toy model Alice can be in one of three locations: $x \in \{0, 1, 2\}$, ordered clockwise over a circle. A cloak here is represented by an interval covering two coordinates, and can be chosen in only three ways either $[0, 1]$ or $[1, 2]$, or $[2, 0]$, hence a pure strategy y for Bob can be chosen in only three ways: with the convention here that y indicates the left-end of the interval we have $y \in \{0, 1, 2\}$ (see Fig.1). Also Charlie has three pure strategies available: $z \in \{0, 1, 2\}$.

We are adopting the assumption that Charlie's attack is effective only if it falls on the real Alice's location, i.e. only if $z = x$ and that its utility in that case is -1 for Bob and +1 for Charlie, i.e. we are adopting the utility functions $v(x, y, z) = -u(x, y, z) = \delta(z-x)$. i.e. in this version of the game we are assuming the sensitivity $s(x)$ is uniform over the landscape, whereas the probability of Alice's location is not: before the start of the game A's location prior $a(x)$ is common knowledge, and the fact that both know the prior is common knowledge as well.

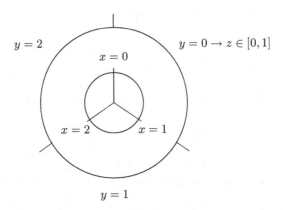

Fig. 1. Toy model with three possible coordinates, $x \in \{0, 1, 2\}$. When Alice is in $x = 1$ Bob can communicate to Charlie either the cloak $[0, 1]$ (conventionally indicated by $y = 0$) or the cloak $[1, 2]$ (conventionally indicated by $y = 1$). If Bob chooses to communicate the message $y = 0$, Charlie will know that Alice is in $[0, 1]$ and will attack either at $z = 0$ or at $z = 1$.

Pure strategies. After Bob has observed Alice's location, he knows the location x with certainty; at this point Bob has two *pure* strategies left: $y = x$ consisting in using the observed x as the lower end of the cloak, and $y = (x - 1) \bmod 2$ consisting in using the observed x as the upper end of the cloak.

After Bob has sent the message y to Charlie also the latter is left with two *pure* strategies (since one coordinate has been ruled out): the first consists in attacking on y (i.e. betting on the possibility $(y = x|x)$ that Bob has taken the clockwise choice $y = x$), the second consists in attacking on $(y + 1) \bmod 2$ (i.e. betting on the possibility $(y = (x - 1) \bmod 2|x)$ that Bob has taken the anti-clockwise choice $y = (x - 1) \bmod 2$).

Mixed strategies. Bob's randomized mixed strategies are defined by different mixes of pure strategies ($y = 0, y = 1, y = 2$), according to different probabilities: however, after the observation of x by Bob, his mixed strategies can be qualified using a single degree of freedom, e.g. if Alice is observed at $x = 1$, then only $y = 1$ and $y = 0$ are possible and the mix between the two possibilities can be expressed by the probability p_1 of adopting strategy $y = 1$, whereas $y = 0$ will be adopted with probability $(1 - p_1)$. With those conventions (see Fig.2) the mixed strategies $\underline{b}(\cdot|x = 0)$, $\underline{b}(\cdot|x = 1)$ and $\underline{b}(\cdot|x = 2)$ will be characterized respectively by the probabilities p_1, p_2 and p_3 as follows

$$b(y|x = 0) = \begin{cases} Pr(y = 0|x = 0) = p_0 \\ Pr(y = 2|x = 0) = (1 - p_0) \\ Pr(y = 1|x = 0) = 0 \end{cases}$$

$$b(y|x=1) = \begin{cases} Pr(y=1|x=1) = p_1 \\ Pr(y=0|x=1) = (1-p_1) \\ Pr(y=2|x=1) = 0 \end{cases}$$

$$b(y|x=2) = \begin{cases} Pr(y=2|x=2) = p_2 \\ Pr(y=1|x=2) = (1-p_2) \\ Pr(y=0|x=2) = 0 \end{cases}$$

Correspondingly, with similar conventions (see Fig.2), Charlie's mixed strategies $\underline{c}(\cdot|y=0)$, $\underline{c}(\cdot|y=1)$ and $\underline{c}(\cdot|y=2)$ will be characterized by the probabilities q_1, q_2 and q_3 as follows

$$c(z|y=0) = \begin{cases} Pr(z=0|y=0) = q_0 \\ Pr(z=1|y=0) = (1-q_0) \\ Pr(z=2|y=0) = 0 \end{cases}$$

$$c(z|y=1) = \begin{cases} Pr(z=1|y=1) = q_1 \\ Pr(z=2|y=1) = (1-q_1) \\ Pr(z=0|y=1) = 0 \end{cases}$$

$$c(z|y=2) = \begin{cases} Pr(z=2|y=2) = q_2 \\ Pr(z=0|y=2) = (1-q_2) \\ Pr(z=1|y=2) = 0 \end{cases}$$

Mixed strategies payoffs. Assume that players B and C adopt respectively the strategy profiles $\underline{b}$ and $\underline{c}$.

Player B's payoff. Suppose that Bob observes Alice at $x=0$, he will adopt the mixed strategy $\underline{b}(\cdot|x=0)$, the expected utility to B of this mixed strategy is

$$\bar{u}(x=0, \underline{b}(\cdot|0), \underline{c}) = \sum_{y=0}^{2} b(y|0) \sum_{z=0}^{2} c(z|y) \, u(0,y,z)$$

however it can be simplified considering that the sum over y has only two non-zero terms terms (relative to $y=0$ and $y=2$), and making use of the zero-sum assumption about the utilities, which leaves only one term in the sum over z:

$$- \bar{u}(x=0, \underline{b}(\cdot|0), \underline{c}) = p_0 q_0 + (1-p_0)(1-q_2) = (q_0 + q_2 - 1)\, p_0 + (1-q_2)$$

similarly (see also Fig.2)

$$- \bar{u}(x=1, \underline{b}(\cdot|1), \underline{c}) = p_1 q_1 + (1-p_1)(1-q_0) = (q_0 + q_1 - 1)\, p_1 + (1-q_0)$$

$$- \bar{u}(x=2, \underline{b}(\cdot|1), \underline{c}) = p_2 q_2 + (1-p_2)(1-q_1) = (q_1 + q_2 - 1)\, p_2 + (1-q_1)$$

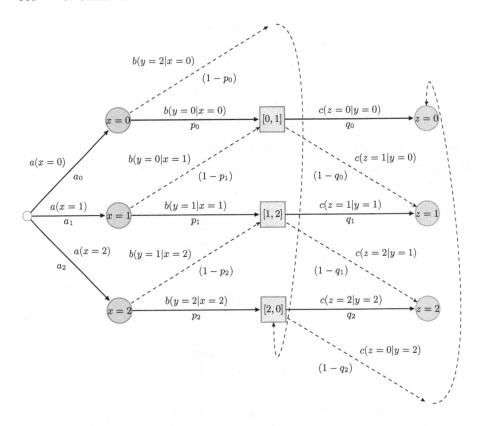

Fig. 2. The Toy model game

Player C's payoff. Charlie cannot observe the location of Alice: before receiving Bob's message he can only rely on the landscape prior $\underline{a}(\cdot) = (a_1, a_2, a_3)$. However after receiving Bob's message in the form of a constant $y = y'$, Charlie is able to update the distribution $a(x)$ to a posterior form $a^*(x) = a(x|y')$ using the Bayes' theorem, so that the ex-post expected utility becomes

$$\bar{v}(\underline{a}^*, y = 1, \underline{c}(\cdot|y = 1)) = \sum_{x=0}^{2} a^*(x)c(z = x|y = 1)v(x, 1, z)$$

with $\underline{a}^*(\cdot) = (a_1^*, a_2^*, a_3^*)$. For instance if Bob signals $y = 1$, which means the cloak extends over the interval $[1, 2]$, leaving 0 outside, then $a^*(0) = a(0|y = 1) = 0$, whereas $a^*(1) = a(1|y = 1)$ and $a^*(2) = a(2|y = 1)$ are given by

$$a^*(1) = \frac{p_1 a_1}{p_1 a_1 + (1 - p_2)a_2} \quad and \quad a^*(2) = \frac{(1 - p_2)a_2}{p_1 a_1 + (1 - p_2)a_2}$$

and Charlie's ex-post expected utility is

$$\bar{v}(\underline{a}^*, y = 1, \underline{c}(\cdot|y = 1)) = a_1^* q_1 + a_2^*(1 - q_1) = \frac{a_1 p_1 q_1 + a_2(1 - p_2)(1 - q_1)}{p_1 a_1 + (1 - p_2)a_2}$$

If Bob signals $y = 0$, which means the cloak extends over the interval $[0, 1]$ leaving 2 outside, then $a^*(2) = a(2|y = 0) = 0$, whereas $a^*(0) = a(0|y = 0)$ and $a^*(1) = a(1|y = 0)$ are given by

$$a^*(0) = \frac{p_0 a_0}{p_0 a_0 + (1 - p_1)a_1} \quad and \quad a^*(1) = \frac{(1 - p_1)a_1}{p_0 a_0 + (1 - p_1)a_1}$$

and Charlie's (ex-post) expected utility is

$$\bar{v}(\underline{a}^*, y = 0, \underline{c}(\cdot|y = 0)) = a_0^* q_0 + a_1^*(1 - q_0) = \frac{a_0 p_0 q_0 + a_1(1 - p_1)(1 - q_0)}{p_0 a_0 + (1 - p_1)a_1}$$

If Bob signals $y = 2$, which means the cloak extends over the interval $[2, 0]$ leaving 1 outside, then $a^*(1) = a(1|y = 1) = 0$, whereas $a^*(2) = a(2|y = 2)$ and $a^*(0) = a(0|y = 2)$ are given by

$$a^*(2) = \frac{p_2 a_2}{p_2 a_2 + (1 - p_0)a_0} \quad and \quad a^*(0) = \frac{(1 - p_0)a_0}{p_2 a_2 + (1 - p_0)a_0}$$

and Charlie's ex-post expected utility is

$$\bar{v}(\underline{a}^*, y = 2, \underline{c}(\cdot|y = 2)) = a_2^* q_2 + a_0^*(1 - q_2) = \frac{a_2 p_2 q_2 + a_0(1 - p_0)(1 - q_0)}{p_2 a_2 + (1 - p_0)a_0}$$

Pure Strategy Equilibria. Here it is easy to verify that there ar no pure strategy equilibria: indeed, in a zero-sum game, the only equilibrium cells of the payoff matrix, should any exist, are the saddle points. One can observe that the payoff matrix (Table 2) has no saddle points: this can be easily checked by taking note of the minima for each column and of the maxima of each row. To be a saddle point a cell has to be the minimum of its row and the maximum of its column: in this game the row minimum is always 0, corresponding to the combination of pure strategies of the two players where the attack is unsuccessful), whereas the column maximum is always 1 and corresponds to Charlie delivering a successful attack.

Since there are no pure strategy equilibria there must be a (unique) Nash equilibrium in the mixed strategies.

Mixed Strategy Equilibria. Mixed strategy equilibria correspond to values of the mixing parameters which induce in the opponent the indifference among the different pure strategy choices. This can be easily translated into a set of linear equations.

Indeed, when Bob's message is $y = 1$ (i.e. the cloak is $[1, 2]$), Charlie's ex-post expected utility is a linear function of the variable q_1, the mixing probability, giving the proportion of times C will attack on 1:

$$\bar{v}(\underline{a}^*, y = 1, \underline{c}(\cdot|y = 1)) = = \frac{[a_1 p_1 - a_2(1 - p_2)]q_1 + a_2(1 - p_2)}{p_1 a_1 + (1 - p_2)a_2}$$

since the variable q_1 is defined on the interval $[0, 1]$ the maxima of the linear function will be at $q_1 = 1$ when it is increasing and at $q_1 = 0$ when it is decreasing; since Bob's probabilities p_1 and p_2 are parameters of the expression, Bob can control the slope: by rendering the slope equal to zero, Bob can force Charlie's payoff to the value of the intercept at the origin, $a_2(1 - p_2)$. A slope equal to zero makes Charlie indifferent between the choice of attacking at $z = 1$ and that of attacking at $z = 2$ and makes perfectly equivalent any conditional mixed strategy $\underline{c}(\cdot|y = 1)$; the condition can be written as $a_1p_1 - a_2(1 - p_2) = 0$ or as $a_1p_1 + a_2p_2 = a_2$. Similarly, the condition on the parameters for inducing Charlie's indifference, when Bob plays $y = 0$ are $a_0p_0 + a_1p_1 = a_1$ and when Bob plays $y = 2$ are $a_2p_2 + a_0p_0 = a_0$. These conditions, together, translate in the vector equation

$$
\begin{bmatrix} 0 & a_1 & a_2 \\ a_0 & a_1 & 0 \\ a_0 & 0 & a_2 \end{bmatrix} \begin{pmatrix} p_0 \\ p_1 \\ p_2 \end{pmatrix} = \begin{pmatrix} a_2 \\ a_1 \\ a_0 \end{pmatrix}
$$

which is solved by the equilibrium parameters:

$$
\hat{p}_0 = \frac{1}{2}(1 + \frac{a_1 - a_2}{a_0}) \qquad \hat{p}_1 = \frac{1}{2}(1 + \frac{a_2 - a_0}{a_1}) \qquad \hat{p}_2 = \frac{1}{2}(1 + \frac{a_0 - a_1}{a_2})
$$

An analogous procedure can be performed over Bob's payoffs, which depend on the parameters q_0, q_1 and q_2,controlled by Charlie. It is easily seen that in order to force Bob into the indifference condition, Charlie has to make equivalent to Bob the choice between the cloak $[1, 2]$ (i.e. the signal $y = 1$) and the cloak $[0, 1]$ (i.e. the signal $y = 0$) when Bob finds Alice in $x = 1$, and so on. This corresponds to Charlie playing as many times ($z = 1|y = 1$) as ($z = 1|y = 0$), in short $q_1 = (1 - q_0)$. The other conditions obtained are $q_2 = (1 - q_1)$ and $q_0 = (1 - q_2)$. In summary Charlie has to adopt the equilibrium values $\hat{q}_0 = \hat{q}_1 = \hat{q}_2 = \frac{1}{2}$. Should Charlie choose a different strategy profile, there would be strategy profiles for Bob that increase Bob's payoff.

Notice that the attack of Charlie prescribed by the equilibrium has to be uniform over the cloak, as in the case of a uniform landscape prior. This is a remarkable result, since it means that the adoption of the equilibrium strategy profile by Bob makes the advantage, provided to Charlie by the landscape constraints, disappear.

4.2   A Game Variant: Non-uniform Sensitivity

The game can be easily reformulated in a slightly richer variant, leading to similar conclusions. To make the game more general we can assume a non-uniform sensitivity $s(x)$ of the landscape. In this case the utilities are $v(x, y, z) = -u(x, y, z) = s(x)\delta(x - z)$. All the corresponding derivation procedure however flows as above.

By adopting the notation $\underline{s} = (s_0, s_1, s_2)$ with $s_i > 0 \ \forall i$, it is straightforward to figure out that there are still no pure strategy equilibria, i.e. no saddle points in the payoff matrix, since the minimum of each column is a zero whereas the maximum of each row is $s_0a_0 + s_1a_1 + s_2a_2$.

The mixed strategy equilibrium conditions for Bob can be obtained by Charlie's indifference conditions: for instance the equalization of the utilities for Charlie choosing to attack on $z = 1$ and and on $z = 2$, when player B move is $y = 1$ can be obtained by choosing values of p_1 and p_2 such that $s_1a_1p_1 = s_2a_2(1 - p_2)$ i.e such that $s_1a_1p_1 + s_2a_2p_2 = s_2a_2$, and so on. As before the problem can be formulated as a vector equation:

$$\begin{bmatrix} 0 & s_1a_1 & s_2a_2 \\ s_0a_0 & s_1a_1 & 0 \\ s_0a_0 & 0 & s_2a_2 \end{bmatrix} \begin{pmatrix} p_0 \\ p_1 \\ p_2 \end{pmatrix} = \begin{pmatrix} s_2a_2 \\ s_1a_1 \\ s_0a_0 \end{pmatrix}$$

which is solved by the equilibrium parameters:

$$\hat{p}_0 = \frac{1}{2}(1 + \frac{s_1a_1 - s_2a_2}{s_0a_0}) \quad \hat{p}_1 = \frac{1}{2}(1 + \frac{s_2a_2 - s_0a_0}{s_1a_1}) \quad \hat{p}_2 = \frac{1}{2}(1 + \frac{s_0a_0 - s_1a_1}{s_2a_2})$$

The corresponding equilibrium adopted by Charlie can be found again equalizing Bob's payoff, corresponding to the two choices available when he finds Alice in each of the three conditions (locations $x = 0$, $x = 1$ and $x = 2$): the equilibrium equations are $s_0q_0 = s_0(1 - q_2)$, $s_1q_1 = s_1(1 - q_0)$ and $s_2q_2 = s_2(1 - q_1)$. Again the equilibrium solution is $\hat{q}_1 = \hat{q}_2 = \hat{q}_0 = 1/2$.

Again the attack of Charlie prescribed by the equilibrium has to be uniform over the cloak, as in the case of a uniform landscape prior. Since sensitivity and probability play in the equations in the same way, the adoption of the equilibrium strategy profile by Bob makes the advantage provided to Charlie by a non-neutral landscape disappear.

4.3   A Generalized 1D Toy Model

Since we did not make any use of the cyclical character of the coordinates, but that of simplifying the notation, we can easily extend the results to a more general 1D model.

If we still consider a cloak of width equal to 2 units, it is straightforward to generalize the game and the corresponding equilibrium to the discrete 1D case where the possible coordinates are the relative integers, i.e. $x, y, z \in Z$. We will denote the probabilities of Alice's location by $\{\cdots, a_{x-1}, a_x, a_{x+1}, \cdots\}$, and the sensitivities by $\{\cdots, s_{x-1}, s_x, s_{x+1}, \cdots\}$.

There will still be no pure strategy equilibria, i.e. no saddle points in the payoff matrix. The mixed strategy equilibrium conditions for player B, obtained by player's C indifference conditions are satisfied by the equilibrium parameters:

$$\hat{p}_x = \frac{1}{2}(1 + \frac{s_{x+1}a_{x+1} - s_{x-1}a_{x-1}}{s_xa_x}) \quad \forall x \quad and \quad \hat{q}_y = \frac{1}{2} \quad \forall y$$

Table 2. The payoff matrix for the toy model game: each of the labels for the rows indicate a pure strategy for player B: the rightmost digit in each label refers to the condition $x = 0$, the next to the condition $x = 1$, the leftmost to the condition $x = 2$; the value of each digit is either zero or one and corresponds to the value of $|x - y|$ (for instance by convention the label 000 means always play $y = 0$ when $x = 0$, always play $y = 1$ when $x = 1$, always play $y = 2$ when $x = 2$). Similar conventions hold for the column labels, which indicate pure strategies for player B: the upper digit in each label refers to the condition $y = 0$, the next to the condition $y = 1$, the leftmost to the condition $y = 2$; the value of each digit is either zero or one and corresponds to the value of $z - y$ (for instance by convention the label 000 means always play $z = 0$ when $y = 0$, always play $z = 1$ when $y = 1$, always play $z = 2$ when $y = 2$). Each cell contains the expected payoff to player C due to the combination of the corresponding row and column pure strategies. The last row contains the payoff minima of the columns, whereas the last column contains the payoff maxima of the rows. One can observe that each row as maximum value equal to one, whereas each column has a minimum value equal to zero: therefore there are no cells which are at the same time the column minimum and the row maximum, i.e. there are no saddle point cells. Therefore there cannot be any pure strategy equilibrium in the game.

| | 0 | 1 | 0 | 1 | 0 | 1 | 0 | 1 | **0** |
| | 0 | 0 | 1 | 1 | 0 | 0 | 1 | 1 | **1** |
	0	0	0	0	1	1	1	1	**2**
0 0 0	1	a_1+a_2	a_0+a_2	a_2	a_0+a_1	a_1	a_0	0	1
0 0 1	a_1+a_2	1	$\cdots$	$\cdots$	$\cdots$	$\cdots$	0	a_0	1
0 1 0	a_0+a_2	$\cdots$	1	$\cdots$	$\cdots$	0	$\cdots$	a_1	1
0 1 1	a_2	$\cdots$	$\cdots$	1	0	$\cdots$	$\cdots$	a_0+a_1	1
1 0 0	a_0+a_1	$\cdots$	$\cdots$	0	1	$\cdots$	$\cdots$	a_2	1
1 0 1	a_1	$\cdots$	0	$\cdots$	$\cdots$	1	$\cdots$	a_0+a_2	1
1 1 0	a_0	0	$\cdots$	$\cdots$	$\cdots$	$\cdots$	1	a_1+a_2	1
1 1 1	0	a_0	a_1	a_0+a_1	a_2	a_0+a_2	a_1+a_2	1	1
2 1 0									
	0	0	0	0	0	0	0	0	

5   Discussion and Conclusions

Several approaches exist to anonymization for data privacy protection. Given background knowledge the anonymized data can undergo inference attacks (a survey of inference attacks can be found in [6]). We frame the data anonymization and the attack in a game-theoretical approach and use a scenario of location privacy protection by cloaking as a case study.

Game Theory, which has been used extensively in fields such as economics, is still only at the beginning of its application to security and privacy problems.

Halpern et al. [9] consider the problem of secret sharing and multiparty computation among rational agents, whereas Abrahm et al. introduce $k-$resilient Nash equilibria [1], for solving Shamir's secret sharing problem. Zhang at al. [12] propose a game theoretic way of measuring the privacy of Privacy Preserving Data Mining (PPDM). Kargupta et al. [11] develop a game-theoretic framework for analyzing PPDM algorithms and outlines a game theoretic solution based on the concept of "cheap-talk". None of those approaches address the non-collaborative game scenario represented by obfuscation. Ettinger [5] introduces a two-player, zero-sum, matrix game for the purpose of modeling the contest between a data-hider and a data-attacker in steganography: however he pictures the game as a simultaneous move game; beside this difference, in information hiding games the data are transformed so that the target data remain private during data mining operations, but the transformation can be reverted, whereas, on the constrary, in the obfuscation games the data are transformed before communication so that part of the information is lost. This make the obfuscation game a different game from the ones mentioned above.

We model the contest between a data-obfuscator and a data-attacker as a two-player, zero-sum, signaling game, with common knowledge of the constraints and payoffs associated to the landscape (representing the background knowledge), then we point to the corresponding Bayes-Nash equilibrium solution, the Perfect Bayes Equilibrium, which can be computed in practical cases by a straightforward procedure, illustrated with a toy game example.

We show how, when the anonymizer is playing the equilibrium strategies the advantage provided to the attacker by the landscape disappears. Furthermore the value of the game, in terms of expected negative utility to the user can be computed in advance so that the anonymizer can tune the size of the cloak so as to fulfill the maximum rate of successful attacks acceptable by the user.

We suggest that the game-theoretical formulation of the obfuscation provided by this paper could be used as the basis for establishing a performance measurement procedure to evaluate obfuscation procedures which can be associated with some utility measure: the game-theoretical equilibrium value of the game could be used as a reference value for the utility; for instance two given obfuscation procedures, thanks to the ratio between their expected utility value and the reference game-theoretical value, could be compared to one-another.

Acknowledgments. This work was supported in part by the EU within the SecureSCM project in the FP7-ICT Programme under contract n.AOR 213531.

References

1. Abraham, I., Dolev, D., Gonen, R., Halpern, J.: Distributed computing meets game theory: robust mechanisms for rational secret sharing and multiparty computation. In: PODC 2006: Proceedings of the twenty-fifth annual ACM symposium on Principles of distributed computing, pp. 53–62. ACM Press, New York (2006)

2. Ardagna, C.A., Cremonini, M., Damiani, E., De Capitani di Vimercati, S., Samarati, S.: Location privacy protection through obfuscation-based techniques. In: Barker, S., Ahn, G.-J. (eds.) Data and Applications Security 2007. LNCS, vol. 4602, pp. 47–60. Springer, Heidelberg (2007)
3. Beresford, A.R., Stajano, F.: Location privacy in pervasive computing. IEEE Pervasive Computing 2(1), 46–55 (2003)
4. Borel, E.: Traite du Calcul des Probabilites et ses Applications, vol. 4(2). Gautier-Villars, Paris (1938)
5. Ettinger, M.: Steganalysis and game equilibria. In: Aucsmith, D. (ed.) IH 1998. LNCS, vol. 1525, pp. 319–328. Springer, Heidelberg (1998)
6. Farkas, C., Jajodia, S.: The inference problem: a survey. SIGKDD Explor. Newsl. 4(2), 6–11 (2002)
7. Fudenberg, D., Tirole, J.: Game Theory. MIT Press, Cambridge (1991)
8. Gruteser, M., Grunwald, D.: Anonymous usage of location-based services through spatial and temporal cloaking. In: MobiSys 2003: Proceedings of the 1st Int. Conf. on Mobile systems, applications and services, pp. 31–42 (2003)
9. Halpern, J., Teague, V.: Rational secret sharing and multiparty computation: extended abstract. In: STOC 2004: Proc. of the 36th annual ACM symposium on Theory of computing, pp. 623–632. ACM Press, New York (2004)
10. Hengartner, U., Steenkiste, P.: Access control to information in pervasive computing environments. In: HOTOS 2003: Proc. of the 9th Conf. on Hot Topics in Operating Systems, Berkeley, CA, USA, p. 27. USENIX Association (2003)
11. Liu, K., Kargupta, H., Das, K.: A game-theoretic approach toward multy-party privacy preserving distribute data mining. Technical Report TR-CS 01 07, Dept. of Computer Science and Electrical Engineering, U.of Mariland (April 2007)
12. Zhang, W.Z.N., Chen, J.: Performance measurement for privacy preserving data mining. In: Ho, T.-B., Cheung, D., Liu, H. (eds.) PAKDD 2005. LNCS (LNAI), vol. 3518, pp. 43–49. Springer, Heidelberg (2005)
13. Samarati, P.: Protecting respondents' identities in microdata release. IEEE Transactions on Knowledge and Data Engineering 13(6), 1010–1027 (2001)
14. von Neumann, J., Morgenstern, O.: The Theory of Games and Economic Behavior. Princeton University Press, Princeton (1944)

Query Rewriting for Access Control on Semantic Web

Jian Li and William K. Cheung

Department of Computer Science
Hong Kong Baptist University, Kowloon Tong, HK
{jli, william}@comp.hkbu.edu.hk

Abstract. Along with describing the web resources with ontology-based meta-data to make them machine-understandable, one also needs to carefully protect Semantic Web data from unauthorized access. This paper presents a query re-writing mechanism for access control so as to avoid leakage of sensitive re-sources in the Semantic Web. We propose to specify the security policies for access restrictions on resources as views declared based on ontologies. Illus-trated examples are presented in the paper for explaining the underlying con-cepts. In addition, bucket-based algorithms are proposed for supporting the query rewriting.

Keywords: Access Control, Semantic Web, Ontology, Query Rewriting.

1 Introduction

The recent proliferation of the Semantic Web has resulted in an increasing amount of on-line resources being semantically annotated to support more accurate search and interoperability. To achieve more effective resources management, development of a number of management systems for semantic web data have been reported in the literature [18,19,20]. One important issue is how to control access to sensitive and private information embedded in the Semantic Web – a highly distributed knowledge repository. This is especially true if the application domains are related to business, health, and national defense. In this paper, we propose a policy-based approach to control access in the context of querying the Semantic Web.

Users' retrieval requirements for resources in the Semantic Web are commonly ex-pressed as queries specified using different entities defined in some ontologies. Given a query submitted to a semantic web data management system, information of the matched web resources should reasonably be expected to return, but sometimes to-gether with sensitive information as well. Using the conventional role-based access control model, some restricted forms of access control can be enforced. However, as the contents of the Semantic Web are abundant and highly dynamical, the use of de-clarative policies for access control is often believed to be more suitable [1]. One intuitive idea to implement the policy-based approach is to rewrite queries by adding restrictions on them so that the rewritten queries will result only the resources which can be accessed according to the access control policies.

The main contribution of this paper is to describe how the query rewriting idea can be carried out in the context of the Semantic Web. We adopt an ontological approach

W. Jonker and M. Petković (Eds.): SDM 2008, LNCS 5159, pp. 151–168, 2008.
© Springer-Verlag Berlin Heidelberg 2008

to specify access control policies as the permissions or forbiddances for subjects accessing to resources. Due to the unambiguous semantics of the policies, automatically query rewriting based on access control policies becomes possible. In particular, we propose algorithms that, given ontology-based conjunctive queries for web resources, can determine 1) the policies relevant to the queries, 2) extract the restrictions expression from the policies, and 3) add them to the queries for rewriting. The issue related to policies conflict resolution is also discussed with respect to the proposed approach.

2 Basic Concepts

The Semantic Web [14] is an extension of the World Wide Web in which on-line resources are expressed in a format that is machine understandable and can be used by software agents, thus permitting them to find, share and integrate information more easily. In the Semantic Web, ontology is to describe or posit the basic entities and relationships within some domains. There are two basic types of entities in ontologies: concept and role. Concepts are the abstract definitions for entities within the domain, whereas roles express the relationships between entities. On-line resources annotated with the labels of concepts are generally termed as **instances** of these concepts (also called classes). Fig. 1 shows a simple ontology about the domain of weapons, where concepts (e.g., "Weapon" and "Missile") are annotated using ellipses, "subclass" roles and other roles (e.g., "HasRange") are annotated using dashed and solid lines respectively, and individual values are annotated using rectangles (e.g., "Liquid Fuel" and "Solid Fuel"). Using this ontology, instance resources of "Missile" can be annotated.

Several markup languages (e.g., RDF [15], OWL [16]) have been proposed for describing ontologies. To retrieve resources described using RDF and OWL, a retrieval requirement should first be expressed as a query using terms defined in some ontologies. For example, Query "$Q(x) \leftarrow Missile(x)$" with the knowledge of ontology O in Fig. 1 is to retrieve all the instance resources under the concept "Missile".

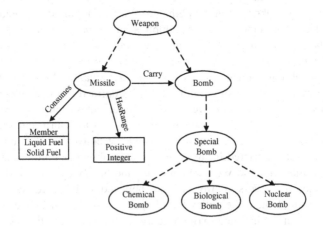

Fig. 1. An ontology for the domain of weapon

3 Access Control Models for Semantic Web

3.1 Policies for Access Control

In this paper, we study access control to instance resources in the Semantic Web when being queried. We proposed the use of access authorization policies to specify the rights of different subjects (e.g., users or other active entities which can initiate access requests) to gain access to the resources.

Definition 1. An **access control model** for the Semantic Web can be defined as a tuple $<O, R, S, P>$, where O is an ontology of the concerned domain; R is the set of instance resources annotated using entities in O; S is the set of subjects which are active entities requesting access to resources and can be defined in O as well; and P is the set of policies specifying when some s in S can gain access to some r in R.

Definition 2. Given an access control model $<O, R, S, P>$, a **policy** p ($p \in P$) is denoted as $<s, v, sign>$, where

$s \in S$ is a subject requesting to gain access to some resources,

v is a **view** that defines a set of tuples with instance resources relevant to p, given as

$v(x_1,...,x_n) \leftarrow c_i(x_i),...,c_j(x_j),r_k(x_{k1}, x_{k2}),...,r_m(x_{m1}, x_{m2}), aps$

with commas between predicates denoting conjunctive relationships, $c_i,...,c_j$ and $r_k,...,r_m$ denoting some concepts and roles in O, $c_i(x_i)$ referring to concept c_i's instances to be bound with variable x_i, $r_k(x_{k1}, x_{k2})$ referring to relation r_k between variables x_{k1} and x_{k2}, and aps denoting a conjunctive expression that consists of additional predicates such as "=", "<", ">", and

$sign \in \{+,-\}$ defines an authorization that grants (for "+") or deny (for "-") subject s access right to the resources as defined by v.

In addition, we define "$c_i(x_i),...,c_j(x_j),r_k(x_{k1}, x_{k2}),...,r_m(x_{m1}, x_{m2}), aps$" to be the **body expression** of v, denoted as $body(v)$, and the variables $\{x_1,..., x_n\}$ appearing in v's head as $head\_variable(v)$. We call v a **safe view** if the variables in $head\_variable(v)$ also appear in $body(v)$. There also exists a case where a subject is only granted access to some of the variables defined in $body(v)$. By allowing this variation in describing views, more flexible authorization rights can be described. To illustrate the flexibility, the followings are some policy examples derived based on Definition 2 and the weapon ontology presented in Fig. 1:

p_1: $<s, v_1, +>$, $v_1(x)$ $\leftarrow$ *Missile(x), Carry(x,y), BiologicalBomb(y)*
p_2: $<s, v_2, +>$, $v_2(x,y)$ $\leftarrow$ *Missile(x), Carry(x,y), BiologicalBomb(y)*
p_3: $<s, v_3, ->$, $v_3(x)$ $\leftarrow$ *Missile(x), Carry(x,y), SpecialBomb(y), HasRange(x,z), z>3000*

Policy p_1 depicts the authorization which grants subject s the permission to gain access to the resources described as missiles that carry biological bombs as their warheads. Although the variable y (for binding with biological bomb instances) appears in the view's body, it does not appear in the view's head and thus the policy does not grant the permission to gain access to the resources of biological bombs. So, while the instances of missiles carrying biological bombs can be retrieved by s, the information about what particular biological bombs being carried is not accessible based p_1. Policy

p_2 distinguishes from p_1 by retaining variable y in the head of its view so that instances of the biological bombs become accessible. Policy p_3 specifies the denial of subject s to gain access to the resources about missiles carrying special bombs with their range over 3000 miles.

3.2 Policy Propagation

As it is common for concepts and roles in the subject ontology and domain ontology to possess hierarchical relationships, the authorization defined in a policy for subject s to resources could also be propagated to other subjects and resources accordingly [7].

Given a policy $<s,v,sign>$ and the condition that s' is an instance or subclass of s (later on denoted as $s' \leq s$), a new policy $<s',v,sign>$ should also be valid. In other words, the authorization right assigned to s as defined by v should also be **propagated** and applied to s'. When compared with some existing policy propagation mechanisms (e.g., [7]), the propagation of the proposed policies is more complicated as the authorizations are here associated with sets of instance resources via **views** instead of merely individual instances. For example, one view can be a "constrained" (to be more formally defined later) version of another one. Also, we can have views containing common instances. How to propagate policies among such "overlapping" views becomes a non-trivial issue. In the remaining part of this subsection, we define formally the notion of constrained views. In Section 3.3, we describe how the detection and resolution of conflicting policies caused by "overlapping" views can be handled.

Definition 3. Given views v and v', v' is a constrained view of v, denoted as $v' \preceq v$, if and only if the set of tuples defined by v'

(1) is equivalent to that of v, or

(2) is a subset of that defined by v, and/or the element set of each tuple in v' is a subset of the counterpart in v.

Lemma 1. *Given views v and v', $v' \preceq v$ if one of the following holds:*
    (1) $body(v') = body(v)$ and $head\_variable(v') \subseteq head\_variable(v)$
    (2) $head\_variable(v') = head\_variable(v)$, all members in $body(v)$ also appear in $body(v')$, and $body(v')$ contains additional constraint expressions which do not appear in $body(v)$.
    (3) $head\_variable(v') = head\_variable(v)$, all members in $body(v')$ are the same as those in $body(v)$ except one $c'(x)$ or $r'(x,y)$ corresponds to $c(x)$ or $r(x,y)$ in $body(v)$, and c' is a subclass of c or r' is a sub-property of r.

Proof. Let R be the set of tuples defined by v. For condition (1) where $body(v') = body(v)$ and $head\_variable(v') \subseteq head\_variable(v)$, the set of tuples defined by view v' will become $R' = \pi_{head\_variable(v')}(R)$ where π denotes a project operation. Then, it is easy to show that the element set of tuples in R' is a subset of that in R, and thus $v' \preceq v$ (by definition). For condition (2) where $body(v')$ contains more constraints than

$body(v)$, R' will be a subset of R and thus $v' \preceq v$ (by definition). For condition (3) with $body(v')$ containing $c'(x) \subseteq c(x)$ or $r'(x,y) \subseteq r(x,y)$, again R' will be a subset of R which completes the proof.

Lemma 2. " $\preceq$ " *is a transitive relation, i.e.,* $v'' \preceq v$ *if* $v' \preceq v$ *and* $v'' \preceq v'$ *hold.*

Proof. Let the set of tuples defined by v, v' and v'' be R, R' and R'' respectively. If $v' \preceq v$ and $v'' \preceq v'$ hold, one can derive that $R' = \pi \ \sigma \ (R)$ and $R'' = \pi \ ' \ \sigma \ '(R')$ where π , $\pi \ '$ correspond to some project operations and σ and $\sigma \ '$ correspond to some select operations. Then, it can easily be shown that $R'' = \pi \ ' \ \sigma \ '(\pi \ \sigma \ (R)) = \pi \ '' \ \sigma \ ''(R)$ for some $\pi \ ''$ and $\sigma \ ''$, which completes the proof.

As the resources associated with view v' are always associated with view v if $v' \preceq v$, the authority of subject s to view v can be propagated to s as its authority to view v'. So the authority propagation for our policies can be refined as: Given a policy $<s,v,sign>$, a new policy $<s,v',sign>$ can be derived if $v' \preceq v$.

The followings are some view examples derived based on the weapon ontology as depicted in Fig. 1:

$v_4(x)$ ← *Missile(x), Carry(x,y), SpecialBomb(y)*
$v_5(x,y)$ ← *Missile(x), Carry(x,y), SpecialBomb(y)*
$v_6(x,y)$ ← *Missile(x), Carry(x,y), BiologicalBomb(y)*
$v_7(x,y)$ ← *Missile(x), Carry(x,y), BiologicalBomb (y), HasRange(x,z), z>3000*

Based on Lemma 1, one can easily derive that $v_4 \preceq v_5$, $v_6 \preceq v_5$ and $v_7 \preceq v_6$. One can also derive that $v_7 \preceq v_5$ based on Lemma 2. In addition, given a policy $<s,v_5,sign>$, new policies $<s,v_4,sign>$, $<s,v_6,sign>$ and $<s,v_7,sign>$ can be derived. The only difference between v_4 and v_5 is the absence of variable y in the head of v_4. As $<s,v_5,sign>$ grants/denies subject s the permission to both instance variables x and y in v_5, same authorization rights should be granted to s for variable x in v_4 too.

3.3 Policy Conflict Resolution

Policy conflicts arise when there are policies which assert conflicting authorizations (permission and denial) for a subject to gain access to identical resources at the same time.

Definition 4. Two policies are conflicting if one grants and the other denies permission for a subject s to gain access to some resource u.

Lemma 3. Policies p ($<s,v,+>$) and p' ($<s',v',->$) are conflicting if there exist subject s'' and non-empty view v'' such that $s'' \le s$, $v'' \preceq v$ and $s'' \le s'$, $v'' \preceq v'$. (see Fig. 2 for an illustration)

Proof. If s"≤ s, v" ≼ v, all instances of s" are also instances of s and the tuple set defined by v" is the subset defined by v. So, policy p (<s,v,+>) should be propagated to s" for granting it access to resources of v". By the same argument, p'(<s',v',->) will deny subject s" to gain access to resource of v". So, two policies p(<s,v,+>) and p'(<s',v',->) are conflicting.

For example, as described in Section 3.1, policy p_2 grants subject s the permission to gain access to resources about missiles carrying biological bombs. Meanwhile, policy p_3 denies subject s to have access to resources about missiles carrying special bombs with their range over 3000 miles. Via propagation of p_3, subject s should be denied to have access to resources about the missiles carrying biological bombs (a subclass of special bombs) with their range over 3000 miles.

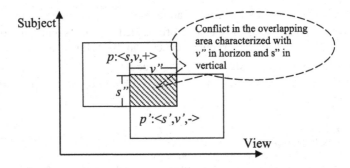

Fig. 2. Policy conflicts are caused when a positively and negatively authorized policies overlap

To resolve policy conflicts, some meta-policy rules based on priority or additional knowledge are normally required. For example, by adopting a priority-based selection strategy, the policy with a higher priority level prevails. Next, the prevailing policy is reserved for the authority definition of the overlapping area as depicted in Fig. 2, and the non-overlapping areas should be properly split and associated with their corresponding policies. Consider the two aforementioned conflicting policies p_2 and p_3. If p_2 is chosen to grant subject s permission to gain access to the resources about missiles carrying biological bombs with their range over 3000 miles, p_3 should be revised and split into two policies with the help of policy propagation as follows:

p_3': <s, v_3, ->, $v_3(x)$ ← Missile(x), Carry(x,y), ChemicalBomb(y), HasRange(x,z), z>3000
p_3'': <s, v_3, ->, $v_3(x)$ ← Missile(x), Carry(x,y), NuclearBomb(y), HasRange(x,z), z>3000

Policies p_3' and p_3'' cover the range of policy p_3 except the overlapping range of p_2 and p_3 as the concept "Special Bomb" in Fig.1 is a union of the concepts "Chemical Bomb", "Biological Bomb" and "Nuclear Bomb". Alternatively, if p_3 is chosen to deny subject s to have access to the overlapping area, policy p_2 should be revised to a new policy p_2', given as:

p_2': <s, v_2, +>, $v_2(x,y)$ ← Missile(x), Carry(x,y), BiologicalBomb(y), HasRange(x,z), z≤3000.

It restricts the permission of subject s to have access to resources about missiles whose ranges are *within* 3000 miles to avoid conflicts with policy p_3.

3.4 Access Decision for Policies

Even after we have propagated policy authorizations and resolved policy conflicts, there still exists the possibility that access rights of some subjects to some resources are neither declared as permitted nor denied according to the policies. Jajodia *et al.* in [10] mentioned two well-known decision mechanisms called "Open" and "Close". Considering whether subject s can gain access to resource u, we call a policy $<s',v,\pm>$ to be **applicable** if u is included in the resources that can be found in view v and $s \leq s'$. **Open (Close) decisions** can be defined as the fact that the access of subject s to resource u is denied (allowed) only if a negative (positive) authorization policy $<s',v,->$ ($<s',v,+>$) is applicable, or allowed (denied) otherwise.

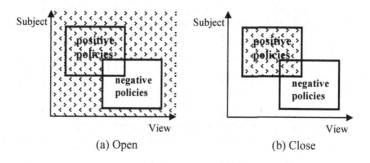

(a) Open   (b) Close

Fig. 3. The scopes of the accesses permitted or denied under different decision mechanisms. The accesses falling in the shaded areas are permitted, or denied otherwise.

Without any policy conflict, the difference between Open and Close decision mechanisms lies on the access rights of subject s to resource u which is neither allowed nor denied by any positive or negative authorization policies. For Open (Close) decision, all the unspecified will be granted (denied) access. In other words, positive (negative) authorization policies need not to be taken into consideration for access control under Open (Close) decision mechanism as shown in Fig. 3. The access is denied (allowed) only when a negative (positive) authorization policy can be applied.

4 Query Rewriting for Access Control

Based on the declarative access control policies introduced in Section 3, we propose algorithms for rewriting queries for Semantic Web data so that sensitive information can be protected from unauthorized access.

Definition 5. A Semantic Web data query Q for retrieving some targeted instance resources is generically defined as:

$$Q(x_1, \ldots, x_n) \leftarrow c_i(x_i), \ldots, c_j(x_j), r_k(x_{k1}, x_{k2}), \ldots, r_m(x_{m1}, x_{m2}), aps.$$

Each retrieved result to the Semantic Web data query takes the form of an n-tuple, that is an order list of instances which satisfies the body (i.e., the right hand side of the arrow sign) of the query. Fig. 4 illustrates w tuples returned (indicated using a box with solid line borders) given a query Q, where each tuple contains n instances corresponding to the variables $x_1,...,x_n$ in the head of Q. If access to the tuples t_1, t_2 and t_w in this result set is denied according to some policy(ies), only the tuples indicated using the box with dashed line will be returned and Q is expected to be rewritten to a new Q' so as to reflect that. As previously described, the proposed policy representation also imposes restriction on variables. According to Fig. 4, if x_1 and x_2 are restricted according to some policies, the resulting tuple set will be shrunk as the box with pointed line and Q is then expected to be rewritten as Q'' to reflect that.

	x_1	x_2	x_3	...	x_{n-1}	x_n	...
...							
t_1	Q				Q''		
t_2							
...	Q'						
...							
t_{w-1}							
t_w							
....							

Fig. 4. An illustration of some rewritten queries

4.1 Query Rewriting Algorithm under Close Decision

In the case of close decision, only positive authorization policies are needed to be considered for access control.

Example 1 (Access Control: Close Decision)
Query from s: $Q_1(x,y) \leftarrow Missile(x),Carry(x,y),SpecialBomb(y)$
Policies: e_{11}: $<s,v_{11},+>$, $v_{11}(x) \leftarrow Missile(x),HasRange(x,z)$, $z<3000$
    e_{12}:$<s,v_{12},+>$, $v_{12}(y) \leftarrow BiologicalBomb(y)$

Query Q_1 in Example 1 is to retrieve the instances of "Missile" that carry "Special-Bomb". There are two positive authorization policies e_{11} and e_{12} to be respected. Policy e_{11} states that only missiles with their range within 3000 miles are accessible for s, and thus it further restrict what instances are allowed to be bound with variable x in Q_1. Policy e_{12} states that only information related to biological bombs can be accessed and this puts restriction on variable y in Q_1. Under the close decision assumption, all the instances cannot be accessed unless they are allowed by some of the positive authorization policies. Policy e_{11} restricts only variable x but have no restriction on y. So, queries with e_{11} applied should NOT be processed. By considering also policy e_{12}, the query Q_1 can be rewritten as:

$Q'_1(x,y) \leftarrow$ Missile(x),Carry(x,y),BiologicalBomb(y), HasRange(x,z), z<3000

where both variables x and y are implicitly governed by policies e_{11} and e_{12}. If the subject s is further explicitly restricted from accessing to any information matched with the variable x or y, Q_1 could also be rewritten as Q'_{11} and Q'_{12}, given as:

$Q'_{11}(x) \leftarrow$ Missile(x),Carry(x,y),SpecialBomb(y), HasRange(x,z), z<3000
$Q'_{12}(y) \leftarrow$ Missile(x),Carry(x,y),BiologicalBomb(y).

Example 2 (Access Control: Close Decision)
Query from s: $Q_2(x,y)$ $\leftarrow$Missile(x),Consume(x,z),Carry(x,y),SpecialBomb(y),z=Liquid Fuel;
Policies:
e_{21}: <s,v_{21},+>, $v_{21}(x,y)$ $\leftarrow$Missile(x), HasRange(x,w), Carry(x,y), NuclearBomb(y), w<3000;
e_{22}: <s,v_{22},+>, $v_{22}(x)$ $\leftarrow$Missile(x), Consume(x,z), HasRange(x,w), w<3000, z = Liquid Fuel;
e_{23}: <s,v_{23},+>, $v_{23}(x)$ $\leftarrow$Missile(x), Consume(x,z), z = Solid Fuel;
e_{24}: <s,v_{24},+>, $v_{24}(y)$ $\leftarrow$ChemicalBomb(y);

Example 2 gives another illustration with a query being governed by four positive authorization policies. Applicable policies include e_{21}, e_{22} and e_{24}. Policy e_{23} is not applicable as it is only related to missiles consuming "Solid Fuel" which is disjoint with "Liquid Fuel" as put in the body of Q_2. The query can be rewritten as the union of the following:

$Q'_{21}(x,y) \leftarrow$ Missile(x), Consume(x,z), Carry(x,y), NuclearBomb(y), HasRange(x,w), z =Liquid Fuel, w<3000;
$Q'_{22}(x,y) \leftarrow$ Missile(x), Consume(x,z), Carry(x,y), ChemicalBomb(y), HasRange(x,w), z =Liquid Fuel, w<3000;

$Q'_{21}(x,y)$ is derived by adding the restrictions described in policy e_{21} to Q. In particular, policy e_{21} restricts variable y to match with not all the instances of "SpecialBomb" but only those of its sub-concept "NuclearBomb" and at the same time with the additional restriction "HasRange(x,w), w<3000" satisfied. Similarly, $Q'_{22}(x,y)$ is derived by adding the restrictions in policies e_{22} and e_{24}. In particular, the concept "Special-Bomb" is restricted to "ChemicalBomb" and additional restriction "HasRange(x,w), w<3000" is added.

The query rewriting process illustrated can be computed automatically. Three main steps are needed for the rewriting. First, policies which are applicable to the query have to be identified. Then, for each applicable policy, their restriction expressions to be added to the query are computed by comparing the policy's view bodies and the query body. Lastly, different combinations of the restriction expressions are computed so that all the variables in Q's head can be covered (i.e., governed by some positive policies) and rewrite the query accordingly.

The detailed query rewriting algorithm based on the close decision mechanism is shown as follows:

Algorithm 1: Query Rewriting Algorithm under Close Decision
Input

Query form s: $Q(x_1,...,x_n) \leftarrow c_i(x_i),...,c_j(x_j),r_k(x_{k1}, x_{k2}),...,r_m(x_{m1}, x_{m2}),aps$;
Policy set: P
Ontology: O

Output

Rewritten query: $Q'(x_1,...,x_{n'}) \leftarrow c_{i'}(x_{i'}),...,c_{j'}(x_{j'}),r_{k'}(x_{k1'}, x_{k2'}),...,r_{m'}(x_{m1'}, x_{m2'}),aps'$;

Process

1. *Create buckets for storing restrictions of applicable policies to the query.*

    For each variable in Q's head, create a bucket for storing (1) the concepts in the body of the query that the variables are associated, and (2) the restriction expressions of the applicable policies' views. See Table 1 for an illustration where each row corresponds to the bucket of a variable, and the concepts and the restriction expressions are stored in two separate main columns.

2. *Identify applicable policies with respect to Q.*

    For each variable x in Q's head, identify its associate concepts by either locating the concept $c(x)$ directly in Q's body or locating x in one of the roles from which the concept of x can be deduced based on the ontological description in O. The same concept identification step can be applied to the variables defined in the view's head of each positive authorization policy p ($<s'$, v, $+>$) in P where $s \leq s'$. Then, if a semantic match can be established between the variable x in Q and those in v, replace the label of the corresponding variable in v by x. In the same way, other variables in v are matched and replaced with their corresponding variables in Q. Let this kind of semantic match between variables be Θ. If no conflict is found in the Q's body and the body of p's view, p will be an applicable policy for Q. Add the view v to the "Views" slot of x's bucket. In the sequel, the view's body after the variable replacement is denoted as $\Theta(body(v))$.

3. *Derive restriction expressions from the applicable policies and fill up the corresponding buckets.*

    For each applicable policy, compare $\Theta(body(v))$ with Q's body to derive the following two types of restrictions on Q and then add the restriction expressions to the corresponding buckets. In particular, the two kinds of restrictions are:

    a) Subsumption Restriction: The scope of each c_i (r_k) in Q should be further restricted if some sub-concept $c_{i'}$ (sub-role $r_{k'}$) is found to appear in $\Theta(body(v))$. Once identified, add the annotation "$c_i \rightarrow c_{i'}$"(or "$r_k \rightarrow r_{k'}$") in "Subsumption Restriction" column of the corresponding bucket(s) and record also the view v.

    b) Additional Restriction: After the subsumption restrictions are handled, locate the remaining expressions in $\Theta(body(v))$ that have not been matched and add them to the "Additional Restriction" column of the corresponding bucket and again record the view v.

4. *Collect appropriate restriction expressions from the buckets and rewrite the query by adding them to the query body.*

    In the buckets, find a minimal set of views $\{v_1,...,v_u\}$ such that all variables in Q's head are covered. The restrictions in their buckets should be free of the concept and property restriction conflicts. Then, collect all subsumption restrictions and additional restrictions from these views' buckets to rewrite Q as follow:

a) Replace c_i or r_k in Q's body with the greatest lower bound[1] of $c_{i'}$ or $r_{k'}$ among all subsumption restrictions "$c_i \rightarrow c_{i'}$" or "$r_k \rightarrow r_{k'}$" in the buckets of the minimal view set.

b) Add all the "Additional Restriction" expressions in the buckets of this view set to Q's body to give Q'.

Repeat this step with different minimal sets of views to get all possible Q', and return $Q^t = \cup Q'$ as the output.

5. *If Step 4 fails, check if Q can be rewritten with a reduced variable set so that some results can still be obtained.*

If it is impossible to find a view set that can cover all variables in Q's head according to the buckets created, the query rewriting will not be possible. There is an option that the query system can be designed to identify some rewritten version of Q with some column(s) of the returned tuple removed. Assume that $\{x_1,...,x_w\}$ is a maximal subset of variables in Q's head where a minimal view set $\{v_1,...,v_u\}$ can be found to cover them, try to construct the body of rewriting query Q' for reduced variable set $\{x_1,...,x_w\}$ in Q's head as in Step 4.

Repeat this step to find all such Q', and return $Q^t = \cup Q'$ as the output.

6. *If Step 5 still fails after all the variables being removed from Q's head, return Φ.*

According to Example 2, v_{21}, v_{22} and v_{23} are related to variable x in Q_2 indicating that the resources to match with are missiles, and v_{21}, v_{24} are related to variable y in Q_2 indicating the resources to match with are special bombs. v_{21} is added to variable x's bucket with the subsumption restriction "SpecialBomb $\rightarrow$ NuclearBomb" that reduces the concept "SpecialBomb" to "NuclearBomb", and the additional restriction is "HasRange(x,w), $w<3000$". v_{23} is not added to variable x's bucket as "z = Solid Fuel" and "z = Liquid Fuel" in Q_2 are disjointed. View v_{21} covers the variables x and y as it appears in both of their buckets, and so are v_{22} and v_{24}. After replacing the predicates in Q_2's body with their restricted concepts and roles, the rewritten queries Q'_{21} and Q'_{22} mentioned above can be obtained by further adding the restrictions from the buckets of $\{v_{21}\}$ and $\{v_{22}, v_{24}\}$ respectively. The query $Q_2^t = Q'_{21} \cup Q'_{22}$ is the final output based on the proposed algorithm for this example.

Table 1. The buckets created for rewriting Q_2 in Example 2

	Concept	Views		
			Subsumption Restriction	Additional Restriction
X	Missile	v_{21}	SpecialBomb →NuclearBomb	HasRange(x,w), $w<3000$
		v_{22}		HasRange(x,w),$w<3000$,
Y	SpecialBomb	v_{21}	SpecialBomb →NuclearBomb	HasRange(x,w), $w<3000$
		v_{24}	SpecialBomb→ Chemical-Bomb	

---

[1] The greatest lower bound of two concepts is considered as the most general sub-concept which is subsumed by both of them. E.g., "Special Bomb" is the greatest lower bound of the concepts "Bomb" and "Special Bomb" according to the ontology shown in Fig. 1.

4.2 Query Rewriting under Open Decision

In contrary to close decision, only negative authorization policies are needed to be taken into consideration for access control with open decision mechanism adopted. Query rewriting with negative authorization policies is different from that with positively authorized policies. To illustrate the differences, two more examples are shown as follow:

Example 3. (Access Control: Open Decision)
Query from s: $Q_3(x) \leftarrow Missile(x)$
Policies: e_{31}: $<s,v_{31},->$, $v_{31}(x) \leftarrow Missile(x), HasRange(x,z)$, $z>=3000$

In Example 3, policy e_{31} denies subject s to have access to missiles with their range over 3000 miles. Access to the missiles with their rangers within 3000 miles is thus permitted under open decision mechanism. So, Q_3 can be rewritten as follow:

$Q'_3(x) \leftarrow Missile(x)$, $HasRange(x,z)$, $z<3000$

Example 4. (Access Control: Open Decision)
Query from s: $Q_4(x,y) \leftarrow Missile(x)$, $Carry(x,y)$, $SpecialBomb(y)$;
Policies: e_{41}: $<s,v_{41},->$, $v_{41}(x,y) \leftarrow Missile(x)$, $Consume(x,z)$, $Carry(x,y)$, $Special$-$Bomb(y)$, $z = Liquid Fuel$;
    e_{42}: $<s,v_{42},->$, $v_{42}(x) \leftarrow Missile(x)$, $HasRange(x,w)$, $w>3000$;
    e_{43}: $<s,v_{43},->$, $v_{43}(y) \leftarrow NuclearBomb(y)$;

In Example 4, all policies e_{41}, e_{42} and e_{43} are applicable and should be considered in rewriting Q_4. Based on policy e_{41}, information related to missiles carrying special bombs and consuming "Liquid Fuel" is NOT ALLOWED for accessed. Based on policy e_{42}, information related to missiles with their range larger than 3000 miles are NOT ALLOWED for access. Also, based on policy e_{43}, missiles carrying nuclear bombs are NOT ALLOWED. The overall set of instances whose access is NOT ALLOWED can be specified by the disjunction of the three "NOT ALLOWED" conditions. For providing access control to the query, the constraints to be directly added should be specifying the *allowable* range of instances. For this open decision case, the allowable range is formed by taking the intersection of the negation of the restrictions derived from the negative policies. Referring to Example 4, the restriction expressions to be added to the query should be the conjunction of the restriction expressions "missiles carrying special bombs and not consuming Liquid Fuel", "missiles with their range within 3000 miles", and "missiles carrying special bombs which are NOT nuclear bombs".

As "NOT nuclear bombs" can result in either "BiologicalBomb" or "Chemical-Bomb", Q_4 can thus be rewritten as the union of the following:

$Q'_{41}(x,y) \leftarrow Missile(x)$, $Carry(x,y)$, $Consume(x,z)$, $HasRange(x,w)$, $BiologicalBomb(y)$, $z \neq$ $Liquid fuel$; $w \leq 3000$;
$Q'_{42}(x,y) \leftarrow Missile(x)$, $Carry(x,y)$, $Consume(x,z)$, $HasRange(x,w)$, $ChemicalBomb(y)$, $z \neq$ $Liquid fuel$; $w \leq 3000$;

Some examples with further restriction on the variable set in Q_4's head are presented as follow:

$Q'_{43}(x) \leftarrow Missile(x), Carry(x,y), Consume(x,z), HasRange(x,w), SpecialBomb(y), z \neq Liquid$
$Fuel; w \leq 3000;$
$Q'_{44}(y) \leftarrow Missile(x), Carry(x,y), BiologicalBomb(y);$
$Q'_{45}(y) \leftarrow Missile(x), Carry(x,y), ChemicalBomb(y);$

Again, the query rewriting process illustrated can be computed automatically. Referring to the illustrated examples, three main steps are needed for the rewriting. First, policies which are applicable to the query have to be identified. Then, for each applicable policy, their restriction expressions to be added to the query are computed by first comparing the policy's view bodies and the query body, and then compute their negation. Lastly, combinations of the restriction expressions derived from each applicable policies are computed for rewriting the query accordingly.

Algorithm 2: Query Rewriting Algorithm under Open Decision
Input
   Query form s: $Q(x_1,...,x_n) \leftarrow c_i(x_i),...,c_j(x_j),r_k(x_{k1}, x_{k2}),...,r_m(x_{m1}, x_{m2}),aps$;
   Policy set: P
   Ontology: O
Output
   Rewritten query $Q'(x_1,...,x_n') \leftarrow c_i(x_i'),...,c_j(x_j'),r_k(x_{k1}', x_{k2}'),...,r_m(x_{m1}', x_{m2}'),aps'$;
Process
   1.   Find applicable policies and create buckets for them to store the restrictions.
   For each negative authorization policy ($<s'$, v, $->$) in P that $s \leq s'$, it is applicable to the query Q if the concept of any variable x in its view's head is semantically related to that of some variable in the head of Q. For each applicable policy, create a bucket to be used for storing restrictions related to its view v. Also, add the variables in Q's head being "governed" by the policy to its "Related Variables" column.
   2.   Match applicable policies' view bodies with the query body.
   Establish a match Θ between the view v of each applicable policy and the query Q as described in Algorithm 1 in Section 4.1.
   3.   Derive restriction expressions from the applicable policies and fill up the corresponding buckets.
   Compare $\Theta(body(v))$ with Q's body. If all concepts in $\Theta(body(v))$ are found to subsume their matched counterparts in Q's body, the policy will for sure deny all the access to instances matched to the variables in Q. Add annotation "Null Result" to v's bucket; or else, find the following two kinds of restrictions from $\Theta(body(v))$:
   a)   "Subsumption Restriction": For each c_i (r_k) in Q with some sub-concept $c_{i'}$ (sub-role $r_{k'}$) identified in $\Theta(body(v))$, compute a set of concept c' which should be subsumed by c and disjointed with $c_{i'}$ forming its negation (based on knowledge in ontology O). Add all the related annotations "$c \rightarrow c'$" or "$+ c'(x)$" to the "Restricted Concepts" column of v's bucket.
   b)   "Additional Restriction": After the subsumption restrictions are handled, locate the remaining expressions and compute their negations. Then add them to the column "Restricted Expression" of v's bucket.

4.   Collect appropriate restrictions from buckets and rewrite the query accordingly

If none of applicable policies deny access of all instances to be matched with the variables in Q (i.e., no annotation "Null Result" exists in any bucket), rewrite Q as follow:

For each row of the buckets, choose one restriction from its "Restricted Concepts" or "Restricted Expression" columns and add it to the column "Restricted Concepts" or "Restricted Expression" in the total bucket accordingly (see Table 2). Repeat that for all the rows. Then, rewrite query Q' by replacing c with c' or adding "$c'(x)$" in Q's body according to annotations as "$c \rightarrow c'$ " or "$+c'(x)$" in the column "Restricted Concepts" of the total bucket and then adding all expressions in the column "Restricted Expression" of the total bucket to Q's body.

Repeat this step to find other ways of revising queries Q', and return $Q^t = \cup\, Q'$ as the final rewritten query.

5.   If Step 4 fails, check if Q can be rewritten with a reduced variable set so that some results can still be obtained.

If it fails to rewrite the query Q with all the variables in Q's head considered, an alternative is to find a rewritten version of Q with a reduced set of variables. In particular, remove all the variables with annotation "Null Result" in their buckets, and then obtain the rewritten query Q' as Step 4 according to the buckets of reduced variable set.

Repeat this step to find all such Q', and return $Q^t = \cup\, Q'$ as the output.

6.   If it fails to find a rewritten query Q' when all variables are removed from Q's head, return Φ.

The buckets created for query Q_4 are shown in Table 2. As the remaining expressions resulted from applying e_{41} and e_{42} to Q_4's body are "Consume(x,z), z = Liquid fuel" and "HasRange(x,w), $w>3000$", we add their negated versions "Consume(x,z), $z \neq$ Liquid Fuel" and "HasRange(x,w), $w \leq 3000$" to v_{41} and v_{42}'s bucket respectively. As the concept "NuclearBomb" in v_{43}'s body conflicts with its super-concept "SpecialBomb" in Q_4's body, we reduce the concept "SpecialBomb" to the disjunction of "BiologicalBomb" and "ChemicalBomb" which is disjointed with "NuclearBomb" and add them to v_{43}'s bucket. The restricted expressions in v_{41} and are added to the

Table 2. The buckets created for rewriting Q_4 in Example 4

View's Buckets			
Views	Related Variables	Restricted Concepts	Restricted Expression
e_{41}:v_{41}	x, y		Consume(x,z), $z \neq$ Liquid Fuel
e_{42}:v_{42}	x		HasRange(x,w), $w \leq 3000$
e_{43}:v_{43}	y	SpecialBomb$\rightarrow$ BiologicalBomb	
		SpecialBomb$\rightarrow$ ChemicalBomb	
Total Bucket			
Restricted Concepts		Restricted Expression	
SpecialBomb$\rightarrow$ BiologicalBomb or SpecialBomb$\rightarrow$ ChemicalBomb		Consume(x,z), $z \neq$ Liquid Fuel HasRange(x,w), $w \leq 3000$	

total bucket as there exists no restriction annotation in their "Restricted Concepts" columns. Also, one of the restrictions "SpecialBomb→ BiologicalBomb" and "SpecialBomb→ ChemicalBomb" in v_{43}'s bucket can be added to the total bucket. The union of the two obtained rewritten queries Q'_{41} and Q'_{42} should be the final output.

5   A Conceptual System Architecture for Supporting Policy-Based Access Control in the Semantic Web

Fig. 5 shows a conceptual system architecture for supporting the proposed policy-based query rewriting mechanism to impose access control on Semantic Web data upon query requests as described in this paper. First, we assume the ontologies which define the user concerned domain have been established and the instance resources in the Semantic Web annotated based on the concepts and roles defined in the ontologies are created manually or with the help of some software agent acting like Web "spider". Besides, we also assume that the security requirements for these resources are specified with the rule-based policies we described.

From the user perspective, their retrieval requests to the web resources are translated into queries taking the form as described in Definition 5 by the personal agent. Before submitting the query to the Semantic Web data store, it should first be rewritten by the query system which relies on the policies stored in a separate policy system, using the query rewriting algorithms as described in Sections 4.1 and 4.2. The rewritten queries are then sent to the query agent to get the information of the resources to be retrieved, with the guarantee that all the access control polices once specified in the policy system will automatically be respected.

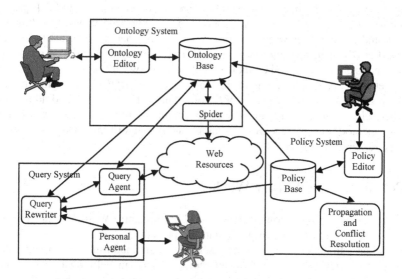

Fig. 5. A conceptual system architecture for supporting the proposed access control model

6 Related Work

Among the existing projects on policy-based access control, Rei [5] is one of the representative ones where a policy language based on OWL-Lite is adopted for trust and security management in a pervasive computing environment. Based on the language, access control policies for allowable actions on particular resources can be expressed as rule-like constraints. Compared with the rule-based policies in Rei [5], the view representation proposed in this paper provides further flexibility in specifying access control policies on instance resources. An overview on more recent requirements and research issues for semantic web policies can be found in [1].

Instead of studying merely access control policies languages, there also exists work that studies ways to control access to ontologies for the Semantic Web. For instance, a policy-based concept-level access control model was presented in [11], in which the control is for access to concept-level entities, such as classes in ontologies. Jain et al. [8] presented an access control model of secure RDF for protecting the RDF data. Policy propagation and conflict resolution are also addressed in their paper. Jeong et al. [9] proposed the use of databases to store the OWL ontologies and users can be controlled to have access to only part of ontologies (also called ontology views). In [6], part of the ontology was suggested to be removed, hidden or modified to protect them from illegal access. Different from security control on ontologies themselves, our work addresses the security issue of resources which are specified using ontologies. Javanmardi et al. [7] studied policy-based protection of concepts and instances in ontologies. Our work is different by the fact that we use of the notion of views to specify the objects to be protected.

Query rewriting with views is an effective way for implementing access control in relational databases. A survey on techniques for answering queries using views can be found in [4], where the bucket algorithm is described. Rizvi et al., in [13], presented techniques of rewriting SQL queries according to authorized views. Lakshmanan et al. [12] studied query answering using views for tree pattern queries. Cautis et al. presented an XML query rewriting approach in [2] for distributed access control, in which queries are modified when they are delivered between agents.

Abel et al. [17] proposed an algorithm for rewriting *SeRQL* queries with policies. It gets all restrictions for the triples in the from-clause of the queries and adds them to the where-clause of the original queries to obtain the rewritten queries. Compared with this method, our queries are rule-based, and our algorithm considers views covering the required resources.

7 Conclusion and Future Work

In this paper, we studied how access control to Semantic Web data can be implemented by rewriting queries. In particular, we presented an access control model, in which authorizations for accessing the resources are defined using rule-based policies. The notion of views on instance resources is adopted in defining policies and the corresponding policy propagation and conflict resolution issues are both addressed in this paper. For controlling sensitive information from leaking via answers to users' queries, a query rewriting approach based on the access control policies is then proposed. Queries rewritten using the proposed algorithms can have their returned results free from policy violated resources information. For future work, we will implement a prototype based on the proposed query rewriting algorithms.

Acknowledgement

This work is partially supported by Faculty Research Grant HKBU FRG/07-08/II-75.

References

1. Bonatti, P.A., Duma, C., Fuchs, N., Nejdl, W., Olmedilla, D., Peer, J., Shahmehri, N.: Semantic Web policies - A discussion of requirements and research issues. In: Sure, Y., Domingue, J. (eds.) ESWC 2006. LNCS, vol. 4011, pp. 712–724. Springer, Heidelberg (2006)
2. Cautis, B.: Distributed access control: A privacy-conscious approach. In: Proceedings of the 12th ACM Symposium on Access Control Models and Technologies, Sophia, Antipolis, France (2007)
3. Duma, C., Herzog, A., Shahmehri, N.: Privacy in the Semantic Web: What policy languages have to offer. In: Proceedings of the 11th IEEE International Workshop on Policies for Distributed Systems and Networks (2007)
4. Halevy., A.Y.: Answering queries using views: A survey. VLDB Journal 2001 10(4), 270–294 (2001)
5. Kagal, L., Finin, T., Joshi, A.: A policy based approach to security for the Semantic Web. In: Fensel, D., Sycara, K.P., Mylopoulos, J. (eds.) ISWC 2003. LNCS, vol. 2870, pp. 402–418. Springer, Heidelberg (2003)
6. Kaushik, S., Wijesekera, D., Ammann, P.: Policy-based dissemination of partial web-ontologies. In: Proceedings of the 2005 Workshop on Secure Web Services (2005)
7. Javanmardi, S., Amini, M., Jalili, R.: An access control model for protecting Semantic Web resources. In: Proceedings of the 2nd International Semantic Web Policy Workshop, Athens, GA (2006)
8. Jain, A., Farkas, C.: Secure resource description framework: An access control model. In: Proceedings of the 11th ACM Symposium on Access Control Models and Technologies, Lake Tahoe, California, USA (2006)
9. Jeong, D., Jing, Y., Baik, D.-K.: Access control model based on RDB security policy for OWL ontology. In: Shi, Y., van Albada, G.D., Dongarra, J., Sloot, P.M.A. (eds.) ICCS 2007. LNCS, vol. 4488, pp. 720–727. Springer, Heidelberg (2007)
10. Jajodia, S., Samarati, P., Sapino, M.L., Subrahmaninan, V.S.: Flexible support for multiple access control policies. ACM Transactions on Database Systems 26(2), 214–260 (2001)
11. Li, Q., Atluri, V.: Concept-level access control for the Semantic Web. In: Proceedings of the 2003 ACM Workshop on XML Security, Fairfax, Virginia (2003)
12. Lakshmanan, V.S.L., Wang, H., Zhao, Z.: Answering tree pattern queries using views. In: Proceedings of the 32nd International Conference on Very Large Databases, Seoul, Korea, pp. 571–582 (2006)
13. Rizvi, S., Mendelzon, A., Sudarshan, S., Roy, P.: Extending query rewriting techniques for fine-grained access control. In: Proceedings of 2004 ACM SIGMOD International Conference on Management of Data, Paris, France (2004)

14. World Wide Web Consortium. Semantic Web, http://www.w3.org/2001/sw/
15. World Wide Web. RDF Vocabulary Description Language 1.0: RDF Schema (December 2003), http://www.w3.org/TR/rdf-schema/
16. World Wide Web Consortium. OWL Web Ontology Language Overview (December 2003), http://www.w3.org/TR/owl-features/
17. Abel, F., Coi, J., Henze, N., Koesling, A.W., Krause, D., Olmedilla, D.: Enabling advanced and context-dependent access control in RDF Stores. In: Aberer, K., Choi, K.-S., Noy, N., Allemang, D., Lee, K.-I., Nixon, L., Golbeck, J., Mika, P., Maynard, D., Mizoguchi, R., Schreiber, G., Cudré-Mauroux, P. (eds.) ASWC 2007 and ISWC 2007. LNCS, vol. 4825, pp. 1–14. Springer, Heidelberg (2007)
18. Broekstra, J., Kampman, A., van Harmelen, F.: Sesame: A generic architecture for storing and querying RDF and RDF Schema. In: Horrocks, I., Hendler, J. (eds.) ISWC 2002. LNCS, vol. 2342, pp. 54–68. Springer, Heidelberg (2002)
19. Wilkinson, K., Sayers, C., Kuno, H., Reynolds, D.: Efficient RDF storage and retrieval in Jena2. In: Proceeding of the 1st International Workshop on Semantic Web and Databases, Berlin (2003)
20. Heflin, J., Hendler, J., and Luke, S.: SHOE: A knowledge representation language for internet applications. Technical Report CS-TR-4078 (UMIACS TR-99-71), Dept. of Computer Science, University of Maryland at College Park (1999)
21. Damiani, E., De Capitani di Vimercati, S., Fugazza, C., Samarati, P.: Extending policy languages to the Semantic Web. In: Koch, N., Fraternali, P., Wirsing, M. (eds.) ICWE 2004. LNCS, vol. 3140, pp. 330–343. Springer, Heidelberg (2004)

On the Facilitation of Fine-Grained Access to Distributed Healthcare Data

Mark Slaymaker, David Power, Douglas Russell, and Andrew Simpson

Oxford University Computing Laboratory
Wolfson Building, Parks Road, Oxford OX1 3QD, United Kingdom

Abstract. As an increasing amount of healthcare-related data is captured in both clinical and research contexts, the drive to provide appropriate access to such data becomes stronger. The very nature of such data means that simplistic approaches to authorisation—be they coarse-grained or role-based—are insufficient: the needs of the domain give rise to requirements for authorisation models capable of capturing fine-grained, expressive access control policies. We describe the development of a framework for the secure sharing and aggregation of healthcare-related data, called *sif* (for service-oriented interoperability framework). In particular, we concentrate on the access control aspects of the system and describe its utilisation of XACML in this respect.

1   Introduction

Recent innovations within the healthcare, IT and research communities have led to the prospect of sharing medical data on a scale that was unimaginable a decade or so ago. The motivation for the collection and sharing of huge amounts of data can be derived both from the delivery of improved research and improved patient care. Within the UK, for example, the National Programme for Information Technology (NPfIT)[1] is delivering a programme for 'computerising' the National Health Service (NHS)—the UK's free-at-the-point-of-service healthcare provider. While the primary focus of NPfIT is improved patient care, there are other aspects to the programme: for example, it is intended that the Secondary Uses Service (SUS) will act as a single repository of data for public health planning and clinical research. Within the US, the caBIG (cancer Biomedical Informatics Grid) initiative[2] is delivering an infrastructure to support the sharing of cancer-related data to facilitate 'bigger and better' research. Both of these systems involve the sharing of large amounts of clinical data to facilitate healthcare delivery and research respectively. In both cases, there are clear security and privacy concerns that underpin the legal and ethical sharing of data.

In this paper we describe a mechanism for facilitating access to, and sharing of, healthcare-related data across organisational boundaries. The mechanism supports the philosophy that data owners should determine access policies and that

---

[1] See www.connectingforhealth.nhs.uk/
[2] See http://cabig.cancer.gov/

W. Jonker and M. Petković (Eds.): SDM 2008, LNCS 5159, pp. 169–184, 2008.

the technology in place to enforce those policies should be sufficiently flexible and fine-grained that the access control requirements of data owners are not compromised. As such, we are sympathetic to the thoughts of [1]: "Although access control is a security service that has been widely studied and applied in healthcare systems such as EMR, the fact is that the most interested parties, the users (both healthcare professionals and patients), are not usually consulted when the access control policies are integrated into these systems, and when the system is integrated within their workflow environments." Further, the need for the consideration of new access control paradigms in this context is recognised in [2], while the need for expressive policies in this context is echoed in a straightforward fashion in [3]: "IT enforced access control policies in medical information systems have to be fine-grained and dynamic."

The mechanism we describe, called *sif* (for service-oriented interoperability framework), has been developed within the GIMI (Generic Infrastructure for Medical Informatics) project [4], the main aim of which is to develop a generic, dependable middleware layer capable of supporting data sharing across disparate sources via fine-grained access control mechanisms, and, in the longer-term, interfacing with technological solutions deployed within the NHS. While the responsibility for middleware development resides with the present authors, collaborators based elsewhere are making use of the middleware to support various applications pertaining to healthcare research, healthcare training, and healthcare delivery. We consider each of these applications below.

The overall aim of Application 1 is to develop medical image algorithms for application to breast and colorectal cancer (with examples including [5]). Via sif, algorithm developers are training their algorithms via the utilisation of data stored in the UK and Italy. Here, sif is being used to provide secure, audited access to legacy data and images from two different sources.

Application 2 is being developed by colleagues at Loughborough University and University College London, and is based on the work of the PERFORMS (Personal Performance in Mammographic Screening) project (the self-assessment programme used by the NHS's Breast Screening Programme) [6]. The application utilises data stored at Oxford, Loughborough, and Unversity College London, with the data comprising demographic information, digitised mammography x-rays, and annotations by experts in the field. The prototype allows an end-user to choose particular cases from any of the three nodes, and, once the selection is made, the application will call through the sif API to query all available data sets. The data returned is a list of cases that exhibit the condition of interest; the user can then select a case to download and view. The functionality requirements here (from the perspective of the middleware) are similar to those for Application 1, with the additional requirement that there is the potential for real patient data—stored on hospital-based PACS (Picture Archiving and Communications System) systems—to be used in the near future.

The self-management of patients with long-term conditions needs to be supported by comprehensive IT systems for disease management, which integrates all relevant information. The team associated with Application 3 (comprising researchers and developers from the Department of Engineering Science at Oxford University and t+ Medical) is engaging in a telemedicine trial involving two GP (General Practitioner) surgeries from the local primary care trust—involving delivering blood-glucose summary data from a telemedicine handset to a GP's desktop. Here, the focus is on transferring large number of small data items in real-time—as opposed to small numbers of large images. While the training-oriented application is concerned with 'pulling' data from a hospital-based system containing patient data, the delivery-oriented application is concerned with 'pushing' data to a GP's system.

While sif has to meet generic requirements pertaining to secure access and transfer, each application also gives rise to unique concerns: the fact that Applications 2 and 3, for example, involve genuine patient data means that issues of confidentiality and privacy are more to the fore than they are in the case of Application 1. In turn, the requirements for Application 3 are even more stringent: while genuine patient data is used for Application 2, it is data that has been 'marked' for training purposes; on the other hand, Application 3 is concerned with supporting patients—and involves unanonymised data.

In Section 2 we describe the background to, and the motivation for, our work. In Section 3 we describe our interoperability framework, sif, concentrating primarily on its ability to capture and enforce fine-grained access control policies. In Section 4 we present a particular example of the use of sif to facilitate access to research data by considering how collaborators are making use of data captured during the e-DiaMoND project [7]. Finally, in Section 5 we summarise the contribution of this paper and describe our ongoing work in this area.

2   Motivation and Background

2.1   The Origins of sif

The requirements for sif have been gathered through experience in two earlier projects (e-DiaMoND [7] and NeuroGrid [8]). In addition, our work has been sympathetic to the legal and ethical obligations associated with the sharing of medical data within the UK; as such, the Data Protection Act,[3] the Human Rights Act,[4] and the recommendations of the Caldicott Report[5] have been of particular concern. Given the focus on UK-oriented issues, the requirements of other countries (such as, for example, those associated with the Health Insurance Portability and Accountability Act (HIPAA)[6] in the United States) have been treated secondarily. Excellent overviews of the general legal and ethical issues pertaining to privacy in digital contexts are given in [9] and [10] respectively.

The architecture upon which sif is based was first described in [11], and is illustrated in Figure 1. Data is accessed via an internal interface, I. The permitted

---

[3] See www.legislation.gov.uk/acts/acts1998/ukpga_19980029_en_1

[4] See www.opsi.gov.uk/ACTS/acts1998/ukpga_19980042_en_1

[5] See www.dh.gov.uk/en/Publicationsandstatistics/Publications/
PublicationsPolicyAndGuidance/DH_4068403

[6] See www.hipaa.org

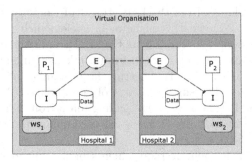

Fig. 1. The sif view of a virtual organisation

access to the data is regulated by a local policy, P. The external interface, E, to the organisation accesses data via the internal interface. The access given to the request for data originating via E is determined by the local policies, P.

The key element of this representation is that each organisation has control over access to the data it holds—which means that the responsibility for policy definition resides with that organisation. As there is no *a priori* statement of what access control *policies* will be implemented, the best that one can do in such circumstances is to offer a system that is flexible and is capable of accommodating varying requirements from different sources. Consequently, there is a need to support flexible and fine-grained access control policies.

It is worth noting that the enforcement of the policies is outside any database management system that an organisation uses. This has the benefit that the same policies can be applied across a number of disparate data sources from different vendors. An additional benefit of this approach is that it can be applied to legacy systems, as a sif-based system effectively acts as a gateway.

2.2   GIMI Authorisation Requirements

The applications described in Section 1 all have specific authorisation-related requirements, and, as the focus of each is different, this means that different concerns arise in each case—with these concerns reflecting the type of data being utilised, as well as the type of application. It is, perhaps, worth considering each in turn. It is worth clarifying that our interest here is in access control requirements; other security aspects—such as those pertaining to trust management, identity management and secure transfer—are not our concern here.

Application 1 is primarily concerned with providing diagnostic information based on image analysis of mammograms. To validate these image analysis algorithms, researchers require access to a large volume of image data. There are two potential sources that this data could come from: data collected specifically for research or data contained in a live healthcare system. Access to both sources of data is restricted, and based on legal and ethical constraints placed on the use and dissemination of the data. If the data is collected for research purposes, the original owner will want to control who the data is passed to and ensure it is done so in accordance with their original ethical approval for collecting and using the data. This would require that only individuals who have signed up to appropriate usage terms be allowed to access any of the data. This could involve the association of particular researchers or groups being associated with particular views or collections of views of the data.

The data could also be extracted directly from live healthcare systems providing appropriate approvals for the proposed data usage are in place. If the data is to be extracted from a live system, it is necessary for the access control mechanism to provide a framework allowing the expression of suitable policies to be captured. The types of policies that have been indicated to the present authors include the following: "only allow researcher Y to see anonomised data pertaining to the following group of patients"; "no researcher may see any data pertaining to the following patients"; "only data pertaining to the following patients may be viewed"; "each researcher has access to a customised list of attributes pertaining to particular patients"; and "a researcher can only see patients involved in a particular trial".

Some clear requirements emerge, including the ability to describe user-centric policies that govern the permitted behaviour that can be undertaken by an individual. Furthermore, it is important that there is support for policies that capture detailed contextual information. To this end, there is a clear need for the ability to support fine-grained access control.

Application 2 is concerned with providing training and assessment to radiologists involved in breast screening; to this end, the application requires access to health-related data, together with data associated with the person undergoing the training or assessment. To facilitate this, the application needs to access data from two different sources. The access to the personal data of the person using the application needs to be restricted to that individual and certain approved others. To achieve this we need to be able to express policies of the following kind: "only the person who the data relates to and their supervisor can see the data"; and "only the person that the data relates to and those approved by the data subject may see the data".

Access to the annotated data sets need to be controlled on the basis of the use to which the data is being put. While it may be appropriate to allow a person undergoing training to 'reveal' the annotations, it would probably be inappropriate to allow someone undergoing assessment to do the same. As such, a requirement that the access control mechanism should allow for access requests to be framed in a way that would distinguish between the two case emerges. To provide the maximum number of cases to use for training radiologists, data needs to be shared between institutions. To facilitate this, institutions have indicated that they need to be able to control who has access to any given annotated training data set. It may be that some of the annotated data is marked as being available to users of a particular institution only. e.g., when being assessed the user can only be assessed on images from an institution other than the one they work at. The scenarios captured relating to this application reinforce the views derived from the requirements of the previous application: namely that there needs to be support for fine-grained, user-centric policies.

The final application area is concerned with supporting the self-management of patients with long-term conditions, such as asthma and diabetes. A first application allows a patient to use their mobile phone to send pertinent information to a central server, where it is recorded; a second application allows GPs to access the data pertaining to their own patients. This gives rise to the requirement that a particular doctor can only view data for their own patients (or, in practice, the patients of the practice for which they work). In addition to developing an application that allows access to the raw data, t+ Medical are providing additional applications that make use of the 'plug-in' facilities of the sif middleware to provide processed data. Access to the various plug-ins also requires restricting to only those who are permitted access to the processed data, which may be because the algorithm is undergoing testing as part of a trial and should therefore not be totally relied upon. To prevent a random doctor misinterpreting the data from an algorithm under test, access to the algorithm needs to be restricted to those involved in the trial and those analysing the trial results.

Given the above, the need to support fine-grained access control policies is clear—as is the requirement for control to reside with the data owner. Additionally, it is important to be able to define access control policies that depend on the actions being performed at that time. This was highlighted by the need for a radiologist undergoing assessment to not have any cases from their own institution contained within the data composing the test set. Further, the long-term conditions application highlights the need for the relationships between the data being accessed and the person accessing it to be expressible.

3   Support for Fine-Grained Access Control in a Distributed Healthcare Context

3.1   sif

sif has been developed to facilitate access to, and aggregation of, data from disparate data sources. As discussed in the previous section, a key principle that underpins sif is the notion that it is the data owner that is responsible for the creation of access control policies.

The sif middleware is comprised of a collection of web services, with only a limited number of the core web services standards, e.g., WS-Security,[7] being utilised. The security provided by WS-Security is enhanced with the use of a 'ticketing system' for delegation, which provides an auditing facility from which it is possible to obtain information on the origin of a request and the route taken to reach a given point within the system. The approach taken has given rise to a portable system, which has been deployed successfully to machines running Linux, Windows XP, IBM AIX, and Mac OS X.

---

[7] See http://www.oasis-open.org/committees/documents.php?wg_abbrev=wss

sif offers support for three types of 'plug-in': data plug-ins, file plug-ins and algorithm plug-ins. By using a standard plug-in interface for each, it is possible to add heterogeneous resources into a virtual organisation via sif; importantly, there is no need for the resource being advertised through the plug-in system to directly represent the physical resource. What is advertised as a single data source may come from any number of physical resources—even another distributed system.

Data plug-ins currently treat all data sources as SQL databases, with the plug-in being responsible for all translations between the native data format and SQL. The plug-in user or application developer can retrieve schemas for known resources; as such, the user of the plug-in is able to perform a join or a union query on data from fundamentally different data sources. From an end-user perspective, a user can request a list of plug-ins and descriptions from the middleware: definitions for a specific plug-in can be retrieved which contain an interface definition. The user can then request action to be taken for a plug-in by sending a request which conforms to the interface definition (the response is also bound by the definition so the response will be in an expected format).

For any user to be able to perform any particular action they must first be permitted to do so by the access control subsystem of the sif middleware. The sif access control decision mechanism is based on Sun's implementation[8] of the OASIS XACML (eXtensible Access Control Markup Language) standard.[9]

3.2   XACML

XACML is an OASIS standard comprising two languages: the *policy language* is used to describe general access control requirements and has standard extension points that allow one to define aspects such as new functions, data types, and logics to combine such entities; the *request/response language* allows one to construct a query to determine whether a particular action should be permitted. Every response contains an answer pertaining to whether the action should be permitted in terms of one of four possible values: *permit, deny, indeterminate* (a decision cannot be made due to a missing value or the occurrence of an error), or *not applicable* (the question cannot be answered by this service).

In order for an application or user to perform some action on a particular data resource, a request is made to the entity that protects that resource—the *policy enforcement point* (PEP). On the basis of several aspects—the requester's attributes, the resource that the requester wishes to perform its action on, what the action is, etc.—the PEP will form a request. This request is then sent to a *policy decision point* (PDP), which analyses the request together with a policy that applies to the request, and determines the appropriate answer, which is returned to the PEP, which, in turn, may then either allow or deny access.

A policy can have any number of *rules*. At the heart of most rules is a *condition*, which is a Boolean function. If the condition evaluates to true, then the rule's *effect*—which is the intended consequence of a satisfied rule (either 'permit' or 'deny')—is returned. In addition, a rule specifies a *target*, which defines:

---

[8] See http://sunxacml.sourceforge.net/

[9] See www.oasis-open.org/committees/xacml/

the set of the *subjects* who can access the resource; the *resource* that the subject can access; the *action* that the subject can undertake on the resource; and the *environmental* attributes that are relevant to an authorisation decision and are independent of a particular subject, resource or action.

Within the request document there exist values of specific attributes that must be compared with the corresponding policy document values in order to determine whether or not access should be allowed. The values of the request attributes are compared with those of the policy document so that a decision can be made with respect to access permission. When many different policies exist, a *policy set document* is defined as a combining set.

A policy set or policy may contain multiple policies or rules, each of which may evaluate to different access control decisions. In order for a final authorisation decision to be made, combining algorithms are used, with *policy combining algorithms* being used by policy sets and *rule combining algorithms* being used by policies. Each such algorithm represents a different means of combining multiple decisions into a single authorisation decision.

When the PDP compares the attribute values contained in the request document with those contained in the policy or policy set document, a response document is generated. The response document includes an answer containing the authorisation decision. This result, together with an optional set of *obligations*, is returned to the PEP by the PDP. Obligations are sets of operations that must be performed by the PEP in conjunction with an authorisation decision; an obligation may be associated with a positive or negative authorisation decision.

3.3 XACML and sif

Each of the individual sif middleware components formulate their own access control requests. The supplied XACML policies are evaluated against the generated request by the sif access control subsystem, a part of the sif security mechanism. The request contains the pertinent information that allows an access control decision to be made.

Access control decisions relating to the requested action are made independently at each node. That is, if a query is requested to be performed on three different nodes, then each of those nodes will determine if access can be granted independently of the other nodes. The processing of a single query is illustrated in Figure 2. Here, the client application communicates with the local sif node via the sif API. In this case, a query is formulated by the application using the API and then passed to the appropriate web service at the local sif node. The web service first checks if the user is permitted to interact with it by making an initial call to the sif security mechanism to get an access control decision. If the interaction is permitted, the query request is forwarded to the query processor. The query processor in turn checks if the user is permitted to execute the requested query by making another call to the the sif security mechanism to get an access control decision. Once the query is processed the results are returned via the mechanism provided in the sif API to the client application.

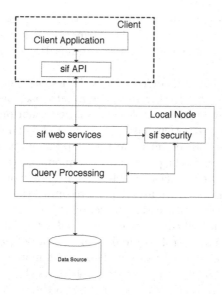

Fig. 2. The processing of a query

The processing of a federated query joining data across multiple data sources and potentially across organisational boundaries is described in detail in [12]. For the purposes of this discussion we can consider a query that is made up of a number of sub-queries, some of which need to be processed by other nodes. The local node splits out the sub-queries and forwards them to the relevant nodes. The ticketing mechanism provides information about the hops taken and who made the request. Each of the nodes that receive a forwarded request check if the originating node is one which they will accept requests from, then, using the originator's details, proceeds to process the request in the way described above. The results of the individual sub-queries are then returned to the local sif node, which combines the results before returning the overall result.

As XACML is designed to be extensible, a number of extension functions have been written to allow finer grained access control than would be possible otherwise. In general terms, these functions evaluate relationships between the subject requesting the access and the resources they are requesting access to. For example, a function establishes that a doctor has a legitimate relationship with a particular patient—either because they are the patient's doctor or the doctor is one of the practitioners working at the clinic at which the patient is registered. Thus, by utilising the facilities provided by XACML and the provision of appropriate extensions it is possible to meet many of the requirements identified by the various applications.

It is, perhaps, worth considering some of the information contained in an access control request, which includes: the user making the request; the resource they wish to interact with; and the action they wish to perform on the resource. Within the sif middleware, the information relating to the user making the request is extracted from their user certificate. This information includes items such as their distinguished name, common name, locality, organisational unit, certificate validity dates, etc.

The resource information included within the request depends entirely upon the resource. For example, if the resource is a database, the data plug-in providing access to that database may decide to forward not only the name of the database but also the query that has been requested to be executed, detailing, for example, the tables and columns that make up the query. In contrast, a plug-in exposing a file system might provide details about the exact file or directory for which access has been requested. The action corresponds to how the user wishes to interact with the previously defined resource: this could pertain to, for example, querying a database, reading a file, or copying a file.

Each of the items described above can be used by a data owner to provide the granularity of access control required in their own policies. The information about a particular user can be used in the subject match block to determine the applicability of that element as well as being used in the evaluation of a condition. Similarly, the information pertaining to the resource and action can also be used.

To provide a useful facility allowing data owners to write sensible policies, a list of attributes associated with the subject, resource and action is provided for each of the standard facilities provided by the sif middleware. A selection of the possible resource/action pairs is presented in Table 1.

For query requests to data-plugins, the SQL is parsed to give schema, table and column information. To avoid indirect accessing of information, columns included in where clauses are also included in the parsed output as are details of any sub-queries. As an example consider the following query.

```
SELECT C1 FROM S1.T1
WHERE C2 = 'Value1' AND C3 IN (SELECT C4 FROM S2.T2)
```

The execution of this query would produce the following resource attributes:

- schema: S1
- schema: S2
- schema.table: S1.T1
- schema.table: S2.T4
- schema.table.column: S1.T1.C1
- schema.table.column: S1.T1.C2
- schema.table.column: S1.T1.C3
- schema.table.column: S2.T2.C4

The policies can be written using the functions defined within the XACML specification, as well as functions provided as extensions that allow additional— and potentially more complicated—evaluations to take place. For instance, a function has been provided to one application to allow the application to determine if a given file is associated with a particular medical trial.

Table 1. Resource/Action pairs for standard facilities

Resource	Action
download	$fileID
upload	fileStore
create	webDav
delete	webDav
modify	webDav
write	webDav
federation	$server
union	databases
join	databases
list	databases
query	$dbName
listAllPlugins	pluginManager
installPlugin	$pluginID
uninstallPlugin	$pluginID
getPluginDefinition	$pluginID
executeAlgorithmPlugin	$pluginID
filePluginGet	$pluginID
filePluginPut	$pluginID
filePluginList	$pluginID

4   An Example

The aim of the e-DiaMoND project was to develop a prototype system that demonstrated the potential for emerging 'grid' technologies to support various breast screening applications, with a particular focus on meeting the needs of the UK's Breast Screening Programme (BSP). As well as the middleware and applications developed during the project, a significant amount of images and patient data was collected. That resource is now being utilised within GIMI to as a data source for the Applications 1 and 2.

Consider the following scenario. Two sites have decided that they wish to share data to allow their researchers access to a large volume of data to help validate image processing algorithms. The two sites, however, do not want to expose all their data to each other; rather, they would prefer to keep certain aspects of the data for internal use only, possibly because of legal and ethical constraints associated with data usage.

Assume that the researchers rA and rB work for organisations oX and oY respectively and that the data sets dP, dQ and dR are available for sharing. Researcher rA wishes to run a query against a database dQ held by organisation oY—and the policies governing the access that rA has are determined by oY. oY has decided that researchers from oX cannot execute a query that includes a reference to schema S, table T and column C in database dQ. This can be achieved by using a rule within an XACML policy such as that given below.

```
<Rule
  RuleId="R_CanNotReadColumnC"
  Effect="Deny">
  <Description>
    People from organisation oX cannot read
    column C in Table T in Schema S in database dQ
  </Description>
  <Target>
    <Subjects>
      <Subject>
        <SubjectMatch
          MatchId="urn:oasis:names:tc:xacml:1.0:function:string-equal">
          <AttributeValue
            DataType="http://www.w3.org/2001/XMLSchema#string">oX</AttributeValue>
          <SubjectAttributeDesignator
            AttributeId="organisation"
            DataType="http://www.w3.org/2001/XMLSchema#string"/>
        </SubjectMatch>
      </Subject>
    </Subjects>
    <Resources>
      <Resource>
        <ResourceMatch MatchId="urn:oasis:names:tc:xacml:1.0:function:string-equal">
          <AttributeValue
            DataType="http://www.w3.org/2001/XMLSchema#string">S.T.C</AttributeValue>
          <ResourceAttributeDesignator
            AttributeId="schema.table.column"
            DataType="http://www.w3.org/2001/XMLSchema#string"/>
        </ResourceMatch>
      </Resource>
      <Resource>
        <ResourceMatch MatchId="urn:oasis:names:tc:xacml:1.0:function:string-equal">
          <AttributeValue
            DataType="http://www.w3.org/2001/XMLSchema#string">S.T.*</AttributeValue>
          <ResourceAttributeDesignator
            AttributeId="schema.table.column"
            DataType="http://www.w3.org/2001/XMLSchema#string"/>
        </ResourceMatch>
      </Resource>
    </Resources>
    <Actions>
      <Action>
        <ActionMatch MatchId="urn:oasis:names:tc:xacml:1.0:function:string-equal">
          <AttributeValue
            DataType="http://www.w3.org/2001/XMLSchema#string">query</AttributeValue>
          <ActionAttributeDesignator
            AttributeId="urn:oasis:names:tc:xacml:1.0:action:action-id"
            DataType="http://www.w3.org/2001/XMLSchema#string"/>
        </ActionMatch>
      </Action>
    </Actions>
  </Target>
</Rule>
```

Of course, this is only a fragment of the overall policy set describing the access control policy of organisation oY, and would appear in a policy that has a target that includes database dQ. The above shows that the following matches need to take place for it to be relevant to the access control decision: subject matching will match anyone with an organisation affiliation of organisation oX; the resource matches if the column S.T.C is requested explicitly or a * is associated with the table, i.e. S.T.*; and the action matches if a query is being requested. The rule will deny access to the resource if that column is part of the query that has been submitted to be run.

A possible request is illustrated below.

```
<Request>
<Subject
  SubjectCategory="urn:oasis:names:tc:xacml:1.0:subject-category:access-subject">
  <Attribute AttributeId="urn:oasis:names:tc:xacml:1.0:data-type:x500Name"
    DataType="urn:oasis:names:tc:xacml:1.0:data-type:x500Name">
    <AttributeValue>
      1.2.840.113549.1.9.1=#16187a6f686dde646f654073646461672e6f782e61632e756b,
      CN=rA,OU=research,O=oX,L=Red Bank,ST=New Jersey,C=GB</AttributeValue>
  </Attribute>
  <Attribute AttributeId="organisation"
    DataType="http://www.w3.org/2001/XMLSchema#string">
    <AttributeValue>oX</AttributeValue>
  </Attribute>
  <Attribute AttributeId="OU"
    DataType="http://www.w3.org/2001/XMLSchema#string">
    <AttributeValue>research</AttributeValue>
  </Attribute>
  <Attribute AttributeId="location"
    DataType="http://www.w3.org/2001/XMLSchema#string">
    <AttributeValue>Red Bank</AttributeValue>
  </Attribute>
  <Attribute AttributeId="country"
    DataType="http://www.w3.org/2001/XMLSchema#string">
    <AttributeValue>GB</AttributeValue>
  </Attribute>
  <Attribute AttributeId="issuer"
    DataType="http://www.w3.org/2001/XMLSchema#string">
    <AttributeValue>
      1.2.840.113549.1.9.1=#161f646f98676c61732e1622e6f782e61632e756b,
      CN=oX Research CA,OU=research CA,O=oX,C=GB</AttributeValue>
  </Attribute>
</Subject>
<Resource>
  <Attribute AttributeId="sql"
    DataType="http://www.w3.org/2001/XMLSchema#string">
    <AttributeValue>select A, B, C from S.T </AttributeValue></Attribute>
  <Attribute AttributeId="schema"
    DataType="http://www.w3.org/2001/XMLSchema#string">
```

```
      <AttributeValue>S</AttributeValue>
    </Attribute>
    <Attribute AttributeId="schema.table"
      DataType="http://www.w3.org/2001/XMLSchema#string">
      <AttributeValue>S.T</AttributeValue>
    </Attribute>
    <Attribute AttributeId="schema.table.column"
        DataType="http://www.w3.org/2001/XMLSchema#string">
      <AttributeValue>S.T.A</AttributeValue>
    </Attribute>
    <Attribute AttributeId="schema.table.column"
        DataType="http://www.w3.org/2001/XMLSchema#string">
      <AttributeValue>S.T.B</AttributeValue>
    </Attribute>
    <Attribute AttributeId="schema.table.column"
        DataType="http://www.w3.org/2001/XMLSchema#string">
      <AttributeValue>S.T.C</AttributeValue>
    </Attribute>
    <Attribute AttributeId="urn:oasis:names:tc:xacml:1.0:resource:resource-id"
              DataType="http://www.w3.org/2001/XMLSchema#string">
      <AttributeValue>dQ</AttributeValue>
    </Attribute>
  </Resource>
  <Action>
    <Attribute AttributeId="urn:oasis:names:tc:xacml:1.0:action:action-id"
              DataType="http://www.w3.org/2001/XMLSchema#string">
      <AttributeValue>query</AttributeValue>
    </Attribute>
  </Action>
</Request>
```

This request would be generated by the query component of the middleware
to be evaluated against the policy containing rule given earlier. The query component adds all relevant details about the query the user wishes to perform on
the database to the request. In this example it includes details about the user
obtained from their certificate, along with the name of the database, the fact a
query action has been requested, and details of columns and tables that make
up the query. The above request results in the following response.

```
<Response>
  <Result ResourceId="dQ">
    <Decision>Deny</Decision>
    <Status>
      <StatusCode Value="urn:oasis:names:tc:xacml:1.0:status:ok"/>
    </Status>
  </Result>
</Response>
```

This means the user is denied from running the query requested because the rule prevents anyone from organisation oX from running a query against dQ that includes the column S.T.C.

This simple example illustrates the ability of the access control mechanism provided within sif to allow the data owner to define policies that control access to individual columns within a data set. With the use of functions that can form part of a conditional statement other restrictions can be added easily.

5   Discussion

We have described the need to support fine-grained access control policies in the context of distributed healthcare applications, and have discussed how this is being brought about within the GIMI project. As an example, we have demonstrated how access to data gathered in the e-DiaMoND project is being facilitated. As the access control provided by sif is outside the control of any DBMS that the data resides in, it provides a way of sharing legacy data without having to modify the data source. sif uses a single connection to the database—but only allow through the requests that the access control policy permits.

The need for expressive access control policies in this context has been discussed elsewhere, with the work of [1], [2] and [3] being examples; practical work that is sympathetic to these drivers includes [13].

Our focus on fine-grained access control policies has led us to use XACML as our language of implementation; in particular, we use the Sun implementation of the XACML standard with custom extensions. With the benefits of expressiveness, though, come the drawbacks of complexity: XACML is a complex language to understand and reason about. The current provision of XACML editors is poor; further, its complexity means that providing assurance that the *right* policies are in place is extremely difficult. We have started work on providing a formal model of XACML to facilitate such analysis. (Related work includes that of [14].) Other limitations of XACML include the type system not catering for the use of recursively defined types, the lack of support for tuples or bags of bags, and the fact that target matching could be more flexible, allowing for the matching of targets based on multiple elements from the target.

We are hopeful that the applicability and accessibility of XACML will continue to improve: due to ethical and legal obligations, the need for fine-grained access control policies is only likely to increase. Our concern in this paper has been the description of the facilitation of fine-grained access control within the GIMI project. Broader concerns, such as the consideration of so-called tracker attacks [15] have been addressed in our more theoretical work (see, for example, [16]). One immediate area of future work will be to transpose this theory into the sif framework to mitigate against the dangers of re-identification as data is aggregated.

Acknowledgments. The work described in this paper was funded by the Technology Strategy Board's Collaborative Research and Development programme.

References

1. Ferreira, A., Cruz-Correia, R., Antunes, L., Chadwick, D.: Access control: how can it improve patients' healthcare? Studies in Health Technology and Informatics, 127 (June 2007)
2. Chinaei, A.H., Tompa, F.W.: User-managed access control for health care systems. In: Jonker, W., Petković, M. (eds.) SDM 2005. LNCS, vol. 3674, pp. 63–72. Springer, Heidelberg (2005)
3. Verhanneman, T., Jaco, L., De Win, B., Piessens, F., Joosen, W.: Adaptable access control policies for medical information systems. In: Stefani, J.-B., Demeure, I., Hagimont, D. (eds.) DAIS 2003. LNCS, vol. 2893, pp. 133–140. Springer, Heidelberg (2003)
4. Simpson, A.C., Power, D.J., Slaymaker, M.A., Politou, E.A.: GIMI: Generic infrastructure for medical informatics. In: Proceedings of CBMS 2005, pp. 564–566 (2005)
5. Tromans, C., Brady, J.M.: A scatter model for use in measuring volumetric mammographic breast density. In: Astley, S.M., Brady, M., Rose, C., Zwiggelaar, R. (eds.) IWDM 2006. LNCS, vol. 4046, pp. 251–258. Springer, Heidelberg (2006)
6. Gale, A.G.: Performs — a self asssessment scheme for radiologists in breast screening. Seminars in Breast Disease: Improving and Monitoring Mammographic Interpretative Skills 6, 148–152 (2003)
7. Brady, J.M., Gavaghan, D.J., Simpson, A.C., Mulet-Parada, M., Highnam, R.P.: eDiaMoND: A grid-enabled federated database of annotated mammograms. In: Berman, F., Fox, G.C., Hey, A.J.G. (eds.) Grid Computing: Making the Global Infrastructure a Reality, pp. 923–943. Wiley Series, Chichester (2003)
8. Geddes, J., Lloyd, S., Simpson, A.C., Rossor, M., Fox, N., Hill, D., Hajnal, J., Lawrie, S., McIntosh, A., Johnstone, E., Wardlaw, J., Perry, D., Procter, R., Bath, P., Bullimore, E.: NeuroGrid: using grid technology to advance neuroscience. In: Proceedings of CBMS 2005, pp. 570–573 (2005)
9. Terstegge, J.: Privacy in the law. In: Petkovic, M., Jonker, W. (eds.) Security, privacy, and trust in modern data management, pp. 11–20. Springer, Heidelberg (2007)
10. Brey, P.: Ethical aspects of information security and privacy. In: Petkovic, M., Jonker, W. (eds.) Security, privacy, and trust in modern data management, pp. 21–38. Springer, Heidelberg (2007)
11. Power, D.J., Politou, E.A., Slaymaker, M.A., Simpson, A.C.: Towards secure grid-enabled healthcare. Software Practice and Experience 35, 857–871 (2005)
12. Slaymaker, M.A., Power, D.J., Russell, D., Wilson, G., Simpson, A.C.: Accessing and aggregating legacy data sources for healthcare research, delivery and training. In: Proceedings of SAC 2008 (2008)
13. Bertino, E., Squicciarini, A.C., Paloscia, I., Martino, L.: Ws-AC: A fine grained access control system for web services. World Wide Web 9(2) (June 2006)
14. Bryans, J.W., Fitzgerald, J.S.: Formal engineering of XACML access control policies in VDM++. In: Butler, M., Hinchey, M.G., Larrondo-Petrie, M.M. (eds.) ICFEM 2007. LNCS, vol. 4789, Springer, Heidelberg (2007)
15. Denning, D.E.: Are statistical databases secure? In: Proceedings of the 1978 National Computer Conference, pp. 525–530. AFIPS Press (1978)
16. Simpson, A.C., Power, D.J., Slaymaker, M.A.: On tracker attacks in health grids. In: SAC 2006. ACM Press, New York (2006)

A Type-and-Identity-Based Proxy Re-encryption Scheme and Its Application in Healthcare

Luan Ibraimi[1], Qiang Tang[1], Pieter Hartel[1], and Willem Jonker[1,2]

[1] Faculty of EWI, University of Twente, The Netherlands
[2] Philips Research, The Netherlands

Abstract. Proxy re-encryption is a cryptographic primitive developed to delegate the decryption right from one party (the delegator) to another (the delegatee). In a proxy re-encryption scheme, the delegator assigns a key to a proxy to re-encrypt all messages encrypted with his public key such that the re-encrypted ciphertexts can be decrypted with the delegatee's private key. We propose a type-and-identity-based proxy re-encryption scheme based on the Boneh-Franklin Identity Based Encryption (IBE) scheme. In our scheme, the delegator can categorize messages into different types and delegate the decryption right of each type to the delegatee through a proxy. Our scheme enables the delegator to provide the proxy fine-grained re-encryption capability. As an application, we propose a fine-grained Personal Health Record (PHR) disclosure scheme for healthcare service by applying the proposed scheme.

Keywords: Proxy re-encryption, Identity-Based Encryption, Personal Health Record.

1 Introduction

Proxy re-encryption is a cryptographic method developed to delegate the decryption right from one party (the delegator) to another (the delegatee). In a proxy re-encryption scheme, the delegator assigns a key to a proxy to re-encrypt all messages encrypted with his public key such that the re-encrypted ciphertexts can be decrypted with the delegatee's private key. Since Mambo and Okamoto first proposed the concept [1], a number of proxy re-encryption schemes have been proposed [2,3,4,5,6]. Proxy re-encryption has many promising applications including access control in file storage [7], email forwarding [8], and law enforcement [3]. With the increasing privacy concerns over personal data, proxy re-encryption, in particular IBE proxy re-encryption schemes (due to their benefits [9]), will find more and more applications. For example, in the healthcare domain, many regulations, such as HIPPA [10], require that the patient is the owner of his personal health record and should control the disclosure policy for his Personal Health Record (PHR). As we show in Section 5, proxy re-encryption is a powerful tool for patient to enforce his PHR disclosure policies.

W. Jonker and M. Petković (Eds.): SDM 2008, LNCS 5159, pp. 185–198, 2008.

1.1   Motivations and Contributions

An observation on the existing proxy re-encryption schemes is that the proxy is able to re-encrypt all ciphertexts from the delegator to the delegatee. As a result, it is difficult for the delegator to implement any further fine-grained cryptographically enforced access control policy for multiple delegation services. Suppose the delegator wants delegatees Bob and Charlie to recover different subsets of his messages. In this case, the delegator can only trust the proxy to enforce his policies by re-encrypting the legitimate ciphertexts. In practice, this trust assumption might be unrealistic (for example, the proxy can be corrupted). To solve this problem, an alternative solution would be that the delegator chooses a different key pair for each delegatee, which is also unrealistic.

Contribution. We propose a type-and-identity-based proxy re-encryption scheme based on the Boneh-Franklin IBE scheme to enable the delegator to implement different access control policies for his ciphertexts against his delegatees. To achieve our goal, in the proposed scheme, the delegator can categorize his messages into different types, and delegate the decryption right of each type to the delegatee through a proxy. One benefit of our scheme is that the delegator only needs one key pair to provide fine-grained re-encryption capability to his proxy. In other words, the delegator only needs one key pair to provide fine-grained access control policies for his ciphertexts against his delegatees. The other benefit is that there is no further trust assumption on the proxy compared to existing proxy re-encryption schemes. However, the proposed scheme works only for the ciphertexts generated by the delegator. As an application, we propose a fine-grained PHR disclosure scheme for a healthcare service by applying the proposed scheme.

1.2   Organization

The rest of the paper is organized as follows: In Section 2 we introduce related work in proxy re-encryption. In Section 3 we briefly review the preliminaries of pairing and IBE. In Section 4 we present our new scheme which enables the delegator to offer fine-grained re-encryption capability to the proxy and prove its security. In Section 5 we propose a fine-grained PHR disclosure scheme as an application of our proxy re-encryption scheme. The last section concludes the paper.

2   Related Work

Mambo and Okamoto [1] first propose the concept of delegation of decryption right in the context of speeding up decryption operations. Blaze *et al.* [2] introduce the concept of atomic proxy cryptography which is the current concept of proxy re-encryption. In a proxy re-encryption scheme, the proxy can transform ciphertexts encrypted with the delegator's public key into ciphertexts that can be decrypted with the delegatee's private key. Blaze *et al.* propose a proxy re-encryption scheme based on the ElGamal encryption scheme [11]. One property of this scheme is that, with the same proxy key, the proxy can transform the ciphertexts not only form the delegator to the delegatee but also from the delegatee to the delegator. This is called the "bi-directional" property in the literature. Bi-directionality might be a problem in some applications, but it might also be a desirable property in some other applications. Jacobsson [4] addresses this "problem" using a quorum controlled asymmetric proxy re-encryption where the proxy is implemented with multiple servers and each of them performs partial re-encryption.

Dodis and Ivan [3] propose a generic construction method for proxy re-encryption schemes and also provide a number of example schemes. Their constructions are based on the concept of secret splitting, which means that the delegator splits his private key into two parts and sends them to the proxy and the delegatee separately. During the re-encryption process the proxy performs partial decryption of the encrypted message using the first part of the delegator's private key, and the delegatee can recover the message by performing partial decryption using the second part of the delegator's private key. One disadvantage of this method is that it is not collusion-safe, i.e. the proxy and the delegatee together can recover the delegator's private key. Another disadvantage of this scheme is that the delegatee's public/private key pair can only be used for dealing with the delegator's messages. If this key pair is used by the delegatee for other encryption services, then the delegator can always decrypt the ciphertexts.

Ateniese et al. [7] propose several proxy re-encryption schemes based on the ElGamal scheme. In their schemes, the delegator does not have to interact and share his private key with the delegatee. The delegator stores two secret keys, a master secret key and a "weak" secret key. The ciphertext can be fully decrypted using either of the two distinct keys. Their scheme is collusion safe, since only the "weak" secret key is exposed if the delegatee and the proxy collude but the master key remains safe. The disadvantage of this scheme is that the delegator has to perform two levels of encryptions, the first level encryption encrypts messages that can be decrypted by the delegator, and the second level encryption encrypts messages that can be decrypted by the delegator and his delegatees. In addition, Ateniese et al. also discuss a number of properties for proxy re-encryption schemes in [7].

The concept of IBE is proposed by Shamir [12]. Unlike a traditional public key encryption scheme, an IBE does not require a digital certificate to certify the public key because the public key of any user in an IBE can be an arbitrary string such as an email address, IP address, etc. IBE becomes practical and popular after Boneh and Franklin [9] propose the first pairing-based scheme. Recently, two IBE proxy re-encryption schemes were proposed by Matsuo [6] and Green and Atteniese [5], respectively. The Matsuo scheme assumes that the delegator and the delegatee belong to the same Key Generation Center (KGC) and use the Boneh-Boyen encryption scheme [13]. The Green-Atteniese scheme assumes that the delegator and the delegatee can belong to different KGCs but the delegatee posesses the public parameter of the delegator's KGC.

3   Preliminary

In this section we briefly review the pairing technique and the concept of IBE.

3.1   Review of Pairing

We briefly review the basis of pairing and the related assumptions. More detailed information can be found in the seminal paper [9]. A pairing (or, bilinear map) satisfies the following properties:

1. $\mathbb{G}$ and $\mathbb{G}_1$ are two multiplicative groups of prime order p;
2. g is a generator of $\mathbb{G}$;
3. $\hat{e} : \mathbb{G} \times \mathbb{G} \to \mathbb{G}_1$ is an efficiently-computable bilinear map with the following properties:
   - Bilinear: for all $u, v \in \mathbb{G}$ and $a, b \in \mathbb{Z}_p^*$, we have $\hat{e}(u^a, v^b) = \hat{e}(u, v)^{ab}$.
   - Non-degenerate: $\hat{e}(g, g) \neq 1$.

As defined in [9], $\mathbb{G}$ is said to be a bilinear group if the group action in $\mathbb{G}$ can be computed efficiently and if there exists a group $\mathbb{G}_1$ and an efficiently-computable bilinear map $\hat{e}$ as defined above.

The Bilinear Diffie-Hellman (BDH) problem in $\mathbb{G}$ is as follows: given g, g^a, g^b, $g^c \in \mathbb{G}$ as input, output $\hat{e}(g, g)^{abc} \in \mathbb{G}_1$. An algorithm $\mathcal{A}$ has advantage ϵ in solving BDH in $\mathbb{G}$ if:

$$\Pr[\mathcal{A}(g, g^a, g^b, g^c) = \hat{e}(g, g)^{abc}] \geq \epsilon.$$

Similarly, we say that an algorithm $\mathcal{A}$ has advantage ϵ in solving the decision BDH problem in $\mathbb{G}$ if:

$$|\Pr[\mathcal{A}(g, g^a, g^b, g^c, \hat{e}(g, g)^{abc}) = 0] - \Pr[\mathcal{A}(g, g^a, g^b, g^c, T) = 0]| \geq \epsilon.$$

Here the probability is over the random choice of $a, b, c \in \mathbb{Z}_p^*$, the random choice of $T \in \mathbb{G}_1$, and the random bits of $\mathcal{A}$ (the adversary is a nondeterministic algorithm).

Definition 1. *We say that the (decision) (t, ϵ)-BDH assumption holds in $\mathbb{G}$ if no t-time algorithm has advantage at least ϵ in solving the (decision) BDH problem in $\mathbb{G}$.*

As in the general group, the Computational Diffie-Hellman (CDH) problem in $\mathbb{G}$ is as follows: given $g, g^a, g^b \in \mathbb{G}$ as input, output $g^{ab} \in \mathbb{G}$. An algorithm $\mathcal{A}$ has advantage ϵ in solving CDH in $\mathbb{G}$ if:

$$\Pr[\mathcal{A}(g, g^a, g^b) = g^{ab}] \geq \epsilon.$$

Definition 2. *We say that the (t, ϵ)-CDH assumption holds in $\mathbb{G}$ if no t-time algorithm has advantage at least ϵ in solving the CDH problem in $\mathbb{G}$.*

Given a security parameter k, a problem (say, BDH) is believed to be intractable if any adversary has only negligible advantage in reasonable time. We usually define a scheme to be secure if any adversary has only a negligible advantage in the underlying security model. The time parameter is usually be ignored.

Definition 3. *The function $P(k) : \mathbb{Z} \to \mathbb{R}$ is said to be negligible if, for every polynomial $f(k)$, there exists an integer N_f such that $P(k) \leq \frac{1}{f(k)}$ for all $k \geq N_f$.*

3.2   Review of Identity Based Encryption

We briefly review the Boneh-Franklin scheme, which, compared with the original scheme [9], is slightly modified in the definition of the message domain and the encryption/decryption procedures (as we show below). Nonetheless, we still call it the Boneh-Franklin scheme.

1. Setup(k) : Run by the KGC, given a security parameter k, the algorithm generates two cyclic groups $\mathbb{G}$ and $\mathbb{G}_1$ of prime order p, a generator g of $\mathbb{G}$, a bilinear map $\hat{e} : \mathbb{G} \times \mathbb{G} \to \mathbb{G}_1$, a master secret key $\alpha \in \mathbb{Z}_p^*$, and a hash function $\mathsf{H}_1 : \{0,1\}^* \to \mathbb{G}$. The public parameter is $params = (\mathbb{G}, \mathbb{G}_1, p, g, \mathsf{H}_1, \hat{e}, pk)$, where $pk = g^\alpha$ is the public key of the KGC.
   In the original Boneh-Franklin scheme, the plaintext space is $\{0,1\}^n$ where n is an integer and there is an additional hash function $\mathsf{H}_2 : \mathbb{G}_1 \to \{0,1\}^n$.
2. Extract(id) : Run by the KGC, given an identifier id, the algorithm outputs the private key $sk_{id} = pk_{id}^\alpha$, where $pk_{id} = \mathsf{H}_1(id)$.
3. Encrypt(m, id) : Run by the message sender, given a message $m \in \mathbb{G}_1$ and an identifier $id \in \{0,1\}^*$ the algorithm outputs the ciphertext $c = (c_1, c_2)$ where $c_1 = g^r$, $c_2 = m \cdot \hat{e}(pk_{id}, pk)^r$, and $r \in \mathbb{Z}_p^*$.
   In the original Boneh-Franklin scheme, $c_2 = m \oplus \mathsf{H}_2(\hat{e}(pk_{id}, pk)^r)$.
4. Decrypt(c, sk_{id}) : Run by the receiver with identifier id, given a ciphertext $c = (c_1, c_2)$ and sk_{id}, the algorithm outputs the message $m = \frac{c_2}{\hat{e}(sk_{id}, c_1)}$.
   In the original Boneh-Franklin scheme, $m = c_2 \oplus \mathsf{H}_2(\hat{e}(sk_{id}, c_1))$.

The same modifications are also made in [5] and they are essential for us to construct proxy re-encryption schemes. Implied by the security proof of the scheme IBP1 in [5], the Boneh-Franklin scheme is semantically secure against an adaptive chosen plaintext attack (IND-ID-CPA) based on the decision BDH assumption in the random oracle model. The IND-ID-CPA security is defined as follows:

The semantic security against an adaptive chosen ciphertext attack (IND-ID-CCA) is modelled by an IND-ID-CCA game. The game is carried out between a challenger and an adversary, where the challenger simulates the protocol execution and answers the queries from the adversary. Specifically, the game is as follows:

1. Game setup: The challenger takes a security parameter k and runs the Setup algorithm to generate the public system parameter $params$ and the master key mk.
2. Phase 1: The adversary takes $params$ as input and is allowed to issue two type of queries:
   (a) Extract query with any identifier id: The challenger returns the private key sk_{id} corresponding to id.
   (b) Decrypt query with any ciphertext c and any identifier id: The challenger runs Extract to generate the private key sk_{id} corresponding to id, and then returns the value of Decrypt(c, sk_{id}).

Once the adversary decides that Phase 1 is over, it outputs two equal length plaintexts m_0, m_1 and an identifier id^* on which it wishes to be challenged. The only constraint is that id^* has not been the input to any Extract query.

3. Challenge: The challenger picks a random bit $b \in \{0, 1\}$ and returns $c^* =$ Encrypt(m_b, id^*) as the challenge to the adversary.

4. Phase 2: The adversary is allowed to continue issuing the same types of queries as in Phase 1. However, it is not allowed to ask a Extract query with the input id^* and a Decrypt query with the input (c^*, id^*).

5. Guess (game ending): the adversary outputs a guess $b' \in \{0, 1\}$.

Definition 4. *An IBE scheme is said to be semantically secure against an adaptive chosen ciphertext attack (IND-ID-CCA) if any polynomial-time adversary has only a negligible advantage against the challenger in the IND-ID-CCA game, where the adversary's advantage is defined to be* $|\Pr[b' = b] - \frac{1}{2}|$.

Definition 5. *An IBE scheme is said to be semantically secure against an adaptive chosen plaintext attack (IND-ID-CPA) if any polynomial time IND-ID-CCA adversary's advantage is negligible when it makes no Decrypt query in the game.*

Apart from semantic security, we can also define the one-wayness for IBE. Formally, we have the following attack game.

1. Game setup: The challenger takes a security parameter k and runs the Setup algorithm to generate the public system parameter *params* and the master key mk.

2. Extraction: The adversary takes *params* as input and is allowed to issue any number of Extract query with any identifier id: The challenger returns the private key sk_{id} corresponding to id. Once the adversary decides that this phase is over, it outputs an identifier id^* on which it wishes to be challenged. The only constraint is that id^* has not been the input to any Extract query.

3. Challenge: The challenger picks a random message m and returns $c^* =$ Encrypt(m, id^*) as the challenge to the adversary.

4. Guess (game ending): the adversary outputs a guess m'.

Definition 6. *An IBE scheme is said to be one-way if any polynomial time adversary's advantage is negligible in the above game, where the adversary's advantage is defined to be* $\Pr[m' = m]$.

4   A Type-and-Identity-Based Proxy Re-encryption Scheme

In this section we propose a type-and-identity-based proxy re-encryption scheme based on the Boneh-Franklin scheme described in Section 3.2. In our scheme, the delegator and the delegatee are allowed to be from different domains, which nonetheless share some public parameters.

- Suppose that the delegator is registered at KGC_1 in a modified Boneh-Franklin IBE scheme ($\mathsf{Setup}_1, \mathsf{Extract}_1, \mathsf{Encrypt}_1, \mathsf{Decrypt}_1$). Users categorize their messages into different types, say $\{t \in \{0,1\}^*\}$; the IBE algorithms are defined as follows:

  - Setup_1 and $\mathsf{Extract}_1$ are the same as in the Boneh-Franklin scheme, except that Setup_1 outputs an additional hash function $\mathsf{H}_2 : \{0,1\}^* \to \mathbb{Z}_p^*$. The public parameter is $params_1 = (\mathbb{G}, \mathbb{G}_1, p, g, \mathsf{H}_1, \mathsf{H}_2, \hat{e}, pk_1)$, and the master key is $mk_1 = \alpha_1$.
  - $\mathsf{Encrypt}_1(m, t, id)$: Given a message m, a type t, and an identifier id, the algorithm outputs the ciphertext $c = (c_1, c_2, c_3)$ where $r \in_R \mathbb{Z}_p^*$,

$$c_1 = g^r, \quad c_2 = m \cdot \hat{e}(pk_{id}, pk)^{r \cdot \mathsf{H}_2(sk_{id}||t)}, \quad c_3 = t.$$

  - $\mathsf{Decrypt}_1(c, sk_{id})$: Given a ciphertext $c = (c_1, c_2, c_3)$, the algorithm outputs the message

$$m = \frac{c_2}{\hat{e}(sk_{id}, c_1)^{\mathsf{H}_2(sk_{id}||c_3)}}$$

  Without loss of generality, suppose the delegator holds the identity id_i and the corresponding private key sk_{id_i}. Apart from the delegator, another party cannot run the $\mathsf{Encrypt}_1$ algorithm under the delegator's identity id_i since he does not know sk_{id_i}.

- Suppose that the delegatee (with identity id_j) possesses private key sk_{id_j} registered at KGC_2 in the Boneh-Franklin IBE scheme, where the public parameter is $params_2 = (\mathbb{G}, \mathbb{G}_1, p, g, \mathsf{H}_1, \hat{e}, pk_2)$, the master key is $mk_2 = \alpha_2$, and $sk_{id_j} = \mathsf{H}_1(id_j)^{\alpha_2}$. For the ease of comparison, we denote the IBE scheme as ($\mathsf{Setup}_2, \mathsf{Extract}_2, \mathsf{Encrypt}_2, \mathsf{Decrypt}_2$) although these algorithms are identical to those described in Section 3.2.

4.1   The Delegation Process

If the delegator wants to delegate his decryption right for messages with type t to the delegatee, the algorithms of the proxy re-encryption scheme are as follows:

- $\mathsf{Pextract}(id_i, id_j, t, sk_{id_i})$: Run by the delegator, this algorithm takes the delegator's identifier id_i, the delegatee's identifier id_j, the type t, and the delegator's private key sk_{id_i} as input and outputs the proxy key $rk_{id_i \to id_j}$, where $X \in_R \mathbb{G}_1$ and

$$rk_{id_i \to id_j} = (t, sk_{id_i}^{-\mathsf{H}_2(sk_{id_i}||t)} \cdot \mathsf{H}_1(X), \mathsf{Encrypt}_2(X, id_j)).$$

- $\mathsf{Preenc}(c_i, rk_{id_i \to id_j})$: Run by the proxy, this algorithm, takes a ciphertext $c_i = (c_{i1}, c_{i2}, c_{i3})$, where

$$c_{i1} = g^r, \quad c_{i2} = m \cdot \hat{e}(pk_{id_i}, pk)^{r \cdot \mathsf{H}_2(sk_{id_i}||t)}, \quad c_{i3} = t,$$

and the proxy key $rk_{id_i \to id_j}$ as input, and outputs a new ciphertext $c_j = (c_{j1}, c_{j2}, c_{j3})$, where $c_{j1} = c_{i1}$ and

$$c_{j2} = c_{i2} \cdot \hat{e}(c_{i1}, sk_{id_i}^{-\mathsf{H}_2(sk_{id_i}||c_{i3})} \cdot \mathsf{H}_1(X))$$

$$= m \cdot \hat{e}(g^{\alpha_1}, pk_{id_i}^{rH_2(sk_{id_i}||t)}) \cdot \hat{e}(g^r, sk_{id_i}^{-H_2(sk_{id_i}||t)} \cdot H_1(X))$$
$$= m \cdot \hat{e}(g^r, H_1(X)),$$

and $c_{j3} = \mathsf{Encrypt}_2(X, id_j)$.

Given a re-encrypted ciphertext c_j, the delegatee can obtain the plaintext m by computing

$$m' = \frac{c_{j2}}{\hat{e}(c_{j1}, H_1(\mathsf{Decrypt}_2(c_{j3}, sk_{id_j})))}$$
$$= \frac{m \cdot \hat{e}(g^r, H_1(X))}{\hat{e}(g^r, H_1(X))}$$
$$= m.$$

4.2   Threat Model

We assume that both KGC$_1$ and KGC$_2$ are semi-trusted in the following sense: they will behave honestly all the time except that they might be curious about the plaintexts for either the delegator or the delegatee; in addition, they are passive attackers. As mentioned in [14], the key escrow problem of IBE can be avoided by applying some standard techniques (such as secret sharing) to the underlying scheme, hence, we skip any further discussion in this paper. The proxy is assumed to be semi-trusted in the following sense: it will honestly convert the delegator's ciphertexts using the proxy key; however, it might act actively to obtain some information about the plaintexts for the delegator and the delegatee. The delegatee may be curious in the sense that it may try to obtain some information about the plaintexts corresponding to the delegator's ciphertexts which have not been re-encrypted by the proxy.

As a standard practice, we describe an attack game for modeling the semantic security against an adaptive chosen plaintext attack for the delegator (IND-ID-DR-CPA security) for our scheme. The IND-ID-DR-CPA game is carried out between a challenger and an adversary, where the challenger simulates the protocol execution and answers the queries from the adversary. Specifically, the game is as follows.

1. Game setup: The challenger takes a security parameter k as input, runs the Setup$_1$ algorithm to generate the public system parameter $params_1$ and the master key mk_1, and runs the Setup$_2$ algorithm to generate the public system parameter $params_2$ and the master key mk_2.
2. Phase 1: The adversary takes $params_1$ and $params_2$ as input and is allowed to issue the following types of queries:
   (a) Extract$_1$ query with any identifier id: The challenger returns the private key sk corresponding to id.
   (b) Extract$_2$ query with any identifier id': The challenger returns the private key sk' corresponding to id'.
   (c) Pextract query with (id, id', t): The challenger returns the proxy key $rk_{id \rightarrow id'}$ for the type t.

(d) $\text{Preenc}^{\dagger}$ query with (m, t, id, id'): The challenger first computes $c = \text{Encrypt}_1(m, t, id)$ and then returns a new ciphertext c' which is obtained by applying the delegation key $rk_{id \to id'}$ to c, where $rk_{id \to id'}$ is issued for type t.

Once the adversary decides that Phase 1 is over, it outputs two equal length plaintexts m_0, m_1, a type t^*, and an identifier id^*. At the end of Phase 1, there are three constraints here:

(a) id^* has not been the input to any Extract_1 query.
(b) For any id', if (id^*, id', t^*) has been the input to a Pextract query then id' has not been the input to any Extract_2 query.
(c) If there is a $\text{Preenc}^{\dagger}$ query with (m, t, id, id'), then (id, id', t) has not been queried to Pextract.

3. Challenge: The challenger picks a random bit $b \in \{0, 1\}$ and returns $c^* = \text{Encrypt}_1(m_b, t^*, id^*)$ as the challenge to the adversary.
4. Phase 2: The adversary is allowed to continue issuing the same types of queries as in Phase 1. At the end of Phase 2, there are the same constraints as at the end of Phase 1.
5. Guess (game ending): the adversary outputs a guess $b' \in \{0, 1\}$.

At the end of the game, the adversary's advantage is defined to be $|\Pr[b' = b] - \frac{1}{2}|$. Compared with the CPA security formalizations in [5,6], in our case, we also take into account the categorization of messages for the delegator. The $\text{Preenc}^{\dagger}$ query reflects the fact that a curious delegatee has access to the the delegator's plaintexts.

4.3   Security Analysis of Our Scheme

We first briefly prove the IND-ID-DR-CPA security of our scheme and then show some other security properties.

Theorem 1. *For the type-and-identity-based proxy re-encryption scheme described in Section 4.1, any adversary's advantage is negligible.*

Proof sketch. We suppose that the total number of queries issued to H_1 and H_2 is bounded by integer q_1 and q_2, respectively[1]. Suppose an adversary $\mathcal{A}$ has the non-negligible advantage ϵ in the IND-ID-DR-CPA game. The security proof is done through a sequence of games.

Game_0: In this game, $\mathcal{B}$ faithfully answers the oracle queries from $\mathcal{A}$. Specifically, $\mathcal{B}$ simulates the random oracle H_1 as follows: $\mathcal{B}$ maintains a list of vectors, each of them containing a request message, an element of $\mathbb{G}$ (the hash-code for this message), and an element of $\mathbb{Z}_p^*$. After receiving a request message, $\mathcal{B}$ first checks its list to see whether the request message is already in the list. If the check succeeds, $\mathcal{B}$ returns the stored element of $\mathbb{G}$; otherwise, $\mathcal{B}$ returns g^y, where

---

[1] For simplicity of description, it is reasonable to assume that the total number is counted for queries with different inputs.

y a randomly chosen element of $\mathbb{Z}_p^*$, and stores the new vector in the list. $\mathcal{A}'$ simulates the random oracle H_2 as follows: $\mathcal{B}$ maintains a list of vectors, each of them containing a request message and an element of $\mathbb{Z}_p^*$ (the hash-code for this message). After receiving a request message, $\mathcal{B}$ first checks its list to see whether the request message is already in the list. If the check succeeds, $\mathcal{B}$ returns the stored element of $\mathbb{Z}_p^*$; otherwise, $\mathcal{B}$ returns u which is a randomly chosen element of $\mathbb{Z}_p^*$, and stores the new vector in the list.

Let $\delta_0 = \Pr[b' = b]$, as we assumed at the beginning, $|\delta_0 - \frac{1}{2}| = \epsilon$.

Game$_1$: In this game, $\mathcal{B}$ answers the oracle queries from $\mathcal{A}$ as follows:

1. Game setup: $\mathcal{B}$ faithfully simulates the setup phase.
2. Phase 1: $\mathcal{B}$ randomly selects $j \in \{1, 2, \cdots, q_1 + 1\}$. If $j = q_1 + 1$, $\mathcal{B}$ faithfully answers the oracle queries from $\mathcal{A}$. If $1 \leq j \leq q_1$, we assume the j-th input to H_1 is $\tilde{id}$ and $\mathcal{B}$ answers the oracle queries from $\mathcal{A}$ as follows: Answer the queries to Extract$_1$, Extract$_2$, Pextract, and Preenc† faithfully, except that $\mathcal{B}$ aborts as a failure when $\tilde{id}$ is the input to a Extract$_1$ query.
3. Challenge: After receiving (m_0, m_1, t^*, id^*) from the adversary, if one of the following events occurs, $\mathcal{B}$ aborts as a failure.
   (a) id^* has been issued to H_1 as the i-th query and $i \neq j$,
   (b) id^* has not been issued to H_1 and $1 \leq j \leq q_1$.
   Note that, if the adversary does not abort then either $1 \leq j \leq q_1$ and $id^* = \tilde{id}$ is the input to j-th H_1 query or $j = q_1 + 1$ and id^* has not been the input to any H_1 query. $\mathcal{B}$ faithfully returns the challenge.
4. Phase 2: $\mathcal{B}$ answers the oracle queries faithfully.
5. Guess (game ending): the adversary outputs a guess $b' \in \{0, 1\}$.

The probability that $\mathcal{B}$ successfully ends is $\frac{1}{q_1+1}$, i.e. the probability that $\mathcal{B}$ does not abort in its execution is $\frac{1}{q_1+1}$. Let $\delta_1 = \Pr[b' = b]$ when $\mathcal{B}$ successfully ends, in which case $|\delta_1 = \delta_0|$. Let θ_1 be the probability that $\mathcal{B}$ successfully ends and $b' = b$. We have $\theta_1 = \frac{\delta_1}{q_1+1}$.

Game$_2$: In this game, $\mathcal{B}$ simulates the protocol execution and answers the oracle queries from $\mathcal{A}$ in the following way.

1. Game setup: $\mathcal{B}$ faithfully simulates the setup phase. Recall that $pk_1 = g^{\alpha_1}$.
2. Phase 1: $\mathcal{B}$ randomly selects $j \in \{1, 2, \cdots, q_1 + 1\}$. If $j = q_1 + 1$, $\mathcal{B}$ faithfully answers the oracle queries from $\mathcal{A}$. If $1 \leq j \leq q_1$, $\mathcal{B}$ answers j-th query to H_1 with g^β where $\beta \in_R \mathbb{Z}_p^*$, and answers the oracle queries from $\mathcal{A}$ as follows: Suppose the input of the j-th query to H_1 is $\tilde{id}$.
   (a) Answer Extract$_1$ and Extract$_2$ faithfully, except that $\mathcal{B}$ aborts as a failure when $\tilde{id}$ is the input to a Extract$_1$ query.
   (b) Pextract query with (id, id', t): If $id = \tilde{id}$, $\mathcal{B}$ returns the proxy key $rk_{id \to id'}$, where

$$g_{t \sim id'} \in_R \mathbb{G}, \quad X_{t \sim id'} \in_R \mathbb{G}_1, \quad rk_{id \to id'} = (t, g_{t \sim id'}, \mathsf{Encrypt}_2(X_{t \sim id'}, id')).$$

Otherwise, $\mathcal{B}$ answers the query faithfully. If id' has been queried to $\mathsf{Extract}_2$, when $X_{t \sim id'}$ is queried to H_1 then $\mathcal{B}$ returns $g_{t \sim id'} \cdot h_{t \sim id'}^{-1}$ where $h_{t \sim id'} \in_R \mathbb{G}$.

(c) $\mathsf{Preenc}^\dagger$ query with (m, t, id, id'): If $id = \tilde{id}$, $\mathcal{B}$ returns

$$r \in_R \mathbb{Z}_p^*,\ X_{t \sim id'} \in_R \mathbb{G}_1,\ c' = (g^r, \hat{e}(g^r, \mathsf{H}_1(X_{t \sim id'})), \mathsf{Encrypt}_2(X_{t \sim id'}, id')).$$

Otherwise, $\mathcal{B}$ answers the query faithfully.

3. Challenge: After receiving (m_0, m_1, t^*, id^*) from the adversary, if one of the following events occurs, $\mathcal{B}$ aborts as a failure.
   (a) id^* has been issued to H_1 as the i-th query and $i \neq j$,
   (b) id^* has not been issued to H_1 and $1 \leq j \leq q_1$.
   Note that, if the adversary does not abort then either $1 \leq j \leq q_1$ and $id^* = \tilde{id}$ is the input to j-th H_1 query or $j = q_1 + 1$ and id^* has not been the input to any H_1 query. In the latter case, $\mathcal{B}$ sets $\mathsf{H}_1(id^*) = g^\beta$ where $\beta \in_R \mathbb{Z}_p^*$, and returns $c^* = (c_1^*, c_2^*, c_3^*)$ as the challenge to the adversary, where:

$$b \in_R \{0, 1\},\ r \in_R \mathbb{Z}_p^*,\ T \in_R \mathbb{G}_1,\ c_1^* = g^r,\ c_2^* = m_b \cdot T,\ c_3^* = t^*.$$

4. Phase 2: $\mathcal{B}$ answers the oracle queries from $\mathcal{A}$ as in Phase 1.
5. Guess (game ending): the adversary outputs a guess $b' \in \{0, 1\}$.

Let θ_2 be the probability that $\mathcal{B}$ successfully ends and $b' = b$. We have $\theta_2 = \frac{1}{2(q_1+1)}$ since $T \in_R \mathbb{G}_1$. Let E_1 be the event that, for some id' and t, the adversary issues a H_2 query with the input $g^{\alpha_1 \cdot \beta} || t$ or $X_{t \sim id'}$ is issued to H_1 while id' has not been issued to $\mathsf{Extract}_2$. Compared with Game_1, Game_2 differs when E_1 occurs. From the difference lemma [15], we have $|\delta_2 - \delta_1| \leq \epsilon_2$ which is negligible in the random oracle model based on the BDH assumption. Note that $(\mathsf{Setup}_2, \mathsf{Extract}_2, \mathsf{Encrypt}_2, \mathsf{Decrypt}_2)$ is one-way based on the BDH assumption and BDH implies CDH.

From $|\theta_2 - \theta_1| \leq \epsilon_2$ and $\theta_2 = \frac{1}{2(q_1+1)}$, we have $|\frac{1}{2(q_1+1)} - \theta_1| \leq \epsilon_2$. In addition, from $|\delta_0 - \frac{1}{2}| = \epsilon$, $|\delta_1 - \delta_0| \leq \epsilon_1$ and $\theta_1 = \frac{\delta_1}{q_1+1}$, we have $\frac{\epsilon}{q_1+1} \leq \frac{\epsilon_1}{q_1+1} + \epsilon_2$. Because ϵ_i ($1 \leq i \leq 2$) are negligible and ϵ is assumed to be non-negligible, we get a contradiction. As a result, the proposed scheme is IND-ID-DR-CPA secure based on the CDH assumption in the random oracle model, given that $(\mathsf{Setup}_2, \mathsf{Extract}_2, \mathsf{Encrypt}_2, \mathsf{Decrypt}_2)$ is one-way. $\square$

Recall that Ateniese *et al.* describe a number of properties for proxy re-encryption schemes [7]. Our scheme possesses the following properties:

- Uni-directional. In our scheme, the delegation key is generated by the delegator, hence it is clear that the delegation is only from the delegator to the delegatee but not from the delegatee to the delegator.
- Non-Interactive. In our scheme, the delegator creates the re-encryption key by himself, neither the delegatee nor any other party is involved.

– Collusion Safe. In our scheme, the delegatee and the proxy together can recover the private key for the type t if the delegator wants to delegate his decryption right for t to the delegatee. We cannot see any damage here since the delegatee is allowed to see the messages encrypted under this key. Apart from this, the delegatee and the proxy together cannot recover the delegator's private key sk_{id_i}; in particular, they cannot recover any key for other message types from Theorem 1.

5 Fine-Grained PHR Disclosure

As mentioned in [16], a Personal Health Record (PHR) contains all kinds of health-related information about an individual (say, Alice). Firstly, the PHR contains medical data from various medical service providers, for example about surgery, illness, family history, vaccinations, laboratory test results, allergies, drug reactions, etc. Secondly, the PHR may also contain information collected by Alice herself, for example weight change, food statistics, and any other information connected with her health. The PHR is helpful for Alice to obtain health care services and monitor her health status, however, a PHR is sensitive information. Inappropriate disclosure of the PHR may cause an individual serious problems. For example, if Alice has some disease and a prospective employer obtains this, then she might be discriminated in finding a job. Alice needs to protect her PHR. It is worth stressing that PHR data may have different levels of privacy concerns. For example, Alice may not be seriously concerned about disclosing her food statistics to other persons, but she might wish to keep her illness history as a top secret and only disclose it to the appropriate person.

There are some possible solutions to guarantee the privacy of Alice's PHR. In one solution, Alice could make her own access control policies for her PHR, store her PHR in plaintext in a database, and rely on this database to enforce her policies. In this case, Alice needs to trust the database fully. Once the database is corrupted all Alice's PHR will be disclosed. As an alternative, Alice could encrypt her PHR and store the ciphertext in a database, and then decrypt the ciphertext on demand. In this case, Alice only needs to assume that the database will properly store her encrypt data, and even if the database is corrupted Alice's PHR will not be disclosed. The problem with this solution is that Alice needs to be involved in every request and perform the decryption. Yet another solution is to use a traditional proxy re-encryption scheme, in which Alice assigns a re-encryption key to the database which re-encrypts the encrypted PHR into encrypted PHR with the requester's public key. In this case, Alice must assume that the database will properly store her encrypt data and that the database performs the re-encryption. If the database is corrupted, some of Alice's PHR may be disclosed to an illegitimate entity based on the fact that the proxy key can re-encrypt all Alice's encrypted PHR. To avoid this problem, Alice needs to have as many key pairs as there are categories of her PHR data.

Using our type-and-identity-based proxy re-encryption scheme, we can construct a fine-grained PHR disclosure scheme for Alice as follows:

1. Alice categorizes her PHR according to her privacy concerns. For instance, she can set her illness history as type t_1, her food statistics as type t_2, and the necessary PHR data in case of emergency as type t_3.
2. For each type of PHR, Alice finds a proxy and stores each type of her PHR in encrypted form using our scheme, and assigns a re-encryption key to the proxy. In practice, this could be a dynamic process. For example, if Alice wishes to travel to the US, then she can find a proxy there and store her encrypted PHR data for emergency case (type t_3) there. Then if Alice needs emergency help in the US, the PHR data can be disclosed on demand by the proxy.

In this solution Alice only needs one key pair to protect her PHR data and can choose the proxy for each category of her PHR data according to her trust and privacy concerns. Since Alice chooses a different proxy for every type of PHR, even if the proxies for certain types of PHR are corrupted, other types of PHR cannot be illegitimately disclosed from Theorem 1.

6   Conclusion

In this paper we propose a type-and-identity-based proxy re-encryption scheme based on the Boneh-Franklin scheme which has been proved semantically secure against a chosen plaintext attack. Our scheme enables the delegator to provide different re-encryption capabilities to the proxy while using the same key pair. This property is showed to be useful in our PHR disclosure scheme, where an individual can easily implement fine-grained access control policies to his PHR data. For future work, it would be interesting to construct type-and-identity-based proxy re-encryption schemes with chosen ciphertext security and to investigate new applications for this primitive.

References

1. Mambo, M., Okamoto, E.: Proxy Cryptosystems: Delegation of the Power to Decrypt Ciphertexts. IEICE Transactions on Fundamentals of Electronics, Communications and Computer Sciences 80(1), 54–63 (1997)
2. Blaze, M., Bleumer, G., Strauss, M.: Divertible protocols and atomic proxy cryptography. In: Nyberg, K. (ed.) EUROCRYPT 1998. LNCS, vol. 1403, pp. 127–144. Springer, Heidelberg (1998)
3. Ivan, A., Dodis, Y.: Proxy cryptography revisited. In: Proceedings of the Network and Distributed System Security Symposium. The Internet Society (2003)
4. Jakobsson, M.: On quorum controlled asymmetric proxy re-encryption. In: Imai, H., Zheng, Y. (eds.) PKC 1999. LNCS, vol. 1560, pp. 112–121. Springer, Heidelberg (1999)
5. Green, M., Ateniese, G.: Identity-based proxy re-encryption. In: Katz, J., Yung, M. (eds.) ACNS 2007. LNCS, vol. 4521, pp. 288–306. Springer, Heidelberg (2007)
6. Matsuo, T.: Proxy re-encryption systems for identity-based encryption. In: Takagi, T., Okamoto, T., Okamoto, E., Okamoto, T. (eds.) Pairing 2007. LNCS, vol. 4575, pp. 247–267. Springer, Heidelberg (2007)

7. Ateniese, G., Fu, K., Green, M., Hohenberger, S.: Improved proxy re-encryption schemes with applications to secure distributed storage. ACM Transactions on Information and System Security (TISSEC) 9(1), 1–30 (2006)

8. Wang, L., Cao, Z., Okamoto, T., Miao, Y., Okamoto, E.: Authorization-Limited Transformation-Free Proxy Cryptosystems and Their Security Analyses*. IEICE Transactions on Fundamentals of Electronics, Communications and Computer Sciences (1), 106–114 (2006)

9. Boneh, D., Franklin, M.K.: Identity-based encryption from the weil pairing. In: Kilian, J. (ed.) CRYPTO 2001. LNCS, vol. 2139, pp. 213–229. Springer, Heidelberg (2001)

10. The US Department of Health and Human Services. Summary of the HIPAA Privacy Rule (2003)

11. ElGamal, T.: A public key cryptosystem and a signature scheme based on discrete logarithms. In: Blakely, G.R., Chaum, D. (eds.) CRYPTO 1984. LNCS, vol. 196, pp. 10–18. Springer, Heidelberg (1985)

12. Shamir, A.: Identity-based cryptosystems and signature schemes. In: Blakely, G.R., Chaum, D. (eds.) CRYPTO 1984. LNCS, vol. 196, pp. 47–53. Springer, Heidelberg (1985)

13. Boneh, D., Boyen, X.: Efficient selective-id secure identity-based encryption without random oracles. In: Cachin, C., Camenisch, J.L. (eds.) EUROCRYPT 2004. LNCS, vol. 3027, pp. 223–238. Springer, Heidelberg (2004)

14. Chen, L.: An interpretation of identity-based cryptography. In: Aldini, A., Gorrieri, R. (eds.) FOSAD 2007. LNCS, vol. 4677, pp. 183–208. Springer, Heidelberg (2007)

15. Shoup, V.: Sequences of games: a tool for taming complexity in security proofs (2006), http://shoup.net/papers/

16. Tang, P.C., Ash, J.S., Bates, D.W., Overhage, J.M., Sands, D.Z.: Personal Health Records: Definitions, Benefits, and Strategies for Overcoming Barriers to Adoption. Journal of the American Medical Informatics Association 13(2), 121–126 (2006)

A Methodology for Bridging between RBAC and an Arbitrary Application Program

Candy Wai-Yue Shum, Sylvia L. Osborn, and He Wang

Dept. of Computer Science, The University of Western Ontario,
London, Ontario, Canada
{wcshum,sylvia,hewang}@csd.uwo.ca

Abstract. Role-Based Access Control (RBAC) models have been available since the early 1990s. However, there is no well-understood methodology for using RBAC with an arbitrary application program. We highlight tradeoffs between the ANSI RBAC model and the Role Graph Model, and also enumerate different versions of each. We then discuss alternatives to bridging between an RBAC model and an ad hoc program. An example of the application of one of the alternatives is given.

1   Introduction

A sound access control system permits an organization to protect, filter and prevent essential and important data from being leaked to unauthorized users. Role Based Access Control (RBAC) is a form of access control that regulates system access by assigning permissions to "roles" rather than individual users within an enterprise [1]. RBAC models were introduced in the 1990s [2,3,4]. There are two distinct forms of RBAC: the ANSI standard model [1] and the Role Graph Model (RGM) [3]. These two RBAC models offer different semantics and different features, which will be discussed in some detail in Section 2.

RBAC has been included in database packages such as Oracle [5], Sybase, and Informix, operating systems such as Solaris [6], Unix systems [7], and Windows 2000 [8], and in enterprise security management systems such as Tivoli [9] and BMC Enterprise Security Station [10]. However, these systems usually have limited versions of RBAC, and one is confined to use the RBAC properties that the system has chosen to include. For software developers implementing arbitrary programs, one choice would be to include an RBAC model within their application. This would add the development of an RBAC model to the effort of implementing the application. What we describe in this paper are several ways to implement or reuse an RBAC tool separately from the application program, and then bridge them at run time so that the application program can use the access control model described by the RBAC system.

There are several reasons why the methodology we are advocating in this paper might be required. The application being contemplated may not be a database application, and using a DB package just to have the RBAC facilities is not the best solution. The company may not be in a position to acquire

W. Jonker and M. Petković (Eds.): SDM 2008, LNCS 5159, pp. 199–208, 2008.

a system like Tivoli, for the cost or perhaps because the company is not big enough to require such a platform. The version of RBAC available in the DB package or through the security management system may not be what is best for the application. No matter what methodology is chosen, the RBAC design should be separated from the software design. The roles in an RBAC design might be used for several applications. Also, the design of the access control model through an RBAC system should be separated from the concerns of the programmer implementing a piece of application software. Populating the roles with users can change over time, whereas the roles might change less frequently.

The purpose of this paper is to help software developers answer two questions: "What kind of RBAC system should I build?" and "How do I use RBAC within an arbitrary software application?" In Section 2 we discuss the ANSI RBAC model and the Role Graph Model, and highlight their differences. Section 3 briefly discusses different RBAC frameworks that can result by combining various components of RBAC models. Section 4 gives a command interface which would be used by an arbitrary software application to check authorizations at runtime, and goes on to discuss alternative architectures for bridging between the RBAC information and the software at run time. A proof of concept application is briefly described. Section 5 contains further discussion and conclusions.

2   RBAC Variations

All RBAC models contain the same basic elements: users, roles and permissions, and the user-role assignment and role-permission assignment relations. They differ in how users are viewed, how much detail is included in the model of permissions, and on how the role hierarchy operations change the hierarchy. In this section we briefly describe the variations of RBAC described in the ANSI RBAC Standard, the components of the RGM, and then compare them.

2.1   ANSI RBAC

The ANSI RBAC Model defines the basic RBAC elements and their relationships. It also discusses four major model variations within RBAC: Core RBAC, Hierarchical RBAC, Static Separation of Duty (SOD) Relations, and Dynamic Separation of Duty Relations. The Core RBAC model defines a minimum collection of RBAC elements, element sets and relations among them. Permissions are assigned to roles by a permission-role assignment relation, PA, and users are assigned to roles by a user-role assignment relation, UA. Additionally, this model includes the concept of sessions which map users to their active roles. Hierarchical RBAC consists of role hierarchies that define inheritance relationships between roles. There are two types of hierarchies: the General Role Hierarchy, and the Limited Role Hierarchy. Limited Role Hierarchies restrict the role hierarchy to a straight line shape. We will assume General Role Hierarchies in what follows. Static Separation of Duty describes user-role assignment constraints pertaining to the user-role assignment relation. Dynamic Separation of Duty describes constraints pertaining to the active roles in a session. The functional specifications in the ANSI Standard use Z-notation to describe the behaviour, pre-conditions and post-conditions of each function. An example for the UserPermissions function within Hierarchical RBAC is:

$UserPermissions(user : NAME, result : 2^{PRMS}) \lhd$
   $user \in USERS;$
   $result = \{r, q : ROLES; \ op : OPS; \ obj : OBJS; \ (op, obj) \in PRMS \mid$
      $(user \mapsto q) \in UA \wedge (q \geq r) \wedge ((op, obj) \mapsto r) \in PA \bullet (op, obj)\} \rhd$

This function retrieves the set of permissions for a given user. The input user is denoted by the name of the user, and the returned set is a set of permissions for this user. The above specifies that this method is valid if the user exists in the system. A permission is added to the result if it is assigned to a role that is assigned to the user, or a role junior to a role assigned to the user.

Core RBAC must always be present. The other three options (role hierarchies, static SOD and dynamic SOD) can be present in all possible combinations, giving 8 different options for sets of RBAC components in an implemented system.

2.2   The Role Graph Model

The RGM is described on three planes: users/groups are on one plane, represented by a group graph; the role hierarchy, or role graph, on a second plane; and permissions on a third plane. The group graph consists of groups, which represent sets of users. Having groups facilitates user-role assignment, as a group can be assigned to a role in one operation. Group membership can be based on some characteristics of the user; for example, in an internet application, as users log in, some credentials they present might automatically place them in a group (according to credit risk or age, for example). Alternatively, groups can be defined to suit the environment; for example, a group representing an Admissions Committee for a university can be made up of both staff and students. The group membership can be altered in the group graph. The UA relation tells us that this group, (and therefore everyone in the group) is assigned to the Admission role. Permissions, in turn, can be assigned to the Admissions role to reflect the operations on relevant data required by this role. In a small setting, each user can be represented as a group of cardinality one. However, if there are thousands of users, then only those users who have individual role assignments should be represented, and other users would appear only in the membership list of a group. A group, then, consists of a unique group name and a unique membership list. There is an edge in the group graph from group g_1 to group g_2 if the member list of $g_1 \subset$ the member list of g_2. Since the member lists are unique, the group graph is acyclic.

In the RGM, the role plane contains the role graph whose nodes are the roles and whose directed edges represent the is-junior relation. Roles consist of a unique name and set of permissions, *rpset*. As well, there is a distinguished role, MaxRole, whose permission set contains all the permissions of all the roles (MaxRole need not be assigned to a user). Permissions sets must be distinct. The permissions directly assigned to a role in PA are called the *direct privileges*[1]; the *effective privileges* of a role, r, consist of the union of the direct privileges and the effective privileges of all the roles junior to r. Effective privileges can also be thought of as derived privileges. The role graph model was initially given together with a number of algorithms to add/delete a role, add/delete an edge, add/delete a privilege [11]. All of these algorithms restore what are called the *Role Graph Properties:*

RGP1: There is a single MaxRole
RGP2: The Role Graph is acyclic
RGP3: For any two roles r_i and r_j, if $r_i.rpset \subset r_j.rpset$, then there must be a path from r_i to r_j.

The permissions plane of the RGM is a model derived from some work for object-oriented databases (OODB) by Rabitti et al. [12]. Permissions are made up of an object, access mode pair. A permission like (printer, use) can have an object part which is indivisible. However, some objects, like an XML document or an object in an OODB, can have a rich structure. Access modes like update might imply read and write. Having a permission on a deeply structured object gives rise to implied permissions on its parts; e.g. the read permission on the root of an XML document implies that the read permission propagates to all the parts of the document. Such propagation is not always appropriate, in which case we "turn it off" by specifying constraints which stop the propagation. Similarly, implications can arise from the access mode; an example of this would be where a user having an update permission on an object means that this user can also read and write this object. Various data structures need to be in place to guide the propagation, representing implications due to object structure and among access modes. Not all access modes are appropriate for all objects (one would not update a printer for example), so there is information about what access modes are valid on what type of object. We assume that if a permission is assigned to a role, all implied permissions are also assigned at the same time [13].

2.3   Comparison of ANSI and Role Graph Models

There are some obvious differences between the ANSI model and the RGM. The ANSI model has only users, no groups. The ANSI model assumes simple permissions, whereas the RGM can have a rich model for permissions. There are major differences in the role hierarchy/role graph which are more subtle. Both models enforce acyclicity in the role hierarchy. In the ANSI model, an edge (relationship) in the role hierarchy, $r_i \rightarrow r_j$, implies inheritance of the assigned permissions from r_i to r_j, or explicitly:

$$r_i \rightarrow r_j \Rightarrow \text{authorized permissions}(r_i) \subseteq \text{authorized permissions}(r_j) \quad (1)$$

In the ANSI model, one can add a role, r_1, with no permissions, and then make another role, r_2, its junior, using AddInheritance. This creates two roles with the

---

[1] In the RGM, the word "privilege" is used; it is a synonym for permission.

same permission sets, albeit different names. This is not allowed in the RGM. In the RGM, by property RGP3, we add an edge, after an operation on the role graph, from r_i to r_j, if the operation has left the permissions of r_i a proper subset of the permissions of r_j. (We remove redundant edges for display of the graph, changing this property to "there must be a path from r_i to r_j.")

$$\forall r_i, r_j, r_i.rpset \subset r_j.rpset \Rightarrow \text{there must be an edge from } r_i \text{ to } r_j \quad (2)$$

We feel that adding such edges provides valuable feedback to the designer of the role graph, in that it shows that, since r_i's permissions are a subset of r_j's, any user assigned to r_j *can* perform all of r_i's permissions. Note that since edges in the role graph also indicate inheritance, equation 2 can be rewritten as:

$$\forall r_i, r_j, r_i.rpset \subset r_j.rpset \Leftrightarrow r_i \rightarrow r_j \quad (3)$$

A longer discussion of these differences with an example can be found in [14]. We can describe the ANSI model as *edges take precedence*, and the RGM as *permissions take precedence*. Both approaches have merit. In the ANSI model, the role hierarchy can be designed before any permissions are assigned to the roles. The designer thus has a clear idea of how the inheritance of permissions should take place and can reflect this understanding in the design. In the RGM, if a role's permissions become a subset of another role's as a result of an operation on the role graph, the role graph is altered to give feedback to the designer. In the ANSI model, then, only the explicit operations involving hierarchy relationships can alter the role hierarchy. In the RGM, all operations can potentially alter the role graph. Another difference involves the uniqueness of permission sets. In the RGM, roles always have distinct effective privilege sets; if two roles which would be created have identical permission sets, the algorithms would be obliged to create a cycle. In the ANSI model, it is possible for two roles to have identical permission sets (they will have distinct names).

3   RBAC Frameworks

In this section we discuss different frameworks for managing RBAC. Here we are assuming that security administrators have an RBAC tool or might be contemplating building one. As we saw in the previous section, there are different RBAC models with different semantics. The ANSI model was presented in a formal way with Z-notation in [1]. We have taken the same notation and specified various forms of the RGM formally as well [15].

Whatever model chosen, there are 5 components: Users, UA, Roles, PA and Permissions. For each of these, there are operations to modify the set, and reporting functions to retrieve information about it. For the ANSI model, Users and Permissions are both simple sets whose members have just a name but no structure. The UA, Roles and PA sets follow the specifications given in [1], which in turn have two variations, one for Core RBAC and one for Hierarchical RBAC.

For the RGM, we can have a simple Users set or one with all the properties of the Group Graph. The Roles set only comes in one version, that given by the role graph properties in Section 2. The Permissions set also can be modeled as a simple set or as a richer model with implications involving complex data and access modes. This gives 4 combinations (simple users set, role graph, simple permissions; group graph, role graph, simple permissions; simple users set, role graph, rich permissions model; and group graph, role graph, rich permissions model). The designer can choose the most appropriate combination, depending on the requirements for the application, in terms of number of users, roles and permissions. For each, there are a few operations which have to be changed to allow for the combinations of features.

With the properties clearly outlined with a formal notation, it is hoped that the implementation of the required RBAC features is straightforward. Currently, we have a prototype with the group and permissions planes fully developed. The function to retrieve the set of permissions for a user, in a system with a simple user set and simple permissions set, but having the role graph rather than the ANSI hierarchical RBAC, is given by the following Z-notation:

$$getPermissionsFromUser(user : NAME; \; result : 2^{PRMS}) \lhd$$
$$\quad user \in USERS;$$
$$\quad roles = \{s : ROLES \mid (user \mapsto s) \in UA \bullet s\}$$
$$\quad result = [\forall (r_i) \in roles, getEffectivePrivilegesFromRole(r_j)] \rhd$$

For getPermissionsFromUser to be valid, the user name given must be in the USERS set. The answer is found by taking all the roles to which the user is assigned according to UA, (the effective privilege sets of these roles contain all privileges assigned to juniors) returning the effective privileges of these roles.

4   Run Time Model

The previous sections have focused on how to design multiple frameworks to create an RBAC system that best fits an industry setting. Once an RBAC system has been developed, one then needs to evaluate how, at run time, an arbitrary software application can actually use the RBAC system for access control. We first describe the run-time interface to RBAC information, then look at some alternative software architectures for gluing a software application to an RBAC model. Finally we describe a sample implementation.

4.1   Run Time Interface

No matter which RBAC version used, the run time design can be standardized as all the alternatives need the same functionality to access the RBAC information. Once the RBAC system has been designed, an application program needs to be able to verify user-privilege combinations in a read-only fashion. The following design can be applied no matter which version of RBAC was used to construct the information. The commands in the interface are listed in Figure 1.

The RBAC design frameworks in Section 3 should contain information retrieval functions for all planes. Therefore, if the same programming team has

Command	Action
Users	
getAllUsersFromSystem	retrieves the list of users from the RBAC system
findUser	checks whether the user is listed in the RBAC system
getRolesFromUser	retrieves the authorized roles from a specific user
getPrivilegesFromUser	retrieves the set of privileges that a specific user has
Roles	
getAllRolesFromSystem	retrieves the list of roles within the RBAC system
findRole	checks if the Role exists in the RBAC system
getUsersfromRole	retrieves the list of users assigned to this role
getPrivilegesFromRole	retrieves the set of privileges from a specific role
Privileges	
getAllPrivilegesFromSystem	retrieves all privileges available from the RBAC system
findPrivilege	checks if a specific privilege exists in the RBAC system
getUsersFromPrivilege	retrieves all users assigned to this privilege
getRolesFromPrivilege	retrieves all roles assigned with this privilege
System	
loadAccessModel	initializes the RBAC system for the application

Fig. 1. Commands in the Run Time Interface

implemented an RBAC system, the run time model interface can be implemented easily by reusing some code. This run-time interface can be used with any of the alternative approaches given below for combining RBAC with applications.

4.2 Alternative Architectures

There are many approaches to bridging the RBAC model and the application domain to actually use RBAC in the software domain. Some alternatives are:

Alternative 1: Embed the whole RBAC system into the application: This alternative is undesirable for several reasons. The security policy is not universally accessible but is buried in one of possibly many applications. If there are changes to the security policy, the application will have to be recompiled. Programmers would have to know about the authorization policy of the organization in order to modify RBAC; this data might be confidential, and is better handled by security or Human Resources personnel. Additionally, if the program is being compromised, confidential information about the organization will be exposed.

Alternative 2: Package the RBAC model and the access data as an independent library, and import that library into the actual application. This architecture is shown in Figure 2(a). This alternative is slightly better than the first; however, the same problem can still occur if the library needs to be updated or a role needs to be modified: the library has to be recompiled and reattached to the application every time, and inappropriate personnel (e.g. programmers) may be required to obtain confidential information in order to maintain and update the program. The programmer would have to implement the run-time interface in Figure 1, calling the library routines to perform the functions.

Alternative 3: The RBAC system and the software application are two independent entities sharing the same data, shown in Figure 2(b). This approach has great advantages over the first two because new security policies can be deployed within the RBAC system without impacting the application. Only authorized personnel have the ability to alter access control information. The location of the access control data must be secure from tampering, in a location where both the RBAC system and the applications can access it. A thin access control module will have to be incorporated into the software application to interpret the access control data properly. If the RBAC system is written by the same team, the required code can be resued from the RBAC system.

Alternative 4: The final approach differs only slightly from the third approach. The RBAC system and the software application are two independent entities. A thin client, shown in Figure 2(c), consisting of the run time model as a library, can be created and attached to the software application. In this design, once a thin client is built, any software applications that require access control can use the library immediately without creation of additional code. As above, one has to ensure that the access data is stored securely.

For the above four alternatives, one can observe that each is a progression to decouple the run time module from the software application. Each case is legitimate depending on the development criteria and the project requirements.

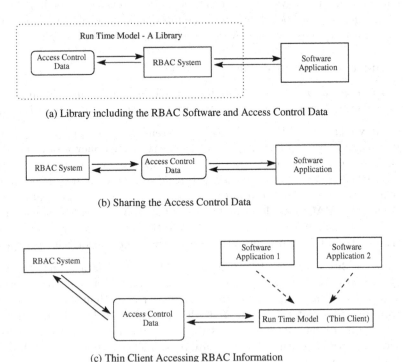

(a) Library including the RBAC Software and Access Control Data

(b) Sharing the Access Control Data

(c) Thin Client Accessing RBAC Information

Fig. 2. Alternatives 2, 3 and 4

The purpose for these run time model designs is to ensure that any software application that requires access control can easily bridge with any existing RBAC system, without tightly coupling the RBAC model into the software application.

4.3   Proof of Concept

We currently have an RBAC development tool, written in Java, which implements the full group graph, role graph and permissions plane functionalities. It writes the RBAC design to disk in an XML format. Embedded within our RBAC tool are methods for loading and verifying the XML.

The first author of this paper works for the Division of Information Technology Serviced (ITS) at the University of Western Ontario. She previously implemented a stand-alone Call Tracker System (in Java) to track calls to ITS and track other projects its employees are involved in. Initially, CT contained all privilege information internally. Users and their teams were stored in a Microsoft SQL Server 2000 database. CT has 92 Java classes, and in total over 37,000 lines of code.

The experiment was to replace the ad-hoc access control initially built into CT with RBAC-based access control. The Role Graph and Permissions plane were designed and input into our RBAC tool; there were 8 roles, and 7 permissions which, after propagation, expanded to 18. Groups were not used. The solution followed the architecture in Alternative 3 above. Because of the availability of the RBAC tool and its code, the commands in the run time interface, given in Figure 1, were implemented very quickly. Then the places in the CT application where access control decisions were made were modified.

5   Discussion and Conclusions

We have discussed details of, and compared two RBAC models which can be used by system developers to describe the access control required in application software. We have also presented different alternatives for using RBAC-specified access control information together with an arbitrary software application. One of these alternatives has been implemented in an actual application.

Having extracted the relevant code from our RBAC tool as part of the proof of concept discussed in Section 4, it would be a small step to package this up as a Java version of the thin client for Alternative 4. We also realize that, with the XML schema that the RBAC tool uses, programmers would have a less attractive, 5th alternative: they could design the RBAC model on paper, and put the results by hand into an XML document to be read by the thin client and thus used with an arbitrary piece of software.

RBAC systems often are enhanced by constraints. Examples are static separation of duty (SSOD), dynamic separation of duty (DSOD) and other constraints dealing with things like location (a user can only activate a role if he/she is in a certain building) or time. SSOD would be handled by role design while the UA is being constructed. Constraints dealing with run time environmental data or currently activated roles need to be evaluated at run time. Additional information needs to be communicated to the access control module, to give data like the location of the user or time of day of the requested access. This would require additional or enhanced commands in the runtime interface shown in Figure 1 to accept additional parameters. However, the alternative architectures discussed in Section 4 are all still valid and would not require any change once the enhanced command set is defined.

We have answered the two questions posed in the introduction. In answer to the question "What kind of RBAC system should I build?", we have described several RBAC models and combinations of features that might be appropriate in different environments, and highlighted their differences. In answer to the second question, "How do I use RBAC within an arbitrary software application?", we have given several alternatives with increasing amounts of separation between the RBAC design system and the application software.

References

1. ANSI: American national standard for information technology - role based access control. In: ANSI INCITS 359–2004. ANSI (2004)
2. Ferraiolo, D., Kuhn, D.R.: Role based access control. In: 15th National Computer security Conference, NIST/NSA (1992)
3. Nyanchama, M., Osborn, S.: Access rights administration in role-based security systems. In: Database Security, vol. VIII, pp. 37–56. North-Holland, Amsterdam (1994)
4. Sandhu, R.S., Coyne, E.J., Feinstein, H.L., Youman, C.E.: Role-based access control models. IEEE Computer 29(2), 38–47 (1996)
5. Loney, K.: Oracle Database 10g: The Complete Reference, 1st edn. McGraw-Hill, Osborne Media (2004)
6. Winsor, J.: Solaris Advanced System Administrators Guide. SunSoft Press, Ziff-Davis Press (1993)
7. Faden, G.: RBAC in unix administration. In: RBAC 1999: Proceedings of the fourth ACM workshop on Role-based access control, pp. 95–101. ACM, New York (1999)
8. Khurana, H., Gavrila, S., Bobba, R., Koleva, R., Sonalker, A., Dinu, E., Gligor, V., Baras, J.: Integrated security services for dynamic coalitions. In: DARPA Information Survivability Conference and Exposition (DISCEX 2003), April 2003, vol. 2, pp. 38–40 (2003)
9. IBM Corporation: Enterprise Security Architecture using IBM Tivoli Security Solutions (2002)
10. BMC Software Inc.: Enterprise Security Station User Guide (Windows GUI) (2002)
11. Nyanchama, M., Osborn, S.: The role graph model and conflict of interest. ACM Transactions on Information and Systems Security 2(1), 3–33 (1999)
12. Rabitti, F., Bertino, E., Kim, W., Woelk, D.: A model of authorization for next-generation database systems. ACM Trans. Database Syst. 16(1), 88–131 (1991)
13. Ionita, C., Osborn, S.: Privilege administration for the role graph model. In: Gudes, Shenoi (eds.) Database & Application Security, pp. 15–25. Kluwer, Dordrecht (2002)
14. Osborn, S.L.: Role-based access control. In: Petkovic, M., Jonker, W. (eds.) Security, Privacy and Trust in Modern Data Management, pp. 55–70. Springer, Heidelberg (2007)
15. Shum, C.W.Y.: Integrating role based access control with application software. Master's thesis, Dept. of Comp. Sci., University of Western Ontario (2008)

An Anonymity Model Achievable Via Microaggregation*

Josep Domingo-Ferrer, Francesc Sebé, and Agusti Solanas

Universitat Rovira i Virgili, UNESCO Chair in Data Privacy, Dept. of Computer
Engineering and Mathematics, Av. Països Catalans 26, E-43007 Tarragona, Catalonia
{josep.domingo,francesc.sebe,agusti.solanas}@urv.cat

Abstract. k-Anonymity is a privacy model requiring that all combinations of key attributes in a database be repeated at least for k records. It has been shown that k-anonymity alone does not always ensure privacy. A number of sophistications of k-anonymity have been proposed, like p-sensitive k-anonymity, l-diversity and t-closeness. We identify some shortcomings of those models and propose a new model called (k, p, q, r)-anonymity. Also, we propose a computational procedure to achieve this new model that relies on microaggregation.

Keywords: Microaggregation, statistical databases, privacy, microdata protection, statistical disclosure control.

1 Introduction

Database privacy can be described in terms of three dimensions, as suggested in [6]: respondent privacy, data owner privacy and user privacy. Respondent privacy is about ensuring the respondents to which the database records correspond that no re-identification is possible. The need for data owner privacy arises in a context with several organizations engaged in collaborative computation and consists of each organization keeping private the database it owns. User privacy refers to the privacy of the queries submitted by users to a queryable database or search engine.

Statistical disclosure control (SDC, [4, 18]) was born in the statistical community as a discipline to achieve respondent privacy. Privacy-preserving data mining (PPDM) appeared simultaneously in the database community [1] and the cryptographic community [11] with the aim of offering owner privacy: several database owners wish to compute queries across their databases in a way that only the results of the queries are revealed to each other, not the contents of each other's databases. Finally, private information retrieval (PIR, [3]) originated in

---

* The authors are with the UNESCO Chair in Data Privacy, but the views expressed in this paper are those of the authors and do not commit UNESCO. This work was partly supported by the Spanish Government through projects TSI2007-65406-C03-01 "E-AEGIS" and CONSOLIDER INGENIO 2010 CSD2007-00004 "ARES" and by the Government of Catalonia under grant 2005 SGR 00446.

W. Jonker and M. Petković (Eds.): SDM 2008, LNCS 5159, pp. 209–218, 2008.

the cryptographic community as an attempt to guarantee privacy for user queries to databases. Although the technologies to deal with the above three privacy dimensions have evolved in a fairly independent way within research communities with surprisingly little interaction, it turns out that some developments are useful for more than one privacy dimension, even if all three dimensions are independent (see [6]). Such is the case for k-anonymity and its enhancements. Thus, improving k-anonymity-related privacy models both conceptually and computationally is an especially relevant objective that will be pursued in this paper. Section 2 is a critical review of k-anonymity and its enhancements. Section 3 presents the (k, p, q, r)-anonymity model. A microaggregation-based heuristic to achieve (k, p, q, r)-anonymity is described in Section 4. Empirical results are reported in Section 5. Finally, Section 6 lists some conclusions and future research issues.

2   A Critical Review of k-anonymity and Its Enhancements

We review in this section the definition and the limitations of the following privacy models: k-anonymity, p-sensitive k-anonymity, l-diversity, (α, k)-anonymity and t-closeness.

2.1 k-anonymity

k-Anonymity is an interesting approach suggested by Samarati and Sweeney [14] to deal with the tension between information loss and disclosure risk. It can also be understood as a kind of indistinguishability, as suggested in [22]. To recall the definition of k-anonymity, we need to enumerate the various (non-disjoint) types of attributes that can appear in a microdata set X:

- *Identifiers.* These are attributes that *unambiguously* identify the respondent.
- *Key attributes.* Borrowing the definition from [5,15], key attributes are those in X that, in combination, can be linked with external information to re-identify (some of) the respondents to whom (some of) the records in X refer.
- *Confidential attributes.* These are attributes which contain sensitive information on the respondent.

Definition 1 (k-Anonymity). *A protected data set is said to satisfy k-anonymity for $k > 1$ if, for each combination of key attributes, at least k records exist in the data set sharing that combination.*

If, for a given k, k-anonymity is assumed to be enough protection for respondents, one can concentrate on minimizing information loss with the only constraint that k-anonymity should be satisfied.

k-Anonymity is able to prevent identity disclosure, *i.e.* a record in the k-anonymized data set will be correctly mapped back to the corresponding record in the original data set with a probability at most $1/k$. However, in general, it may fail to protect against attribute disclosure.

2.2 p-Sensitive k-Anonymity

In [17], an evolution of k-anonymity called p-sensitive k-anonymity was presented. Its purpose is to protect against attribute disclosure by requiring that there be at least p different values for each confidential attribute within the records sharing a combination of key attributes. The formal definition is as follows.

Definition 2 (p-Sensitive k-anonymity). *A data set is said to satisfy p-sensitive k-anonymity for $k > 1$ and $p \leq k$ if it satisfies k-anonymity and, for each group of tuples with the same combination of key attribute values that exists in the data set, the number of distinct values for each confidential attribute is at least p within the same group.*

An attacker trying to obtain the confidential value for a given record that has been linked to the p-sensitive k-anonymous data set will not be able to determine which of the p different values inside the group is the corresponding one. p-Sensitive k-anonymity may cause a huge data utility loss in some data sets. In some cases, p-Sensitive k-anonymity is insufficient to prevent attribute disclosure due to the skewness attack and the similarity attack.

2.3 l-Diversity

Like p-sensitive k-anonymity, l-diversity [12] attempts to solve the attribute disclosure problem that can happen with k-anonymity.

Definition 3 (l-Diversity). *A data set is said to satisfy l-diversity if, for each group of records sharing a combination of key attributes, there are at least l "well-represented" values for each confidential attribute.*

According to [12] "well-represented" can be defined in several ways:

1. *Distinct l-diversity.* There must be at least l distinct values for the confidential attribute in each group of records sharing a combination of key attributes.
2. *Entropy l-diversity.* The entropy of a group G for a particular confidential attribute with domain C can be defined as

$$H(G) = - \sum_{c \in C} p(G, c) \log p(G, c)$$

   in which $p(G, c)$ is the fraction of records in G which have value c for the sensitive attribute. A data set is said to satisfy entropy l-diversity if for each group G, $H(G) \geq \log l$.
3. *Recursive (c, l)-diversity.* This model makes sure that the most frequent values do not appear too frequently and the least frequent values do not appear too rarely. Let m be the number of values of the confidential attribute in a group G and r_i, for $1 \leq i \leq m$, be the number of times that the i-th most frequent value appears in G. Then G is said to satisfy recursive (c, l)-diversity if $r_1 < c(r_l + r_{l+1} + \cdots + r_m)$. A data set is said to satisfy recursive (c, l)-diversity if all of its groups satisfy recursive (c, l)-diversity.

Distinct l-diversity may be vulnerable to skewness and similarity attacks in the same way p-sensitive k-anonymity is. Regarding entropy l-diversity and (c, l)-diversity, both models aim at preventing skewness attacks, but the risk of similarity attacks still remains. All three variants may introduce high information loss in some cases.

2.4 (α, k)-Anonymity

(α, k)-Anonymity was proposed in [19] as follows:

Definition 4 ((α, k)-Anonymity). *A data set is said to satisfy (α, k)-anonymity if it is k-anonymous and, for each group of records sharing a combination of key attributes, the proportion of each sensitive value is at most α, where $\alpha \in [0, 1]$ is a user parameter.*

For $\alpha = 1/k$, this model becomes k-sensitive k-anonymity. This model prevents attribute disclosure (an upper-bound of α on the probability of a correct attribute value estimation is provided) but skewness and similarity attacks are still possible. High information loss may also be incurred during the anonymization procedure.

2.5 (k, e)-Anonymity

Models discussed in this section so far are designed for categorical confidential attributes. In [23], the following model is proposed for numerical attributes:

Definition 5 ((k, e)-Anonymity). *A data set D is said to satisfy (k, e)-anonymity if, given D and any public database P, any association cover that an attacker can derive satisfies: (i) the size of the association cover is no less than k; (ii) the range of the confidential attribute values in the association cover is no less than e.*

Clearly, what is called association cover in Definition 5 can be assimilated to a group of records sharing a combination of key attribute values.

(k, e)-Anonymity tries to overcome the similarity attack described above by requiring a minimum range in the values of the confidential attribute. Besides potentially inflicting a substantial information loss to the data, this model does not guard against skewness attacks.

2.6 t-Closeness

In [10], a new privacy model called t-closeness is defined as follows.

Definition 6 (t-Closeness). *A data set is said to satisfy t-closeness if, for each group of records sharing a combination of key attributes, the distance between the distribution of the confidential attribute in the group and its distribution in the whole data set is no more than a threshold t.*

t-Closeness solves the attribute disclosure vulnerabilities inherent to previous models (i.e. skewness attack and similarity attack). However, some criticisms can be made to t-closeness:

- No computational procedure to enforce t-closeness is given.
- If such a procedure were available, it would greatly damage the utility of data. The only way to decrease the damage is to increase the threshold t, that is, to relax t-closeness.

2.7 Other Models

The models discussed so far share with k-anonymity the lack of assumptions on the intruder's capabilities or the public databases available to the intruder. If such assumptions are made, a number of other evolutions of k-anonymity can still be found in the recent literature: m-confidentiality [20], personalized privacy preservation [21] and (c, k)-safety [13]. These evolutions are mentioned for completeness, but our focus will be to enhance the k-anonymity-like models recalled in the previous sections, which do not make assumptions about the intruder.

3 The (k, p, q, r)-Anonymity Model

From the lessons learned on the limitations of the models described in Section 2, we can define a new model as follows:

Definition 7 $((k, p, q, r)$**-Anonymity**)**.** *A data set is said to satisfy (k, p, q, r)-anonymity if it is k-anonymous and satisfies that:*

- *It is p-sensitive only for those groups where values of confidential attributes appear whose relative frequency is less than q in the overall data set.*
- *For groups where p-sensitivity holds, the ratio between the within-group variance of confidential attributes and their variance over the entire data set is at least r.*

The rationale of the model in Definition 7 is explained in the rest of this section. The variance for numerical attributes is the standard statistical variance. For categorical attributes (ordinal or nominal), specific variance definitions are needed, which can be found in [7] and [9].

(k, p, q, r)-Anonymity guarantees k-anonymity for the key attributes in the data set. Regarding the confidential attributes:

- It guarantees p-sensitivity in those groups where "rare" values of a confidential attribute are present (with relative frequency less than q).
- Disclosure of non-rare values of confidential attributes is not considered a privacy problem. The advantage of suppressing the p-sensitivity requirement for very frequent confidential attribute values is that smaller groups (of size closer to the lower bound k) are feasible, which causes less data utility loss as far as key attributes are concerned. In this data utility respect, the new model outperforms p-sensitive k-anonymity, l-diversity, (α, k)-anonymity, (k, e)-anonymity and t-closeness which may all yield in very large

groups, because they attempt to prevent attribute disclosure even for very frequent values of the confidential attribute.
- Finally, enforcing a lower bound for the within-group variance of confidential attributes is meant to thwart the similarity attack which is possible against k-anonymity, p-sensitive k-anonymity, l-diversity, (α, k)-anonymity and (k, e)-anonymity.

4   A Heuristic for (k, p, q, r)-Anonymity

In this section we present a computational procedure to achieve (k, p, q, r)-anonymity for data sets with numerical key attributes and one confidential attribute. Let $x_1, x_2, \ldots, x_n$ be the records in the original data set X. Let L be the confidential attribute and Q be the set of key attributes. Let $x_j(Q)$ denote the projection of record x_j on its key attributes and $x_j(L)$ denote the projection of record x_j on its confidential attribute.

The proposed heuristic procedure is as follows:

1. Label as 'sensitive' those records in X whose confidential attribute takes a value appearing less than $q \cdot n$ times in X. Let $Y \subseteq X$ be the subset of sensitive records;
2. Compute $Var := Variance(Y(L))$;
3. Compute $MinVar := r \cdot Var$;
4. **While** $NotEmpty(Y)$ **loop**

   (a) Let C be a new empty group;
   (b) Let x_s be a random sensitive record from Y;
   (c) Add x_s to C and remove it from Y and X;
   (d) **While** elements in $C(L)$ do not satisfy p-sensitivity **loop**
      i. Take $x_t \in X$ such that $x_t(Q)$ is the nearest record to $x_s(Q)$ which:
         - contributes to the compliance of p-sensitivity by $C(L)$;
         - increases $Variance(C(L))$ if added to C;
      ii. If no record satisfying the above two conditions is found, take x_t such that $x_t(Q)$ is the nearest record to $x_s(Q)$ that contributes to the compliance of p-sensitivity by $C(L)$;
      iii. Add x_t to C and remove it from X (and from Y if $x_t \in Y$);
      end loop
   (e) **While** $Variance(C(L)) < MinVar$ **loop**
      i. Take $x_t \in X$ such that $x_t(Q)$ is the nearest record to $x_s(Q)$ which increases $Variance(C(L))$ if added to C;
      ii. Add x_t to C and remove it from X (and from Y if $x_t \in Y$);
      end loop
   (f) **While** $Cardinality(C) < k$ **loop**
      i. Take x_t such that $x_t(Q)$ is the nearest record to $x_s(Q)$ which keeps $Variance(C(L)) \geq MinVar$ if added to C;
      ii. Add x_t to C and remove it from X (and from Y if $x_t \in Y$);
      end loop
   (g) **If** $(Variance(Y(L)) < MinVar)$ or (p-sensitivity of $Y(L) < p$) **then**
      i. Add the remaining records from Y to C;
      ii. Remove from X all records in Y;
      iii. Remove all records from Y;

    iv. **If** $(Variance(C) < MinVar)$ **then**

        Remove from C those records not having a 'sensitive' value and return
        them to X;
      end if
    end if
(h) Add C to partition P;
end loop

5. Apply MDAV [8] to build a k-partition of records in X and add the MDAV-generated groups to P;
6. Microaggregate the records, that is, for $i = 1$ to n replace $x_i(Q)$ by the centroid of $C_i(Q)$, where C_i is the group in P to which x_i has been assigned.

Each iteration of Step (4) constructs one group containing 'sensitive' records. These groups are those that must satisfy the constraints given by parameters k, p, q and r. Such constraints are satisfied by the loops nested inside Step (4):

- Each new group C is initialized by assigning a random 'sensitive' record to it (Substep (4c));
- Next, Substep (4d) is iterated until C satisfies p-sensitivity, this is, the records in C contain at least p different values for the confidential attribute; if possible, records to be added to C are chosen so that they increase the variance of $C(L)$;
- After that, Substep (4e) ensures the variance of $C(L)$ is at least the one specified by parameter r; this step iterates until this condition is satisfied;
- Then, Substep (4f) is iterated until C has at least k records (in this way, the constraint specified by k is satisfied); once we get out of this loop, C is guaranteed to satisfy the properties of the (k, p, q, r)-anonymity model;
- Finally, Substep (4g) checks that the remaining records in X will be able to form a new group satisfying the model; if this is not the case, they are added to the last group C.

Once no more 'sensitive' records are left in X, the remaining ones are clustered at Step (5) using the MDAV heuristic [8]. Finally, Step (6) replaces each record x_i with its microaggregated version.

5   Empirical Results

In this section, empirical results on the proposed heuristic are reported and compared with those obtained with k-anonymization (based on microaggregation [8]) and p-sensitive k-anonymization (based on the random initial point variant of the microaggregation heuristic [16]). The information loss is reported as $100 \cdot SSE/SST$, where SSE is the within-groups sum of squares and SST is the total sum of squares. A synthetic data set obtained from the "Census" benchmark file [2] has been used. In our first experiment we have used a data set with 1080 records. Each record has 12 continuous numerical key attributes that have been standardized. The confidential attribute takes integer values in the range from 1 to 10; the attribute has been initialized so that each value appears

Table 1. Information loss of our (k, p, q, r)-anonymity heuristic for $k = 5$, $p = 4$, $q = 0.2$ and different values of r

r	0.1	0.3	0.5	0.7	0.9
$Inf.loss$	11.98	12.09	13.01	30.85	68.518

Table 2. Information loss under several models for several values of k and p and fixed $q = 0.2$ and $r = 0.5$ (unskewed confidential attribute)

k	p	k-anonymity	(k, p, q, r)-anonymity	p-sensitive k-anonymity
3	2	5.58	11.87	7.24
4	3	7.52	11.58	9.81
7	5	11.53	14.69	14.42

in exactly 108 records. Parameter q was set to 0.2 so that all values of the confidential attribute were considered as 'sensitive'. Table 1 shows the information loss of (k, p, q, r)-anonymity for $k = 5$ and $p = 4$ and different values of parameter r. As expected, information loss increases with r. This is due to the fact that higher values of r force the heuristic to form groups with a higher variance of its confidential attribute. The higher r, the more constrained are groups, which increases information loss. The k-anonymous version of the data set used had an information loss of 9.21 and the k-anonymous p-sensitive version had 12.31.

Using the same data set of the previous experiment and for fixed $q = 0.2$, $r = 0.5$ and different values of k and p, a second experiment was carried out to compare the information loss incurred by k-anonymity, p-sensitive k-anonymity and (k, p, q, r)-anonymity. Results are shown in Table 2. It can be seen that k-anonymity presents the lowest information loss. The reason is that it is the model with least restrictions. For p-sensitive k-anonymity and (k, p, q, r)-anonymity the information loss is roughly similar; strictly speaking it is a bit higher for (k, p, q, r)-anonymity due to the additional constraint introduced by parameter r which forces a minimum variance of the confidential attributes in a group.

In the third experiment, we modified the distribution of the values of the confidential attribute. Values from 1 to 9 appeared 10 times each while value 10 appeared 990 times. We took $q = 0.2$, so that records with confidential value 10 were considered 'non sensitive' by the (k, p, q, r)-heuristic. The results are shown in Table 3. It can be seen that (k, p, q, r)-anonymity outperforms p-sensitive k-anonymity.

Table 3. Information loss under several models for several values of k and p and fixed $q = 0.2$ and $r = 0.5$ (skewed confidential attribute)

k	p	k-anonymity	(k, p, q, r)-anonymity	p-sensitive k-anonymity
3	2	5.58	9.47	16.42
4	3	7.52	12.13	22.72
7	5	11.53	18.97	30.42

6   Conclusions and Future Research

We have presented (k, p, q, r)-anonymity as a new security model which outperforms most current security models in the literature: it guarantees p-sensitivity for rare values and offers protection against the similarity attack, one of the most difficult to thwart. The model behaves in a pragmatic way (no p-sensitivity for frequent values) in order to reduce information loss. The only attack for which no defense is offered is skewness, but we have shown that such an attack can only be countered at the expense of a very substantial information loss (using the t-closeness model). Future research will involve designing other heuristic procedures, which can accommodate non-numerical quasi-identifiers and can deal with more than one confidential attribute.

References

1. Agrawal, R., Srikant, R.: Privacy preserving data mining. In: Proceedings of the ACM SIGMOD, pp. 439–450 (2000)
2. Brand, R., Domingo-Ferrer, J., Mateo-Sanz, J.M.: Reference data sets to test and compare SDC methods for protection of numerical microdata., European Project IST-2000-25069 CASC (2002), http://neon.vb.cbs.nl/casc
3. Chor, B., Goldreich, O., Kushilevitz, E., Sudan, M.: Private information retrieval. In: IEEE Symposium on Foundations of Computer Science (FOCS), pp. 41–50 (1995)
4. Dalenius, T.: The invasion of privacy problem and statistics production. An overview. Statistik Tidskrift 12, 213–225 (1974)
5. Dalenius, T.: Finding a needle in a haystack - or identifying anonymous census records. Journal of Official Statistics 2(3), 329–336 (1986)
6. Domingo-Ferrer, J.: A three-dimensional conceptual framework for database privacy. In: Jonker, W., Petković, M. (eds.) SDM 2007. LNCS, vol. 4721, pp. 193–202. Springer, Heidelberg (2007)
7. Domingo-Ferrer, J., Solanas, A.: A measure of variance for nominal attributes (manuscript, 2008)
8. Domingo-Ferrer, J., Mateo-Sanz, J.: Practical data-oriented microaggregation for statistical disclosure control. IEEE Transactions on Knowledge and Data Engineering 14, 189–201 (2002)
9. Domingo-Ferrer, J., Torra, V.: Ordinal, continuous and heterogeneous k-anonymity through microaggregation. Data Mining and Knowledge Discovery 11(2), 195–212 (2005)
10. Li, N., Li, T., Venkatasubramanian, S.: t-Closeness: privacy beyond k-anonymity and l-diversity. In: Proceedings of the IEEE ICDE (2007)
11. Lindell, Y., Pinkas, B.: Privacy preserving data mining. In: Bellare, M. (ed.) CRYPTO 2000. LNCS, vol. 1880, pp. 36–53. Springer, Heidelberg (2000)
12. Machanavajjhala, A., Gehrke, J., Kiefer, D., Venkatasubramanian, S.: l-Diversity: privacy beyond k-anonymity. In: Proceedings of the IEEE ICDE 2006 (2006)
13. Martin, D.J., Kiefer, D., Machanavajjhala, A., Gehrke, J.: Worst-case background knowledge for privacy-preserving data publishing. In: Proceedings of the IEEE ICDE 2007 (2007)

14. Samarati, P., Sweeney, L.: Protecting privacy when disclosing information: k-anonymity and its enforcement through generalization and suppression., Tech. Report, SRI International (1998)
15. Samarati, P.: Protecting respondents identities in microdata release. IEEE Transactions on Knowledge and Data Engineering 13(6), 1010–1027 (2001)
16. Solanas, A., Sebé, F., Domingo-Ferrer, J.: Micro-aggregation-based heuristics for p-sensitive k-anonymity: one step beyond. In: Extending Database Technology, EDBT 2008 (2008)
17. Truta, T.M., Vinay, B.: Privacy protection: p-sensitive k-anonymity property. In: 2nd International Workshop on Private Data Management PDM 2006. IEEE Computer Society Press, Los Alamitos (2006)
18. Willenborg, L., DeWaal, T.: Elements of Statistical Disclosure Control. Springer, Heidelberg (2001)
19. Wong, R.C.-W., Li, J., Fu, A.W.-C., Wang, K.: (α, k)-Anonymity: An enhanced k-anonymity model for privacy-preserving data publishing. In: Proceedings of the KDD 2006 (2006)
20. Wong, R.C.-W., Fu, A.W.-C., Wang, K., Pei, J.: Minimality attack in privacy preserving data publishing. In: Proceedings of the VLDB 2007, pp. 543–554 (2007)
21. Xiao, X., Tao, Y.: Personalized privacy preservation. In: SIGMOD Conference 2006, pp. 229–240 (2006)
22. Yao, C., Wang, L., Wang, X.S., Jajodia, S.: Indistinguishability: The Other Aspect of Privacy. In: Jonker, W., Petković, M. (eds.) SDM 2006. LNCS, vol. 4165, pp. 1–17. Springer, Heidelberg (2006)
23. Zhang, Q., Koudas, N., Srivastava, D., Yu, T.: Aggregate query answering on anonymized tables. In: Proceedings of the IEEE ICDE 2007, pp. 116–125 (2007)

Engineering Privacy Requirements in Business Intelligence Applications

Annamaria Chiasera, Fabio Casati, Florian Daniel, and Yannis Velegrakis

Department of Information Engineering and Computer Science
University of Trento, Italy
{chiasera,casati,daniel,velgias}@disi.unitn.it

Abstract. In this paper we discuss the problem of engineering privacy requirements for business intelligence applications, i.e., of eliciting, modeling, testing, and auditing privacy requirements imposed by the source data owner on the business intelligence applications that use these data to compute reports for analysts. We describe the peculiar challenges of this problem, propose and evaluate different solutions for eliciting and modeling such requirements, and make the case in particular for what we experienced as being the most promising and realistic approach: eliciting and modeling privacy requirements on the reports themselves, rather than on the source or as part of the data warehouse.

Keywords: privacy, business intelligence, outsourcing, compliance, provenance, reports, meta-reports.

1 Introduction

With the rapid increase in the amount of people's data that is gathered and exchanged electronically, the problem of information privacy is rapidly gaining attention. Dozens of public and private organizations now hold bits and pieces of our personal information, subject to a variety of more or less explicit privacy agreements and government laws. At the same time, business intelligence (BI) applications are gaining popularity, consistently with the desire of officials of public and private companies to monitor, analyze, understand, and eventually improve business processes and better serve customers and citizens. BI applications typically extract data from multiple data sources, clean them to ensure data quality and consistency to the possible extent, transform them, and then generate various kinds of reports used by managers and officials to analyze the performed processes.

From a privacy perspective, this scenario poses interesting and very concrete research challenges. The first is that data sources used by BI application often reside in different systems, different departments, even in different companies. This implies that data in the sources of the BI applications is subject to different constraints, both because it was collected under different privacy agreements with the citizens in the first place, but also because the different institutions may further regulate the use of the information they obtained.

The second (and biggest) issue is to define the privacy requirements the BI application must obey when processing the data provided by the source. Privacy laws and

W. Jonker and M. Petković (Eds.): SDM 2008, LNCS 5159, pp. 219–228, 2008.

agreements are typically defined at a very high level and with a certain degree of "fuzzyness". However, the BI developers need to know which data can be extracted from the source databases, whether these data can be used to clean/refine data from other providers (e.g., entity resolution), which report users can view the data, whether data can be shown in aggregate form, at which level of aggregation, and so on. This degree of precision is needed to know how to *develop* and *test* the BI application and also how to *audit* and to resolve possible *disputes*.

Current privacy policy languages like P3P 16 and access control languages like IBM's EPAL or OASIS' XACML [3] allow one to express privacy requirements in terms of the authorized purposes for the use of the data. Purpose-based access control mechanisms as proposed with P-RBAC [10] extend standard RBAC approaches with the notion of purpose, condition for data usage, and obligations. Privacy policy languages and purpose-based access control languages are of general applicability and can be used in different contexts where data are released to third parties. However, their generality makes it hard to express actionable privacy requirements that are directly "testable" and "verifiable" along the BI data lifecycle [11].

In this paper we study the problem of engineering privacy requirements in BI applications. Specifically, we study different ways in which precise, testable and auditable requirements can be agreed upon with the source owners and then modeled as part of the BI application. We explore different and possibly complementary options, including ways to define privacy requirements via privacy metadata coupled with the source data, or coupled with the warehouse data, or coupled with reports, and we conclude that defining engineering requirements directly on reports is viable alternative to conventional approaches.

2 Privacy in Outsourced Business Intelligence Environments

Our research originated from projects developed in our area with the local governments, hospitals, and social agencies, where BI reports are needed by those institutions to have a comprehensive view of provided treatments, to evaluate the quality of delivered processes, and to compute reimbursements. Figure 1 illustrates such a scenario. The arrows in the figure illustrate information and data flow.

Any information provided by or related to a patient is typically considered sensitive personal information and as such, any retain, processing, or presentation should respect the privacy of the patient. Privacy restrictions are provided at multiple levels. First, they may be provided by the patients themselves. As patients visit a health-care center, they sign a consent agreement specifying how their personal information can be treated by the health-care institution. These restrictions accompany the provided data and are illustrated in Figure 1 as *privacy level agreements* (PLAs) or privacy requirements (we will use these terms interchangeably, as the PLA constitute requirements, from a privacy perspective, for the BI developer). The provided information is enhanced at the health-care location (the actual *data provider*, from the perspective of the BI provider who delivers the BI solution) by additional data on the treatment offered. Both kinds of data are provided to the BI applications, and PLAs between the institutions are defined for both. In addition, policies on usage and retention of patient data may also be regulated by local and national laws [22, 23].

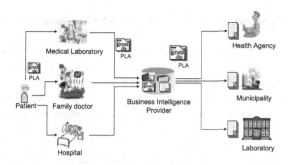

Fig. 1. A privacy-aware business intelligence outsourcing scenario

The *BI provider* extracts, integrates and transforms data that is then loaded on a data warehouse, from which reports are extracted and delivered to the BI users (e.g. reports combining data on usage of prescription drugs and their costs to identify differences in usages and prices, and what causes such differences). The BI provider needs to guarantee that the data it stores, the transformations it performs on that data, and the content of the reports delivered to the users (the co-called *information consumers*) it generates are all complying with the PLAs. It is thus important, and also in the interest of the BI provider, that PLAs are precise, that the BI solution can be tested against them and that it can be audited by third-party auditing agencies.

Most common and in particular such *outsourced BI* scenarios raise several important privacy-related challenges: i) precisely eliciting privacy requirements, ii) integrating privacy requirements from multiple data sources, iii) making requirements analysis robust to changes in the reports, and iv) enforcing and auditing privacy.

Eliciting sufficiently precise PLAs. This refers to the identification of privacy constraints the source whishes to impose by discussing privacy issues with data sources and customers. With the term "sufficiently precise" here we mean formal or semi-formal description of the PLAs that are unambiguous (so that developers know the implementation requirements), that are testable, and that are auditable.

PLA integration. This challenge is related to the integration of multiple privacy requirements from different sources and checking for their compliance in data transformations and reporting.

Robustness of the requirements. While ETL and data warehouse tend to be relatively stable, BI reports are in constant evolution. It is very common to add new reports or modify existing ones, especially in the period after the initial deployment.

Enforcing and auditing privacy. Once requirements (expressed as PLAs) are collected, we have to face the problem of how to implement a solution that i) enforces them and ii) supports monitoring and auditing to detect violations.

In this paper we focus on the elicitation and the precise modeling of robust requirements. These are cornerstone problems since the other challenges can be addressed only after requirements have been engineered. We experienced this to be one of the hardest aspects in any practical BI application we have developed.

3 Privacy Requirements Engineering at the Data Source

A typical way to specify privacy is by defining constraints on the data at the moment that the data is provided, i.e., having the privacy constraints defined at the source level. There are multiple ways one can achieve this goal. One is to leverage UML or some language among those used extensively in the requirements engineering community, for instance, i* [18]. These languages are expressive enough, but hard to use, and due to the fact that they have been to a large extend ignored by modeling techniques, their integration into a data management solutions is not an easy task. An alternative option is to model the PLAs in terms of meta-data that accompany the data and controls its access and use. The advantage of this approach is the metadata can be easily defined and can accompany the data throughout transformations [17]. The meta-data can be part of the data model, typically as data annotations [19][20].

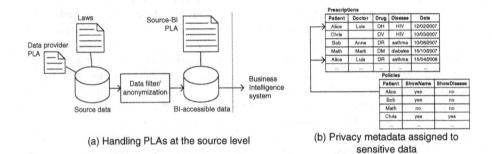

(a) Handling PLAs at the source level   (b) Privacy metadata assigned to sensitive data

Fig. 2. PLAs at the data source level

A solution we are currently developing [21] is the use of intensional associations between data and metadata. The idea is that metadata is stored in completely different tables from the data. Since no modification is required on the data, no disruption of the existing systems functionality occurs. Furthermore, the privacy requirements data can be of any level of structural richness and complexity since it is not accessed by the existing data source applications. The association between the data and metadata is specified in the form of generic queries that serve as intentional descriptions. For instance, the aforementioned privacy restriction may be implemented by a query that selects among all the patients in the database those that have been diagnosed HIV-positive. The advantage is that if a new HIV patient is inserted in the database, for instance, his/her data is automatically associated to the aforementioned privacy restriction without any need for additional modification.

A different approach is the exploitation of the notion of views. In particular, to disallow access to the base tables but define views on top of them with different permissions and operators in each one. The use of views has the additional advantage that it can combine information that is distributed across different tables, thus defining privacy restrictions on the integrated information would have never been possible by defining restrictions on the individual base tables [5].

Alternatives or complements to the use of views as an access control mechanism include automatic *query rewriting* techniques, such as those found in commercial databases like Oracle Virtual Private Database (VPD) or in the Hippocratic Database (HDB) [2]. Apart from controlling the access to the data, the data delivered to BI providers may additionally undergo a *data anonymization* procedure that eliminates sensitive data that could be used to drill down from the provided data to the data of an actual individual (Figure 2(a)). Known anonymization techniques are those based on *k-anonymity* [12] or *l-diversity* [9].

An important issue that needs to be decided when privacy requirements are defined at the source level is how the privacy requirements are used. On one hand, the data source can restrict access to its data one when that access does not violate the privacy restrictions. In other words, the source is responsible for ensuring the PLA compliance. On the other hand, the source can expose to the BI provided all its data, but provide along with the data the PLA. In that case the BI provider will be responsible for the privacy enforcement, but the source will have no control over it. The choice depends on the level of trust to the BI provider. However, experience with real scenarios has shown that the decision is typically based on the IT skills at the data source, with smaller organizations always going for the first option.

A different challenge when defining privacy at the source level is to decide the level of privacy that is needed and to explain to the source owner the privacy requirements. Typically, the managers in charge of privacy are unaware of the details and the meaning of the data in the tables, something that is very often true even for the IT personnel. Furthermore, the schema may be too complex and may make difficult to understand which requirements to model exactly, and how. Furthermore, there is always the risk of "over-engineering" the requirements, i.e., while the source may have a large and complex database, the BI provider may only need a part of that information and for a limited use.

4 Privacy Requirements Engineering at the Warehouse

Instead of defining the privacy requirement at the source level, an alternative is to do so at the warehouse level, i.e., in terms of the data warehouse (DWH) schema and ETL operations. As shown in Figure 3(a), the implementation of PLAs at the DWH/ETL level occurs via meta-data in the DWH and annotations on the ETL procedures that feed the data warehouse. Typically, but not necessarily, before loading the actual warehouse and in order to reduce the complexity of ETL, data is extracted from the data sources and stored in a so-called *staging area* .

Metadata can also be used here to allow the specification of privacy restrictions over tables, rows, or fields, joins or aggregations. Techniques for modeling fine-grained authorizations in *data cubes* can also be used [14]. Restrictions on data disambiguation, correction, and cleaning procedures, can be expressed as annotations to the ETL flows, or to high level views of such flows. Figure 3(b) illustrates how PLAs associated with the ETL procedures can restrict the operations that are allowed on the source tables.

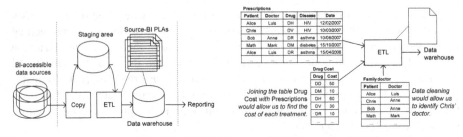

(a) Handling PLAs at the warehouse and ETL level   (b) PLAs accompanying ETL procedures

Fig. 3. PLAs at the DWH and ETL level

Specifying privacy at the DW level has certain advantages as opposed to specyfing it at the source. First, the schema is typically easier to understand, and second, the risk of over-engineering is reduced as the source owner can clearly see which data is used and in which form is stored. By having the restrictions directly on the warehouse data and the ETL, the source owners are guaranteed that the data warehouse schema, though which only their data can be exposed to others, is guaranteed to preserve the privacy. Furthermore, restrictions can be posed also on the ETL processes performed by the warehouse. This allows the BI provider to explain all the ways in which the user's information is used and explicitly ask for permission. The malicious approach of hiding these issues relying on the owners' lack of knowledge of the possible uses of the information does not pay in the long run.

Related work has focused mostly on privacy-preserving data integration [6][7], whose usage, in the case of ETL, for instance, may indeed be part of the requirements. Also, *data perturbation* may be used to modify the data in input, adding noise in such a way that the statistical distribution and the patterns of the input data are preserved and the quality of aggregate reports or mined results is not compromised, even if derived from altered data [13]. *Cryptographic* techniques can be used to scramble the data, again without compromising the possibility of computing aggregates or mining data [13].

Both the task of eliciting privacy requirements with the source owners and later testing PLAs once they have been agreed upon can be supported by *provenance* or *lineage* techniques, that capture the origins of data [17] and facilitate privacy and compliance management. Specifically, provenance traces the necessary meta-data required in compliance checking (i.e., auditing) to understand the data transformations. Widom focuses on lineage and uncertainty in Trio [15] and on non-annotation-based lineage for ETL transformations in [8]. The work described in [1] instead proposes an annotation-based approach to provenance in which elements at the sources (tables, rows, fields) are referred to by means of unique identifiers and provenance annotations (*where-provenance*) is propagated along transformations like copy, insert, and update, commonly used in *curated databases* (databases maintained via a large amount of manual labor). The previous works are not specific to the problem of privacy metadata, but nonetheless they provide techniques that could easily be adapted to our outsourced BI context.

A limitation of defining PLAs at the data warehouse level is that one needs to expose the data warehouse schema to the source owners. More than a confidentiality problem, the challenge here is that the data warehouse is the result of significant data processing and it may be difficult to present and explain to owners the meaning of the various terms – as in all integration problems one of the key challenges is understanding what the various fields mean. Furthermore, we notice that the problems discussed for modeling PLAs at the source level (e.g., complexity and over-engineering) are reduced, but yet not eliminated.

5 Privacy Requirements Engineering on Reports

As discussed, collecting privacy requirements in form of privacy metadata associated with either the source data or the warehouse data and ETL procedures demands significant expertise from the source owners. Engineering privacy requirements directly on the actual reports, instead, hides implementation details and allows the source owners to see exactly which information is shown to which user. It is therefore much easier for them to discuss and define PLAs as annotations on the reports themselves (Figure 4 (a)), typically in terms of which reports are allowed. We have experienced that fact that an interactive discussion of final reports with the data source owners enhances the mutual understanding and enables the BI provider to elicit a complete, precise, and easily testable and auditable set of privacy requirements. Testability is particularly important as source owners, auditors, and BI providers can (relatively) easily detect if development and executions are not compliant with the PLAs. Furthermore, there is no risk of over-engineering, i.e., only the PLAs that are actually needed are specified.

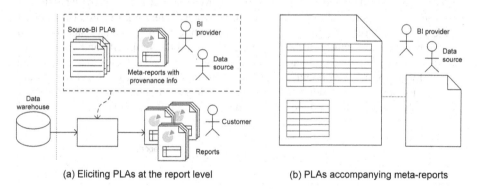

(a) Eliciting PLAs at the report level   (b) PLAs accompanying meta-reports

Fig. 4. PLAs at the report level

Defining privacy on the reports does not make us exempt from defining PLAs also based on how data is used during transformation. In addition, it is important to show on the reports where each report data item comes from, and what happens when the same data element can be obtained from multiple sources. The interaction between the BI provider and the data source can be assisted by a privacy requirements elicitation tool with a simple graphical user interface (GUI), which enables the BI provider to explain the provenance of each data element and the transformations/integrations it goes through. Privacy requirements will then be collected and formalized directly in the tool by annotating reports and provenance schemes. An intuition of how meta-reports can be annotated is given in Figure 4(b). In general, annotations can include i) who can access a certain attribute, ii) what are the aggregation requirements on a table (how many base elements should be present before the aggregation), iii) anonymization requirements on an attribute, iv) join permissions/prohibitions, that is, the permission or prohibition to join information from multiple data sources (even belonging to the same owner) and v) integration permission, that is, the permission to use information to clean/resolve data from other owners. These requirements can be again expressed in intensional form, and in fact sometimes it is necessary to do so as they are instance specific. For example, a PLA may express that in a patient-related column, medical examinations results can be shown only for patients that are not HIV positive. HIV can be a separate column in the same report that is used only for purposes of defining PLAs, even if it is not made visible to users.

On the negative side, this approach has two main limitations: the first is that we need to share with the source owners the reports we deliver to users. The second is that the evolutionary nature of the reports themselves makes PLAs less stable. This is due to the fact that collected requirements are defined on each specific report, thus losing their validity with the evolution of the report. Furthermore, interactions and agreements with source owners are needed each time a new report is defined. This can be a significant limitation as the number of reports in a BI application is very high (having dozens or even hundreds of reports is common even in relatively small applications) and as some BI solutions also give users the ability to create new reports.

To overcome these drawbacks, we use *PLA meta-reports* in the discussion with the data sources, instead of concrete instances of individual reports. Meta-reports represent tables or views over the data warehouse that contain data that can be used to define reports. As depicted in Figure 4(a), we envision that the BI provider will discuss such meta-reports directly with the source owners. Meta-reports are also a subset of the actual reports. The idea is that they constitute an intermediate step between the complexity and stability of the data warehouse, and the simplicity and volatility of the final reports (Figure 5). Meta-reports typically contain wide tables that contain the same information used to populate the final reports. Notice that the meta-reports are intended to facilitate PLA definitions. In general they are not expected to be materialized or to be used as intermediate steps in the generation of the actual reports.

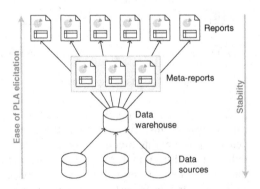

Fig. 5. PLA definition at different levels of abstraction

Once meta-reports are approved by the data sources they will be used not only as a reference for the implementation of privacy requirements compliant ETL procedures but also as a set of test cases on which the design of the cleaning and reporting activities could be tested before they are actually put in operation on the real data.

Each time a new report is created or an existing one is modified, PLAs on the meta-reports are used to determine if the new report is privacy-compliant. This can be often done easily as the reports can, at least conceptually, be expressed as a subset or view over a meta-report.

One of the main challenges in the development of meta-reports for the elicitation of privacy requirements is the identification and implementation of a minimal yet exhaustive set of meta-reports that is able to provide for the necessary flexibility to cope with a continuously changing set of final reports without requiring a new elicitation of requirements. It is further crucial to identify an adequate level of granularity for each of the meta-reports, so as to be able to elicit requirements that are precise enough to derive compliant reports from them, but still immediately understandable by the data source, in order to prevent misunderstandings. In other words, the design challenge here is how many meta-reports to define and how close they should be to the complexity of the data warehouse or the simplicity of the reports. At one extreme, the data warehouse can be viewed as a particularly complex case of meta-reports or universe, just like reporting tools allow the report universe to be the data warehouse itself. In fact, we can take this argument even further and observe that there is a continuum from the PLAs defined on the sources, data warehouse, meta-reports, and reports, going at increasing levels of simplicity and volatility of the PLA definitions.

6   Discussion and Comparisons of the Proposed Solutions

In this work we discussed various approaches to privacy requirements engineering. We described the problem of PLAs in outsourced BI applications, describing why the problem is important from a business perspective and challenging from a research point of view. We also emphasized the differences of this problem with respect to traditional privacy or access control problems. We believe this is still a research void, as we are not aware of systems in the BI arena where privacy policies are tested before they are put in operation in the system. Errors in capturing the intentions of the source owners and data providers with the definition and implementation of the privacy requirements are discovered only when the system is released and it is too late to avoid the disclosure of sensitive data. The problem is more and more pressing, though very often it is underestimated even by data owners, until the various issues and their complexity are made explicit to them.

The work is in its infancy, with a number of fascinating research challenges waiting to be addressed. These challenges range from defining languages and models for annotations and PLAs for BI applications, to identifying ways to support the generation of meta-reports, to defining methodologies for interacting with the source owners in order to quickly converge to a set of PLAs, to even methods for translating PLAs into internal data structures that can be used for automated privacy management support at design time or runtime.

References

1. Vansummeren, S., Cheney, J.: Recording Provenance for SQL Queries and Updates. IEEE Data Eng. Bull 30(4), 29–37 (2007)
2. Agrawal, R., Grandison, T., Johnson, C., Kiernan, J.: Enabling the 21st century health care information technology revolution. Commun. ACM 50(2), 34–42 (2007)
3. Anderson, H.: A comparison of two privacy policy languages: EPAL and XACML. In: SWS 2006, pp. 53–60. ACM Press, New York (2006)
4. Antón, I., Bertino, E., Li, N., Yu, T.: A roadmap for comprehensive online privacy policy management. Commun. ACM 50(7), 109–116 (2007)
5. Bertino, E., Sandhu, R.: Database security-concepts, approaches, and challenges. IEEE Transactions on Dependable and Secure Computing 02(1), 2–19 (2005)
6. Bhowmick, S.S., Gruenwald, L., Iwaihara, M., Chatvichienchai, S.: PRIVATE-IYE: A framework for privacy preserving data integration. In: ICDEW 2006, p. 91. IEEE, Los Alamitos (2006)
7. Clifton, C., Kantarcioğlu, M., Doan, A., Schadow, G., Vaidya, J., Elmagarmid, A., Suciu, D.: Privacy-preserving data integration and sharing. In: DMKD 2004, pp. 19–26. ACM Press, New York (2004)
8. Cui, Y., Widom, J.: Lineage tracing for general data warehouse transformations. The VLDB Journal 12(1), 471–480 (2003)
9. Machanavajjhala, J., Gehrke, D.K., Venkitasubramaniam, M.: l-diversity: Privacy beyond k-anonymity. ACM Trans. Knowl. Discov. Data 1(1), 1556–4681 (2007)
10. Ni, Q., Trombetta, A., Bertino, E., Lobo, J.: Privacy-aware role based access control. In: SACMAT 2007, pp. 41–50. ACM Press, New York (2007)
11. Rizzi, S., Abelló, A., Lechtenbörger, J., Trujillo, J.: Research in data warehouse modeling and design: dead or alive? In: DOLAP 2006, pp. 3–10. ACM Press, New York (2006)
12. Sweeney, L.: Achieving k-anonymity privacy protection using generalization and suppression. Int. J. Uncertain. Fuzziness Knowl. -Based Syst. 10(5), 571–588 (2002)
13. Verykios, V.S., Bertino, E., Fovino, I.N., Provenza, L.P., Saygin, Y., Theodoridis, Y.: State-of-the-art in privacy preserving data mining. SIGMOD Rec. 33(1), 50–57 (2004)
14. Wang, L., Jajodia, S., Wijesekera, D.: Securing OLAP data cubes against privacy breaches. In: IEEE Symposium on Security and Privacy, pp. 161–175. IEEE, Los Alamitos (2004)
15. Widom, J.: Trio: A system for integrated management of data, accuracy, and lineage. In: CIDR 2005, pp. 262–276 (2005)
16. Wenning, R., Schunter, M. (eds.): The Platform for Privacy Preferences 1.1 (P3P1.1) Specification. W3C Working Group Note (November 2006),
   http://www.w3.org/TR/P3P11/
17. Tan, W.: Research Problems in Data Provenance. IEEE Data Engineering Bulletin 27(4), 45–52 (2004)
18. Dehousse, S., Liu, L., Faulkner, S., Kolp, M., Mouratidis, H.: Modeling Delegation through an i*-based Approach. In: IAT 2006, pp. 393–397 (2006)
19. Chiticariu, L., Tan, W.C., Vijayvargiya, G.: DBNotes: a post-it system for relational databases based on provenance. In: SIGMOD 2005, pp. 942–944 (2005)
20. Geerts, F., Kementsietsidis, A., Milano, D.: iMONDRIAN: A Visual Tool to Annotate and Query Scientific Databases. In: Ioannidis, Y., Scholl, M.H., Schmidt, J.W., Matthes, F., Hatzopoulos, M., Böhm, K., Kemper, A., Grust, T., Böhm, C. (eds.) EDBT 2006. LNCS, vol. 3896, pp. 1168–1171. Springer, Heidelberg (2006)
21. Srivastava, D., Velegrakis, Y.: Intensional associations between data and metadata. In: SIGMOD 2007, pp. 401–412 (2007)
22. Italian's Data Protection Code, DL n. 196/30 (June 2003)
23. European Directive 1995/46/EC, OJ L 281, p. 31 of 23.11.1995

Author Index